MORALS AND MARKETS
The Development of Life Insurance in the United States

MORALS AND MARKETS
The Development of Life Insurance in the United States

Viviana A. Rotman Zelizer

Columbia University Press
New York and London
1979

As a dissertation this book was awarded the Bancroft Dissertation Award by a committee of the faculty of the Graduate School of Arts and Sciences of Columbia University.

Library of Congress Cataloging in Publication Data

Zelizer, Viviana A Rotman.
Morals and markets.

Bibliography: p.
Includes index.
1. Insurance, Life—United States—History.
2. Insurance, Life—Social aspects—United States—History. I. Title.
HG8951.Z44 368.3'2'00973 78-31205

Columbia University Press
New York Guildford, Surrey

For my mother, Rosita Weill de Rotman and my father, S. Julio Rotman, who would be my great friends even if they were not my parents.

Contents

Acknowledgments

In his essay on *Faithfulness and Gratitude,* Simmel pointed out that "only when we give first are we free, and this is the reason why, in the first gift, which is not occasioned by any gratitude, there lies a beauty, a spontaneous devotion to the other . . . which cannot be matched by any subsequent gift."[1] The advice and support of Professors Sigmund Diamond and Bernard Barber, their human and intellectual generosity are "first gifts" I shall never be able to repay adequately. This study started as a paper in the seminar of Professor Diamond at Columbia University, where he introduced me to the uses of the historical method in sociological research. Even while teaching at Tel-Aviv University in Israel, Professor Diamond found time to correct with great care the manuscripts I mailed to him. His many substantive comments and editorial suggestions, and his thoughtful words of encouragement were of great value to my work.

I met Professor Barber during my first semester of graduate work at Columbia and have been inspired by his work ever since. Many of the theoretical perspectives of this book are based on Professor Barber's classes, his writings, and our private conversations. His intellectual clarity and breadth of sociological knowledge, coupled with an endless patience with my questions and doubts, were crucial factors in my completion of this book.

For their encouragement and extremely helpful comments on particular issues I am also indebted to Professors Robert K. Merton, David J. Rothman, and Jonathan Cole, and to Dr. John W. Riley, Jr. I am particularly thankful to Professor Irving Louis Horowitz of Rutgers University who read several chapters of the manuscript and helped me so much with his enthusiasm and keen insights. I am also deeply grateful for the generous financial assistance I received during my five years of graduate work from Columbia University and the National Institute of Mental Health. I appreciate as well the encouragement of the American Council of Life Insurance.

I have been fortunate in having the assistance of Helen L. Stevens in typing the manuscript. Elizabeth McGregor kept the household running with love and efficiency. My husband, Jerry, and my son, Julian, were good partners. Finally, I want to thank Professor Harry C. Bredemeier of Rutgers University and Dr. Susanne Schad-Somers who first inspired me to study sociology.

Introduction

Insurance historians have puzzled over the pattern of diffusion of life insurance in the United States. An unusually slow pace of development during the earlier part of the nineteenth century contrasts sharply with the industry's sudden overwhelming success after the 1840s. Zartman noted in 1909: "The tremendous development which took place so suddenly in American life insurance has never been satisfactorily explained."[1] Sixty years later, Stalson was still repeating: "That something momentous took place in American life insurance beginning in 1843 all serious students are agreed; yet no one . . . has given intensive study to that important phenomenon."[2] Existing interpretations remain inconclusive, limited by a predominant concern with the economic aspects of the diffusion of life insurance. Economists and economic historians monopolize the field of insurance, while sociologists for the most part have ignored it.[3] The analysis of life insurance as a social innovation and not simply an economic institution, presents a significant opportunity for the application and extension of important sociological concepts and methods.

This book is primarily concerned with the noneconomic aspects of economic behavior, using as an example the major cultural and ideological factors involved in the legitimation of life insurance. After examining the actual rate and mode of diffusion of the industry in the United States, we turn to some of the typical limitations and errors of current economic interpretations of life insurance history. The role of cultural variables is then tested by a comparative analysis, first, of cross-cultural consistency in the pattern of diffusion of life insurance and, second, of variability between types of insurance in the United States. For example, on the first point, the cultural variable of ideological resistance to life insurance obstructed its growth in most other nations. And, on the second point, while fire and marine insurance, culturally valued on grounds of obvious economic rationality, developed rapidly and easily in the United States, life insurance here developed later and more slowly. What made life insurance so uniquely controversial?

Opposition to life insurance resulted largely from a value system that condemned a strictly financial evaluation of human life. The establishment of monetary equivalents for those aspects of the social order, such as death, life, human organs and other generally ritualized items or behavior considered sacred and therefore, beyond the pale of monetary definition, is a central theoretical concern of this study. Social scientists have done much theorizing about the "cash nexus," but, strangely, have done little research on the area. The first full translation of Simmel's penetrating analysis of personal and monetary values in his *Philosophie des Geldes* has appeared only recently. With a few exceptions, this work had been previously ignored in the sociological literature. The absorption of many social scientists with "market" models and the notion of economic man led them to disregard certain complexities in the interaction between the market and human values. The latter defy the impersonal, rational, and equalizing influence of market exchange. Titmuss's imaginative cross-national comparison of voluntary and commercial systems of providing human blood for transfusions stands as a lone effort to consider this conflict in depth. His book argues that commercial systems of distributing blood are not only less efficient than voluntary blood donation but, more important, they are morally unacceptable and dangerous to the social order. Transform blood into a commercial commodity, says Titmuss, and soon it will become "morally acceptable for a myriad of other human activities and relationships also to exchange for dollars and pounds."[4] Dissatisfied with the consequences of market exchange, Titmuss is persuaded that only reciprocal or gift forms of exchange are suitable for certain items or activities; among others, blood transfusions, organ transplants, foster care, and participation in medical experimentation. His resistance to the laws of the marketplace is not unique. Already in his early writings, Marx was concerned with the dehumanizing impact of money. In *The Economic and Philosophic Manuscripts,* Marx deplored the fact that in bourgeois society human life is easily reduced to a mere salable commodity; he pointed to prostitution and the sale of persons which flourished in his time as ultimate examples of this degrading process.[5] Similarly, Peter Blau, despite his predominantly market model of social behavior, states that "by supplying goods that moral standards define as invaluable for a price in the market, individuals prostitute themselves and destroy the central value of what they have to offer."[6] Using love and salvation as examples, Blau suggests that pricing intangible spiritual benefits leaves only some unwholesome by-product; not love but prostitution, not spiritual blessing but simony.* Life insurance raises the issue of es-

* Cooley formulated another, different perspective on the "moral problem" created by the fact that "pecuniary values fail to express the higher life of society." Although accepting that human values such as love, beauty, and righteousness were not traditional market commodities, Cooley rejected the permanent segregation of pecuniary values into a special,

tablishing monetary equivalences for sacred things in its sharpest terms; how does one determine a fixed dollar amount for death? Institutional effects on cultural values are explored as well through an analysis of the impact of life insurance on prevailing attitudes and definitions of death and dying.

Changing cultural definitions of risk and gambling also had an effect on the development of life insurance. In the earlier decades of the nineteenth century, traditional economic morality and a deterministic religious ethos condemned life insurance as a sacrilegious speculative venture. The emergent voluntaristic religious outlook and the entrepreneurial economic morality of the latter part of the century legitimated the life insurance enterprise. The stigma of insurance as gambling was erased.

Two socio-structural variables are also used in our analysis. First, the strains of shifting from a gift-type of social exchange in assisting the bereaved to an impersonal market system of exchange are explored. Life insurance revolutionized the management of death. Friends, neighbors, and relatives, who had relieved the economic misery of the eighteenth century widow, were replaced by the proud efficiency of a profit-making bureaucracy. The protection of widows and orphans, however, was not easily reduced to pure economics. Second, analysis of the changing marketing techniques used by life insurance companies during the nineteenth century shows their attempts to cope with the simultaneous goals of business and altruism. Agents were caught in the ambivalence, torn between a self-image as missionaries and a public image as greedy salesmen. The occupational status of life insurance agents serves as an indicator of public response to the industry. The concept of "dirty work" is utilized to analyze the role characteristics and low occupational prestige of life insurance agents.

The concern of this book goes beyond a historical narrative of the development of life insurance. The primary purpose is to explore, using previously unanalyzed aspects of that history, the more general sociological problem of the impact of noneconomic factors on economic behavior and the more specific problem of the cultural and structural dilemma created by putting death on the market.

---

inferior province of life. His alternative was the enhancement of monetary evaluation; precisely by encouraging "the translation into it of the higher values . . . the principle that everything has its price should be rather enlarged than restricted" Charles H. Cooley, "The Sphere of Pecuniary Valuation," *American Journal of Sociology* (September 1913), 19:188–203.

My study is based on a qualitative analysis of historical documentary sources. I attempt to include an extensive and diversified set of different kinds of data. Among the primary sources consulted were advertising booklets published by life insurance companies, insurance journals and magazines, early treatises and textbooks on insurance, life insurance agents' training manuals and their memoirs. Although these sources represent predominantly the life insurance industry and not its customers, they provide important indicators of public opinion. The most prevalent objections against life insurance were repeatedly discussed and carefully answered by contemporary advertising copy. Primary sources outside the life insurance industry were consulted as well, among them nineteenth-century business periodicals and general magazines, widows' and marriage manuals, booklets written by critics of life insurance, and a series of government documents. In general, these sources were analyzed in accordance with classical methods of historical inquiry, but theories and concepts developed in sociology, as well as in history, helped formulate the design of the research and the questions to be answered.

MORALS AND MARKETS
The Development of Life Insurance
in the United States

Chapter 1
Historical and Economic Background

> There is a curious and interesting chapter in the history of life insurance in the United States yet to be written. The story of its early struggles, trials and conflicts, when small and feeble was its day.[1]

In 1977 there was an estimated total of over two trillion dollars of life insurance in force in the United States. Life insurance purchases during that year alone amounted to 360 billion. Behind these overwhelming figures of contemporary financial success lies a long history of struggle and opposition. At the outset, life insurance was considered "detrimental" to the interests of the country.[2] It was reported with "wonder in gossips" that only a handful of persons had got their lives insured.[3] One of the earliest life insurance agents later recalled: "It was exceedingly difficult to attract the attention or excite interest in the minds of that class of persons for whom its benefits were intended."[4] As late as 1853, a *New York Times* editorial contended that: "He who insures his life or health must be victim of his own folly or other's knavery."[5] Observers were puzzled: "In a country combining all the elements calculated to demand the extended use of [life] insurance . . . how does it happen that it is so seldom employed?"[6] It took well over half a century for Americans to accept life insurance. The first company was organized in 1759, yet not until the 1840s did life insurance begin selling in any significant degree. Then, suddenly, in the span of a few years, its rate of growth became astonishingly high. At the beginning of the nineteenth century there were not more than 100 policies in force in the entire United States. By 1844 one company alone issued 796 policies in its first nineteen months of operation.[7] In 1815 the courts were still debating the legal validity of a life insurance contract.[8] A third of a century later, a judge declared: "Life insurance has now become a very extensive business and is regarded as highly beneficial to the community."[9] Amidst a plethora of writings on insurance, two major questions remain unanswered: what explains the strong and prolonged resistance of Americans to buying life insurance and what accounts for its unusually rapid success in the 1840s.[10] In the search for answers, two time periods will be considered: the first four decades of the nineteenth century, which cover the struggle of life insurance to establish itself in America and the sources of opposition to it; and the later decades of that century when life insurance was already successfully established. The study will deal with the major cultural variables that obstructed the growth of life insurance in the earlier part of the nineteenth century, assessing as well those changes that allowed for its expansion later in the century. Divisions in time between changing cultural values and ideologies, however, are never absolute in reality. Although different values tended to be dominant at different times, during fairly long periods one can find them coexisting. We are, therefore, dealing with gradual cultural change, tracing roughly the rise in favorable conditions for the adoption of life insurance.

American life insurance first appeared in the informal atmosphere of the coffeehouses, where during the early part of the eighteenth century, merchants and traders met to discuss business matters. Private marine underwriters would occasionally issue short-term life policies for their clients. They were mostly "ransom" policies, granted exclusively for extraordinary risks, as in the case of merchants who traveled to Europe or the West Indies. The first formal life insurance organization was the Corporation for Relief of Poor and Distressed Widows and Children of Presbyterian Ministers, set up in 1759 by the Presbyterian Synods in New York and Philadelphia to insure the lives of their ministers. A similar institution was organized in 1769 by the Episcopalian ministers. These organizations have an ambiguous historical status. They are business corporations for some historians, but many others consider them as only "half-charitable, half-insurance" institutions that served as the link between individual and corporate forms of life underwriting.[11] A financial history of the United States excludes the Presbyterian fund from a list of early corporations on the basis that it was established "for other purposes than business."[12] In fact, both the Episcopal and the Presbyterian corporations were structured very much as life insurance companies, except that they dealt with a specialized clientele and received gift contributions for their funds. However, these additional monies were only to assist nonsubscribers and regular coverage was provided by the established rates. The clergy were "singularly remiss" in embracing the opportunities of their associations.[13] Organizers of the Episcopal Fund assured that "it was not the fault of the Corporation that its benefits were not more generally sought by the clergy. The Corporation took all pains, direct and indirect, to invite contributions."[14]

Many insurance companies were formed during the last decade of the eighteenth century; 29 charters, for example, were granted between 1794 and 1799. Although these were fire and marine companies, at least 5 among them were chartered also to underwrite life risks. With one exception, life insurance business remained a "dead letter."[15] The exception was the Insurance Company of North America, founded in 1794. At first, that company simply followed the practice of individual underwriters and insured lives only for extraordinary risk.* Finally in 1795, the company decided to "undertake some plan for insurance on lives."[16] They were so unsuccessful that no more than half a dozen policies had been issued by November 1799. In 1817, the company dropped life insurance altogether. Another frustrated attempt at life insurance was made in the late eighteenth century by William Gordon, who published a carefully outlined plan for a society making provision for widows in Boston. Nothing ever resulted from it.[17]

The Pennsylvania Company for Insurance on Lives and Granting Annuities was incorporated in Pennsylvania in March, 1812. It was America's first commercial life insurance company organized on a scientific basis to offer policies to the general public.† Between 1812 and 1840 other companies were started with the power to issue life insurance.‡ Business was so bad, however, that most of them abandoned the field

*Two ship captains were insured against capture during two separate voyages from Philadelphia to London and from Baltimore to Oporto or Lisbon. Charles K. Knight, "History of Life Insurance to 1870," p. 66. In essence, these were not so much life insurance policies as "marine risks of a fatal accident nature." J. A. Fowler, *History of Insurance in Philadelphia for Two Centuries*, p. 623.

†A British company opened an agency in Philadelphia in 1807 but was quickly eliminated by a decision from the state legislature (1810) prohibiting all out-of-state insurers. In 1810, Philadelphia blacks founded an African Insurance Company, that dissolved in 1813 from lack of response. W. Weare, *Black Business in the New South*, p. 7.

‡Between 1836 and 1840 several older companies revived their life privileges again unsuccessfully. Nichols comments that "had the bright promises of 1835 been realized it is possible that the beginning of life insurance as a recognized business in America might have dated seven years earlier." Walter S. Nichols, *Insurance Blue Book, 1876–77*, pp. 37–38.

within a few years. The Union Insurance Company, for example, incorporated in New York in 1818, never sold more than 12 policies, and these were bought by its officers and directors.[18] The Pennsylvania Company (1812), the Massachusetts Hospital Life Insurance Company (1818), the New York Life and Trust Company (1830) and the Girard Life Insurance, Annuity and Trust Company (1836) were the four major companies of that period.

Despite their strenuous efforts, not even these companies were able to do more than a modest amount of life insurance business. The weakness of the life insurance business before 1840 can be clearly seen when compared to the successful development of the trust business. Trust companies accepted money or securities in trust, a field previously occupied by private parties. The need for trusteeship arose primarily when a wealthy man became either too old or disabled to manage his property successfully, or when after his death the property was willed to a widow, sisters, or minor children considered incompetent to care for it. Corporate fiduciaries managed property for the benefit of the beneficiaries.* The charters of the Pennsylvania, Massachusetts, New York Life, and Girard companies gave them power to do trust business, and their trust departments flourished while life insurance floundered. It was an unexpected development, for these companies had anticipated doing most of their business with life insurance. The Massachusetts Hospital Life Insurance Co. started its life insurance and trust business in 1818. In 1823, it collected $696 worth of life insurance, while its trust business yielded almost $70,000. In 1827, it issued only 35 life policies, but almost 304 annuities and endowments in trust. By 1830, the trust business of the company amounted to almost $5 million.† Dr. Nathaniel Bowditch, the actuary, informed the Board in 1826: "The business of life insurance . . . is at

* Legally, a trust is defined as "a fiduciary relationship in which one person is the holder of the title to property, subject to an equitable obligation to keep or use the property for the benefit of another." George C. Bogert, *Trusts*, 4th ed. (St. Paul, Minn.: West, 1963), p. 1. The titleholder is the trustee and the person receiving the benefit is the beneficiary. See Marvin Sussman, Judith N. Cates, David T. Smith, *The Family and Inheritance.* On the historical development of trust companies, see Gerald T. White, *A History of the Massachusetts Hospital Life Insurance Company.*

† The case of the Massachusetts Co. is typical of the other three. Between 1813 and 1841, the Pennsylvania Co. never had more than 210 insurance policies in force. The top number of policies for the Girard between 1837 and 1841 was 278. The New York Life reached a maximum of 889 policies between 1830 and 1841. Owen J. Stalson, *Marketing Life Insurance*, pp. 65, 88, 97.

present very small and the whole force of the institution tends toward the trust establishment."[19] The failure to sell life insurance was commented on, and lamented by the organizers of the companies as well as by the national and foreign press and even legislatures. Looking back on the frustrations of the early years of life insurance one of the first directors of the Union Insurance Company wrote in 1873:

> The subject was then but little understood. The late Prof. Renwick of Columbia College was elected actuary and every effort made for one or more years to induce parties to take out policies, but without success. . . . The life insurance department was abandoned and the few policies were cancelled by their owners. It was by many good people regarded at that time as wicked to insure their lives.[20]

Journals in the United States and abroad commented on the reluctance of the American people to purchase life insurance. "It has long been to us a matter of surprise that so little attention is paid in this country to the insurance of lives . . . ," said the *New Orleans Courier* in 1836.[21] *Hunt's Merchants' Magazine* and the *Edinburgh Review* agreed: "Strange to say, it [life insurance] has never been popular in the United States." "Life Insurance, though introduced, cannot be said to flourish among our American descendants."[22] The Board of Directors of the Pennsylvania Company could but concur:

> The Directors regret very much that owing to that kind of prejudice that is generally found to exist among all novel establishments . . . the business transacted by the company has been extremely limited in its extent.[23]

Even legislators reflected on the unexpected failure of life insurance companies to inspire public confidence.[24]

This history of abortive efforts and unsuccessful companies suddenly changed in the 1840s into a story of breathtaking success: "Men who witnessed it were puzzled at the rapidity with which the growth took place."[25] The revolution of the forties, as it is now referred to, has mesmerized many into dating the beginnings of American life insurance in 1840. Historical accounts condense over half a century of defeats into a few understated lines of brief acknowledgment. This historical selectivity has resulted in a bibliography that mostly documents success; perhaps that is why so little is known about resistance to life insurance.*

* Nineteenth-century insurance historians were less reluctant to deal with the "dark days" and the "precarious and miserable existence" of the first life insurance companies that "after a few years of fruitless toil expired of absolute starvation." "Life Insurance Profession

What happened to life insurance between 1840 and 1859 can best be captured through numbers. In 1840 there were 15 life insurance companies in the United States and the estimated amount of total insurance in force was under $5 million. By 1860, there were 43 companies and almost $205 million of insurance in force. In terms of individual companies' achievements, the Mutual Life Insurance Co. of New York went from less than four and a half million dollars of insurance in force in 1845, to $40 million in 1860. Between 1845 and 1860, the Mutual Benefit Life Insurance Company (New Jersey) grew from $2 million to $25 million dollars of insurance in force. Their successful experience was duplicated by most of the other companies. After 1859, despite periodic setbacks, the story of life insurance is that of the consolidation of success. The Civil War did not arrest the growth of the industry. Quite the contrary; 75 new companies were organized between 1859 and 1867, and by the end of the war in 1865 life insurance in force in the United States was more than three times the amount of 1860.*

The development of the insurance press closely mirrors the economic fate of the industry. Until the 1840s only life insurance companies were interested in printing life insurance literature and little was published beyond their booklets and advertisements. There were no insurance trade journals and the general press mostly ignored the subject. As one writer put it: "The necessity had not arisen for life insurance literature . . . the theme appeared unpromising and [one] with which there was so little public sympathy."[26] With public response improving and sales rising, life insurance in the 1840s finally became newsworthy. Articles about it began appearing regularly in the press, particularly in the leading business publications. By 1854, *Hunt's Merchants' Magazine* incorporated among its regular features a Journal of Insurance. *Tuckett's Monthly*, the first insurance journal, was published in 1852. It was followed by the *Insurance Monitor* in 1853 and the *United States Insurance Gazette* in 1855. The first editorial of *Tuckett's Monthly* pointed to the "extensive"

---

and Life Insurance Literature—Their Rise and Progress," *United States Insurance Gazette* (May 1861), 13:7. One writer criticized insurance men who "remember only the prosperity of the present and forget the hard struggle by which that prosperity was attained." William T. Standen, *The Ideal Protection*, p. 228.

* The greatest percentage increase ever to occur in the amount of total insurance in force in the United States was between 1845 and 1850. It was a 571 percent increase from $14,256,000 to $96,687,000. Stalson, *Marketing Life Insurance*, pp. 286, 784. See also R. Carlyle Buley, *The Equitable Life Assurance Society of the United States*, p. 77.

interest in life insurance that had created the need for some means of printed communication. The introductory issue of the *United States Insurance Gazette* similarly stated: "The press, the mercantile classes and the public have turned their attention to the theory and practice of insurance and the cry is now, give us more light and information on the subject."[27] Press coverage of life insurance grew extensively. Its opponents felt that the relationship between life insurance and the press had become too cozy, and complained: "Insurance companies have so patronized religious and secular press [that] . . . scarcely a paper will admit into its columns any articles discussing or calling into question the principles of life insurance."*

* George Albree, *The Evils of Life Insurance*, p. 15. See also Elizur Wright, *Church of the Holy Commissions* (New York, 1877). In this booklet, which was a searing indictment of the commission system of agency compensation, Wright indicated, "for the last seven or eight years . . . it has been very difficult to get published, in any newspaper of wide circulation, any searching criticism . . . of life insurance companies."

Chapter 2
The Persistent Puzzle

Existing interpretations of life insurance history have been more often the result of fertile imagination than of systematic research. A lack of sophisticated theoretical grounding and solid empirical support has been compounded by two additional flaws. First, most explanations rely too heavily on a single supposedly crucial factor to account for the fluctuations of life insurance history; both the initial failure and the later spellbinding success of the industry. A second problem is their economic bias. Cultural factors are dismissed as second-class explanatory variables, useful only to provide anecdotal flavor to otherwise arid narratives.[1] My book attempts to: (1) introduce cultural and ideological, as well as selected socio-structural variables vital to life insurance history; (2) show how economic variables, although insufficient by themselves, constitute necessary elements of a multivariate explanatory model.

This chapter, then, examines the interpretations of other historians; it uncovers their inaccuracies but also points out their contribution to the understanding of life insurance history in the United States.

The following variables will be discussed:

Life Insurance Development

External Factors	Internal Factors
Economic growth	Marketing techniques
Urbanization	Structure of the companies

Life Insurance Development (*Continued*)

External Factors	Internal Factors
Mortality	Quality and price of policies
Actuarial knowledge	Economic security of companies
Attitude of government and jurists	Knowledge of life insurance principles
Purchasing power of the population	

1. Economic Development

The country's stage of economic growth has been considered among the foremost determinants of life insurance development. From this standpoint, the early troubles of life insurance have been seen as the result of "inadequate commercial and financial development."[2] The great economic expansion of the 1840s explains the boom of life insurance at that time.* Rostow first signaled the years between 1843 and 1859 as critical for American economic history. Significantly, his "take-off" date coincides with the "take-off" date for life insurance. The latter reaches, however, its period of "extravagant" growth between 1857 and 1867, before industrialization became, in Rostow's words, a more "massive and statistically . . . impressive phenomenon."[3] In 1867, American life companies surpassed one billion dollars of insurance in force.

Rostow's many critics, while attacking his general theory, do not basically challenge his timetable. Almost all recent economic historians agree that the rate of economic growth experienced a significant acceleration somewhere between 1815 and 1860 and more specifically between 1843 and 1857. North claims that this acceleration began before the 1840s, between 1823 and 1843. He still refers to an economic revival that began in 1843, however, and concludes that the pace of industrialization only became significant in the 1840s and early fifties. David suggests a series of economic "outbursts" instead of one take-off, but still regards the 1840s as one such critical period.[4]

This propitious economic environment of the 1840s partially explains the growth of life insurance at that time.

* By becoming a major mechanism for capital accumulation, life insurance in turn contributed to further economic growth. S. Bruchey, *The Roots of American Economic Growth: 1607–1861*, p. 143.

2. Purchasing Power of the Population

While it may seem logical to assume that life insurance did not sell because the general purchasing power of the population was too low, Stalson, Smith, and White dismiss this argument. By the beginning of the nineteenth century, particularly in the major eastern cities, economic life was sufficiently complex and individual capital large enough to justify the formation of life insurance companies. Not only was the amount of private capital and personal fortunes rapidly rising but there was also an increase in the total number of people having capital.*

The success of the trust business and savings banks also suggests that life insurance was financially feasible at the beginning of the nineteenth century. The prosperity of the trust life insurance companies has already been mentioned. As to savings banks, White tells how the Provident Institution for Savings, chartered in Boston in 1816, quickly flourished "beyond the expectations of its founders."[5] Within five years, the deposits of the bank were $600,000, the surplus $6,200, and the interest 1 percent quarterly. A savings bank opened in Baltimore in 1818 and three more were started in 1819 in Boston, New York, and Portland. During the next ten years, their number rapidly increased and in Massachusetts alone 17 banks were chartered. By 1840 there were 79,000 depositors in savings banks in the United States, owning $14 million of deposits. By 1850 there were 251,000 depositors with over $43 million in deposits. The availability of money among members of the middle class—who later became the best customers of life insurance—is revealed by the difficulty that savings banks had in limiting their accounts to the "frugal poor." The organization of the Massachusetts Hospital Life Insurance Co. responded to the increasingly pressing necessity for financial management of the expanding middle-class funds.[6]

* Smith shows that the aggregate value of houses and lands in seventeen states increased, as a group, almost threefold between 1799 and 1815, from $620 million to $1,632 million. (Price level rises only accounted for part of the increase.) James G. Smith, *The Development of Trust Companies in the United States*, p. 231. Taylor also refers to a rise in standards of living in 1799–1806. Quoted by Paul David, "The Growth of Real Product in the United States Before 1840," p. 154. See also J. Owen Stalson, *Marketing Life Insurance*, p. 54.

3. Urbanization

In 1811, a committee of the Pennsylvania House of Representatives reported that life insurance was "particularly necessary in the city and large towns."[7] Historians consider that the passage from the predominantly rural *Gemeinschaft,* close-knit eighteenth-century community to a more impersonal and urbanized *Gesellschaft* type of society, created the need for life insurance. North writes:

> The self-sufficiency of the family unit in an agricultural and domestic economy gave way to the economic interdependence of an industrial capitalist order. . . . The creation of a large section of the population without property and dependent on a money income . . . resulted in family insecurity. Life insurance was a contrivance to mitigate this insecurity.[8]

Urban dependence on daily wages has been particularly linked to life insurance. In the 1850s a legal textbook predicted: "As the class of persons dependent on a fixed income will be multiplied, the business of assuring lives will rapidly increase."[9] The greater success in England of life insurance was often attributed by contemporaries to a larger population dependent on a life income.[10] Current studies show that, independently of wealth, fewer people carry life insurance in rural areas than in urban areas. One 1956 study, for example, found that the percentage of insured farm operators was lower than for any other occupational group.[11] The acceleration of urbanization coincided in many states with the growth of life insurance. The percentage of people living in urban areas doubled between 1840 and 1860, with the greatest increase occurring in New York and Philadelphia, two cities in leading insurance states.[12] The first life insurance companies were organized in such heavily populated cities as New York, Philadelphia, Boston, and Baltimore, all leading centers of economic development and industrialization. This could suggest a spurious relation between urbanization and life insurance, with economic growth its major determinant. Just as urbanization has an independent effect on economic growth, however, it also seems to influence independently the growth of life insurance.

4. Actuarial Knowledge

For Davis and North, the successful innovation of life insurance in the United States "awaited the construction of an adequate mortality table." [13] Others, however, claim that the scientific and technological basis necessary for life insurance existed already by the end of the eighteenth century.[14] There is much controversy regarding what constitutes sufficient actuarial knowledge. Trenerry argues that the Romans developed life insurance despite their limited actuarial knowledge. He points to the existence of life insurance in Europe in the sixteenth and seventeenth centuries at a time when probability theory was hardly understood and in nations "no better equipped with [actuarial] knowledge than the Romans." [15] MacLean agrees that "scientific data of an advanced type is not absolutely necessary to write life insurance of a sort." [16]

The first mortality table was constructed in 1662 by Graunt in London.* In 1693 Edmund Halley presented to the Royal Academy an "Estimate of the Degree of Mortality of Mankind, drawn from curious tables of the births and funerals at the city of Breslau." † It is considered the first scientific mortality table. The development of mortality tables gradually became connected to the growth of life insurance in England. At first, the latter fed on data obtained from general population statistics, namely the Northampton and Carlisle tables.‡ In order to determine adequate premium rates, the companies began to keep accurate and reliable records of their own mortality experience. Soon life insurance became the source of new and more sophisticated actuarial knowledge. The first life table constructed on the basis of insurance data was completed in 1834 by the actuary of the Equitable Assurance of London.

Life insurance concerns led to the construction of the first American

* An earlier table existed in A.D. 364 among the Romans: Ulpian's table.

† These records were collected by the Prebendary of Breslau to dispel a common superstition about mortality in the seventh and ninth years of a person's life. He collected a list of 5,869 deaths from which he tabulated those that fell in the fateful years and those in between, proving there was no particular difference between them. August Meitzin, *History, Theory and Techniques of Statistics*. The sources of superstitious beliefs regarding death and dying will be discussed in chapter 4.

‡ The Northampton table, constructed in 1793 by Richard Price, contributed to the prosperity of life companies in an unexpected way. It greatly overestimated death rates, thereby yielding large profits for the companies. On the other hand, it hurt the annuity business badly.

mortality table in 1793. Edward Wigglesworth, its author, needed the information to organize a Congregational Ministers' Fund. Through the American Academy of Arts and Sciences he distributed 500 questionnaires on population statistics in Massachusetts and New Hampshire, and collected 62 bills of mortality containing records of 4,893 deaths.[17] No other native tables were constructed until 1814, when the Pennsylvania Company prepared two life-expectancy tables.*

American life insurance companies had the benefit of the English experience. English mortality tables were found to be safe, particularly as they tended to overestimate death rates. The Presbyterian and Episcopalian Funds relied on the Scottish mortality experience,† while the Pennsylvania Co. and the Massachusetts Hospital Life Insurance Co. used the Northampton table. From the 1830s to the 1860s, American companies based their premiums on the Carlisle table. Not until 1868 did Sheppard Homans, using the records of the Mutual Life Insurance Co., produce the first comprehensive table of American mortality, the American Experience table.[18]

The development of actuarial knowledge cannot be assigned a major role in determining the fate of life insurance in the United States. Similar English tables were used during both lean years and the successful decades. The major breakthrough in actuarial knowledge occurred in 1868, long after life insurance had established itself as a successful business.

5. Mortality Rates

The hypothesis that excessive mortality obstructed the progress of life insurance gained popularity in the early decades of the nineteenth century by reinforcing the exaggerated accounts of American insalubrity and

*This disinterest in life tables has been related to the apathy towards life insurance at that time. James H. Cassedy, *Demography in Early America*, p. 256.

†The Scottish data were calculated by the Widow's Fund of the Church of Scotland in 1744 using Halley's table. The Presbyterian and Episcopalian funds took additional precautions; ministers were forbidden to increase their insurance after joining the fund, to prevent older men from doing so. Full benefits were not paid unless fifteen annual premiums had been collected. See Shepard B. Clough, *A Century of American Life Insurance*, p. 23.

mortality then prevalent in Europe.* Contemporary analysts agree on the high incidence of mortality but dispute its effects. While some blame epidemics for the failure of insurance, others consider that premium rates were sufficiently high to protect the companies, which were also safeguarded by various residence, travel, and occupational restrictions imposed on policyholders. Buley reports that the recurrent epidemics of yellow fever, smallpox, and Asiatic cholera did not affect the actuarial calculations of the early American life companies. Fowler confirms that the Pennsylvania Co. remained unscarred by cholera outbreaks in that state.[19]

Systematic analysis of nineteenth-century mortality patterns have been undertaken only recently, and some of the findings suggest that mortality increased in the decades preceding the Civil War. This undercuts the argument that reduced mortality rates contributed to the expansion of life insurance during 1840 to 1860.

Yasuba argues that the probably higher death rate of the 1820s was a consequence of rapid urbanization.[20] Rising death rates in larger cities such as New York, Philadelphia, and Boston were already suggested by Jaffe and Lourie's 1830 life table.[21] Given that life insurance developed precisely in those cities, this fact again disrupts the link between high mortality and low insurance sales. This link is further upset by Buley and Keller's assumption that increased mortality contributed to the growth of life insurance during Civil War years by focusing "on the transience of life in the most dramatic possible way."†

In sum, the evidence on mortality rates is still too inconclusive and its

* Gilbert Chinard, "18th-Century Theories on America as a Human Habitat," pp. 27–57. The reverse was more probably true. A comparison by Wigglesworth between life expectancy rates of Massachusetts and Halley's Breslau table found that Americans lived longer. Walter S. Nichols, *Insurance Blue Book, 1876–77*, p. 15. For an explanation of earlier misperceptions and exaggerations of mortality rates by colonial Americans, see Maris A. Vinovskis, "Angels' Heads and Weeping Willows: Death in Early America," in Michael Gordon, ed. *The American Family in Social-Historical Perspective* (New York: St. Martin's Press, 1978), pp. 546–63.

† Morton Keller, *The Life Insurance Enterprise, 1885–1910*, p. 17. R. Carlyle Buley, *The Equitable Life Assurance Society of the United States*, p. 82. O'Donnell points to the "paradoxical" increase in life insurance applications in Philadelphia early in the nineteenth century, precisely when the city's death rate had doubled as a result of the arrival of germ-carrier overseas ships. Terence O'Donnell, *History of Life Insurance in Its Formative Years*, p. 441.

links to life insurance development too tenuous to rely on mortality as a decisive explanatory variable.

Still another demographic development with a possible impact on life insurance is the progressively widening gap between female and male mortality throughout the nineteenth century; mortality rates of females declined more rapidly. While the expectation of life at birth in Massachusetts for 1850 was 38.3 for males, it was 40.5 for females. By 1900 it became 48.23 for males but 51.08 for females. This had the effect of reducing the number of males in the total population; the number of states reporting an excess of females, for example, doubled between 1790 and 1900.[22] The longer expectation of life for women intensified the problem of economic security after their husbands' death.

6. Attitude of Government and Jurists

While the American public carried on a prolonged resistance to life insurance, their government and legal structures backed it almost immediately. The importance and uniqueness of this support becomes clear in a comparative perspective. In many European countries, governments and legislatures bitterly opposed, and at times banned, life insurance. After listening to various committee reports on the subject, the House of Representatives of Pennsylvania concluded in 1811 that life insurance "would be highly beneficial to many descriptions of citizens throughout the state."[23] An 1852 Assembly Document from New York State described life insurance customers as the "most prudent and cautious of our citizens."[24] Kimball points to the readiness of Wisconsin legislatures to grant special charters for the organization of insurance companies between 1838 and 1871.[25]

The legality of life insurance contracts was debated for the first time in 1815 in Massachusetts during the earliest life insurance case. The positive ruling of the court was of great significance for life insurance history. It declared:

> It has been made a question in the argument whether a policy of assurance upon a life is a contract which can be enforced by the laws of this state. It is true that no precedent has been produced from our own records of an action upon a policy of this nature. . . . By the common principles of law, however,

all contracts fairly made upon valuable consideration which infringe no law and are not repugnant to the general policy of the laws, are valid.

The judge perceived nothing in the contract "unfriendly to the morals or interests of the community." *

Governmental support was not only determined by morality. State governments were quick in perceiving that life insurance was a potential source of important revenue either through taxation or for charitable purposes, as in the case of the Massachusetts Hospital. Handlin points out that state governments were also interested in life insurance as an institution that could alleviate their responsibility to care for dependents.[26] The point was made by the House of Pennsylvania as early as 1811 when it saw that life insurance "might be the means of preventing many families of industrious tradesmen and others from becoming chargeable on the public charity." [27]

7. Marketing Techniques

The insurance "revolution" of the 1840s coincided with the organization of a powerful agency force by the newly established mutual companies. This chronological simultaneity grants credibility to the argument that the clue to the success of life insurance is to be found in the history of its marketing techniques. A firm believer in this hypothesis is Stalson, who criticizes other historians for giving too much attention to mortality tables and the founding dates of companies while ignoring "the astonishing influence that selling method has on life insurance development."[28] His *Marketing Life Insurance* is devoted to setting the record straight. Once this pivotal role is granted to marketing techniques, the development of life insurance can be neatly divided into preagent and postagent eras. Its failures were the result of passive methods of selling; its success, the work of agents. Stalson and White insist that had the Massachusetts Hospital Life Insurance Co. been at all sales-minded, it could

* Lord vs. Dall, *12 Mass. Reports 115.* William Dall, the defendant, sold a $5,000 policy on the life of Jabez Lord who was traveling from Boston to South America, naming his sister Nancy beneficiary. When the claim arose, Dall contested on the grounds that the contract of life insurance was illegal, that Nancy Lord did not have sufficient insurable interest in the life of her brother, and that Lord had deviated from his route.

have easily developed a flourishing life insurance business. To prove that life insurance was "waiting to be sold" after 1840, Stalson compares the policies of the Massachusetts Hospital Life Insurance Co. and the Pennsylvania Co. with those of the New York Life Insurance Co. This last company hired agents primarily to assist their customers in general financial matters, but they also became involved in selling insurance.* The New York Life sold more policies than the other two. Since the three companies offered almost identical rates and conditions, only the presence of agents can account for the success of the New York Life. Stalson and White also contend that it was the superior marketing practices of the mutuals that drove the earlier stock companies out of business. They overlook, however, their own evidence that in the early 1840s business was good even for companies that hired no agents. Some stock companies dropped life insurance because they had become primarily involved in other more lucrative concerns, such as trusts, capital investment, and the emerging commercial bank business.[29]

Agents were not magically effective under all circumstances. *A Brief History of the Mutual Life Insurance Company of New York*, published in 1857, refers to the decision of the first Board of Trustees to issue no policies until they had 250 initial subscribers to insure their lives. Yet: "Such was the apathy of the community, so little the interest then felt in the subject that although active and able agents were employed . . . 10 months elapsed before the list was complete." The effectiveness of agents is indisputable. It cannot, however, become a convincing explanatory variable until we find the reasons for its effectiveness. One must seek the changes in public receptivity that permitted agents' success, and investigate what made them indispensable to life insurance while hardly crucial to marine or fire insurance sales.†

8. Structure of the Companies

With the founding of the Mutual Life Insurance Company in 1842, mutuality replaced stock companies as the prevailing form of corporate

*Active soliciting only began with the mutuals.

†Even Stalson admits this at one point: "In the general quickening tempo of our living during the 'forties' and 'fifties,' I do not doubt that life insurance would have received a

organization of life companies. Between 1843 and 1847, seven major mutual life insurance companies were organized; by 1860, 34 companies had been started on a mutual basis.* *Stock companies* are organized by stockholders for their own profit. They raise the necessary capital and guarantee payment of the policies. In *mutual companies*, there is no initial capital stock and funds are built from premiums paid by policyholders. Policyholders divide all profits and also share in the management of the company. These differences between the two types of companies are relative. In essence, they are both mutuals, since "the payments of all participants aid each participant in case of need."[30] In practice, many stock companies offered dividends and many mutuals instituted fixed premiums. The extent of real influence by policyholders is also similarly limited. Even in the earlier and smaller companies, trustees did most of the decision making. The companies stressed mutuality in their advertisements. In 1846, the directors of the *Mutual Benefit Life Insurance Co.* reported:

> This very unprecedented business for so short a time, shows the greatly increased attention the subject of Life Insurance has obtained, and presenting in an extraordinary degree the preference for the purely Mutual system.[31]

Contemporary observers also credit the success of life insurance in the 1840s to their new organizational mold. From an economic perspective, mutuality meant the possibility of starting a company without a large amount of capital. This was particularly important at a time when few investors were eager to sink their money in uncertain enterprises.

Profitsharing also attracted policyholders who saw life insurance for the first time not simply as protection, but as an investment. From a noneconomic standpoint, mutuality emerged as the "proper" form for life insurance, considering the sacred nature of its responsibilities. Some supported it "for the sake of morality" and because it was "free from all selfish principles."[32] It is also suggested that mutuality was socially appropriate for the 1840s, a time of many cooperative undertakings, such as Brook Farm in New England and Robert Owen's New Harmony in Indiana.

---

larger share of public attention . . . even though we had not had the mutualizing and marketing development which came from within the industry." Stalson, *Marketing Life Insurance*, p. 228.

*Stock companies were not totally displaced by the mutuals. Some of the new companies in the forties were stock companies. Between 1859 and 1867, seventy-five new companies were organized, only two mutuals. Stalson, *Marketing Life Insurance*, p. 286.

For Stalson, however, mutuality was only a "helpful tool" to the more significant selling programs: "Mere mutuality, no matter how perfectly achieved, could never have won life insurance the following which aggressive marketing programs have."[33]

9. Economic Safety of the Companies

Early companies felt that a major obstacle to their expansion was the notion that they were financially unstable institutions engaged in hazardous speculations. Company publications repeatedly reassured the public of the safety of their operations. The introductory remarks of the first booklet published by an American life insurance company—the Pennsylvania Co., in 1814—already certified: "This institution is founded upon a solid and responsible basis possessing a capital adequate to meet all the engagements for the performance of which it may at any time hereafter be pledged."[34] It remained a concern through the 1840s. The Mutual Life Insurance Co. repeated that "no fears need be entertained for the ultimate safety of all contracts for insurance."[35] A quotation by Arthur De Morgan, actuary of the Equitable of London received wide circulation: "There is nothing in the commercial world that approaches even remotely to the security of a well established and prudently managed life assurance company."[36] Companies competed for business on the basis of their financial security. Some publicized a special fund that would "in no case be liable for the other debts, contracts, liabilities and engagement of the said company" other than life insurance.[37] Stock companies claimed that their system "guarantees a security for the payment of claims which the mutual plan lacks."[38]

The actual financial stability of the companies until 1850 should have sufficed to convince skeptics. There were no life insurance failures in the United States before 1850. The companies achieved this financial solvency despite limited sales. For instance, The Massachusetts Hospital Life Insurance Co. showed no losses in its first fifteen years and a total profit exceeding $50,000, and yet few policies were issued. Many of the companies incorporated between 1790 and 1842 discontinued their life insurance business, but without leaving unmet obligations.[39]

The financial stability of life insurance was not seriously threatened by the economic crises of 1837 and 1857. In Philadelphia, several hundred policies for hundreds of thousands of dollars were sold in 1837. Although the 1857 panic was started by the Ohio Life Insurance and Trust Company, this company had left the life insurance business long before then. The crisis did not break any of the established life companies.[40]

Since life insurance failures only began after 1850, they are meaningless as an explanation of low sales in the first half of the century. Public apprehension and its perception of life insurance as a hazardous enterprise, albeit unwarranted, may, however, have obstructed the progress of the enterprise.

10. Knowledge of Life Insurance Principles

Insurance histories often suggest that people did not buy policies because they did not understand the principles of life insurance.* On the other hand, Stalson claims that: "There was enough understanding of insurance in 1814 for agents to have built on in their advocacy with possible buyers."[41] From the establishment of life insurance to our own days, this has remained a controversial issue. Life insurance has been called an "Egyptian mystery,"[42] and a "riddle wrapped in a mystery inside an enigma."[43] It is claimed to be "impenetrable to logic"[44] and "almost as mysterious as love."[45] One writer considers: "There is nothing of equal monetary importance to the American public upon which ignorance is so widespread and phenomenally profound as it is upon the subject of life insurance."[46] Hendrick concludes that this is part of the "psychology of the trade."[47] The industry accuses the public of apathy.† In 1874, the *New York Daily Tribune* wrote: "If it were real estate instead of insurance that he was buying, he would carefully read and consider every word of the deed that conveyed it, would perhaps ask a lawyer to examine it. . . . How many people ever take life insurance with similar precau-

* T. R. Jencks, "Life Insurance in the United States," p. 9. More knowledge is not always correlated with greater acceptance of an innovation. For instance, the science and literature of life insurance were more developed on the European continent, but its business prospered better in England.

† A prominent insurance textbook considers that a life insurance policy is "simplicity itself." Joseph MacLean, *Life Insurance*, p. 178.

tions?"[48] The echo of this complaint reverberates through the years. In 1950, the comment was made that few people would willingly admit that they cannot understand the automobile business or the railroads or banks. Towards life insurance, however, they adopt "the peculiar position that ignorance is bliss."[49] That same year, a poll showed that over 90 percent of insurance owners neither read nor fully understood their policies.[50] In 1973, a study conducted by the Institute of Life Insurance found most people still "relatively uninformed about life insurance."[51] Other recent data confirm consumers' ignorance of the various policies available, the various options, the provisions in the contracts and price variations. The survey data further suggest that "most have no great interest in voluntarily acquiring additional information."*

Consumers lay the blame on the companies, complaining that their operations are abstruse and their contracts unintelligible. A leading consumer advocate, Herbert S. Dennenberg, accused life insurance companies of "inflicting confusion on the public with policies the public cannot understand."[52] In 1974, a *New York Times* article announced that while the Bible scored 67 in a readability test, and Einstein's relativity theory scored 18, insurance contracts score 10 or less.[53] The unnecessary complexity of modern contracts certainly discourages careful reading and contributes to public apathy. The same lack of information existed in the nineteenth century, however, when policies were much simpler documents, often a page long.[54] It had already concerned the mutuals as early as the 1840s; they included extensive material in their booklets on the principles of life insurance. The evidence makes it difficult to argue that lack of clarity was responsible for public apathy to life insurance before the 1840s. An increase in product knowledge, moreover, does not necessarily produce a positive change in consumer behavior toward life insurance. In their analysis of the role of knowledge in the diffusion of innovations, Rogers and Shoemaker conclude that "knowing about an innovation is often quite a different matter from using the idea."[55] Atti-

***Life Insurance Consumers* (Hartford, Conn.: Life Insurance Agency Management Association, 1973), p. 25. Joseph M. Belth, professor of insurance at Indiana University rejects current attempts to simplify the language of policies. In his testimony to the Senate Subcommittee on Antitrust and Monopoly of the Senate Judiciary Committee, Belth stated, "nobody's going to read it anyway." "New Policy Arises in Insurance Field: Language that is Readable," *New York Times*, August 11, 1976, p. 70. His colleague, Professor John D. Long suggests that companies should no longer issue policies; only wallet-sized cards or receipts.

tudes towards an innovation frequently intervene between the knowledge and decision functions. It is likely that ignorance of life insurance principles was as much a consequence of resistance to insuring lives as its cause.*

11. The Life Insurance Policy

Rates. Extravagant rates have been considered an obstacle to the early development of life insurance. It was said in the 1840s: "Many persons in New England and Massachusetts itself . . . resort to New York, Philadelphia and Baltimore for their life insurance . . . to obtain it at lower rates."[56] The Massachusetts Hospital Life Insurance Co. had no competitor in New England and no pressure to lower its rates. According to the legislative act of its incorporation, it was granted a monopoly in the life insurance business in exchange for an annual payment to the Massachusetts Hospital of one-third of the net profits from its life business.†

* Another reason why people did not read their insurance policies is that they are contracts of "adhesion," unilaterally drafted by one of the parties involved in the contractual relationship. The insured merely adheres to it with little choice as to its terms. On contracts of adhesion, see Edwin W. Patterson, *Cases and Materials on the Law of Insurance*, p. 646. Standardized contracts represent the rationalization of the contractual technique in the industrial economy, replacing individualized contracts which became dysfunctional to the expansion of business. Some existed, however, as early as the eighteenth century. Pothier in his *Traité du contrat d'assurance*, described the use of standardized policies for marine insurance in France:

'The agents had printed [policies] . . . in which one only had to fill in the name and characteristics of the vessel, the merchandise, the premium and the names of the contracting parties; and in which they inserted all imaginable clauses for their own advantage. The insured who received the [policy] only inquired the amount of the insurance and the price of the premium, signed them without paying any attention to the inserted clauses, which they did not understand. . . ." Quoted in M. Garcia-Amigo, *Condiciones Generales de los Contratos*, p. 16. My own translation.

Early life insurance contracts in the United States were already standardized. For a copy of the earliest Massachusetts Hospital Life Insurance Company policy from 1823, see Stalson, *Marketing Life Insurance*, pp. 736–37.

† The monopoly feature in itself was a deterrent to life insurance development in New England. Prospective stockholders were reluctant to share one-third of the net profits with the hospital. It was later decided that profit-sharing would take place after stockholders were paid a simple interest of 6 percent on their investment. Gerald T. White, *A History of the*

Mutuals reduced premium rates by several dollars. Stock companies charged approximately $32.80 for a nonparticipating life policy, while the new mutuals offered participating policies for $27.50 (age 35, rate per $1,000).[57] Mutuals also reduced the net cost of a policy by offering dividends. They lowered the cash outlay necessary for new applicants by accepting premium payment upon a part cash and part note system.* Rate reductions and other economic attractions of the mutuals, however, were not dramatic enough to change by themselves the pace of the industry. The case of the Girard Life Insurance Co. shows dividends were no magical solution. Although the Girard was the first company to offer dividends to the public, it sold no more policies than the regular stock companies.†

Policy contract. The policy offered by life insurance companies until 1860 hardly differed from the first policy of the Pennsylvania company in 1813, except for the dividends in participating companies.‡ The mutuals in the 1840s inherited without modifications the contracts of their unsuccessful predecessors. Their only guarantee was to pay the beneficiary, sixty days after having received due notice and proof of the death of the insured. Company booklets vowed to deal fairly in the case of lapsed policies or other eventualities, but these promises did not formalize into contract provisions. Nothing changed until 1861, when the efforts of Elizur Wright resulted in the first nonforfeiture law in Massachusetts. As a result, companies could no longer appropriate as theirs the premiums already paid by withdrawing members but had to provide single premium term insurance for as long a period as the value of the policy would pay.

Massachusetts Hospital Life Insurance Company, p. 10; Buley, *The Equitable Life Assurance Society*, p. 31; Jencks, "Life Insurance in the United States," 119.

* The note system was later subjected to severe criticism from those who felt that it destroyed the financial stability of companies whose assets consisted of personal notes rather than cash.

† Predictably, Stalson considers rates and dividend appeal secondary to selling techniques. North similarly concludes that selling techniques were more important than rates in the late nineteenth century. He attributes the greater success of the high-priced tontine policies over far less expensive regular policies issued by solid, responsible insurance companies, to the aggressive marketing techniques of the leading companies which sold tontines. Douglass C. North, "Capital Accumulation in Life Insurance between the Civil War and the Investigation of 1905," p. 52.

‡ The pioneering Presbyterian policies already contained most of the provisions. Alexander Mackie, *Facile Princeps: The Story of the Beginning of Life Insurance in America*, pp. 2, 6.

Companies were required by law to pay the claim if death took place within the term insurance period. In 1880, a stronger Massachusetts law guaranteed a cash surrender value for every life policy after the payment of two annual premiums. An incontestability clause was added to the contract in 1864,* and a period of grace was legally established in 1898. Since all these improvements are post-1860, they can hardly account for a transformation in business that occurred almost two decades earlier.

After examining a variety of explanations of the diffusion of life insurance, one is left with an incomplete picture and many unanswered questions. Several factors, namely the degree of economic growth and urbanization, were admittedly necessary prerequisites for its development, while others contributed to the industry's growth either directly or indirectly. Yet part of the story remains untold. The impact of noneconomic variables on the adoption of life insurance has never received serious consideration. Before turning to the United States, Chapter III examines the impact of noneconomic variables on the adoption of life insurance in other countries and in different types of insurance.

* This clause limits the time during which a company can contest the truth of an applicant's statements. Previously, life insurance companies were free to forfeit a policy for almost any inaccuracy in the information of the insured, however trivial or unintentional.

Chapter 3
A Comparative Perspective

> We daily insure our property against fire and other casualty for a certain period, no disaster happens—we paid our money but for the satisfactory and strengthening feeling of security, and yet we renew our policies. Why not do the same in life insurance?[1]

> We know that in some places the ideas of healthy morality have been so sullied and stifled by the evil spirit of commerce that insurance on the lives of men has been authorized. But such arrangements have always been forbidden in France.[2]

The diffusion of American life insurance was more than a matter of economics or sophisticated actuarial tables. The business challenged deeply institutionalized values relating to death and concerning the role of Providence in the social order. It defied as well a set of cultural and religious beliefs and ideas on risk and gambling. The relationship between cultural variables and life insurance can be tested by means of comparative analysis between types of insurance. People's values and ideologies were not involved to the same extent with sunken ships or burnt property as they were with death. It should be determined whether the absence of cultural resistance speeded up the adoption of fire and marine insurance. If so, it would strengthen the hypothesis attributing the slow and difficult development of life insurance to the influence of cultural factors. Other questions are raised. Was the connection between cultural response and the growth of life insurance significant in other nations, with different cultural backgrounds?[3]

The development of fire and marine insurance in the United States was considerably easier than that of life insurance. Introduced only a few decades earlier than life insurance, fire and marine had developed firm roots by the end of the eighteenth century, with 33 companies doing both fire and marine business. Eighty-six insurance charters were granted by the various states between 1794 and 1810.* In 1811, there were 11

* Some of these companies were authorized to issue life insurance but never did. Walter S. Nichols, *Insurance Blue Book, 1876–1877*, p. 12.

marine insurance companies in Philadelphia alone. By 1841, while life insurance in Boston did not reach $5 million, the city had $50 million in fire risks and about $39 million in marine insurance.[4]

These early fire and marine insurance companies were, for the most part, financially successful. The directors of Connecticut's first insurance company, incorporated only in 1795, were already boasting in 1814 of its prosperous business.[5] The Massachusetts Mutual Fire Insurance Company organized in 1797, had over $14 million of insurance in force by 1855.[6]

Marine insurance was the first type to be established, and it developed with "inconceivable rapidity," becoming so profitable "that it may truly be said to have laid the foundation of many fortunes in our country." As early as 1721, it was said to be "very much for the Ease and Benefit of the Merchants and Traders."[7] In that year, John Copson opened in Philadelphia the first marine insurance office. The demand grew, and by 1750, offices operated in Boston, Philadelphia, New York, and other commercial centers. Marine policies were also being sold extensively by private underwriters. The Insurance Company of North America became the first incorporated marine office in 1794.* By 1798, it was collecting nearly $1,500,000 in premiums from Philadelphia alone.[8]

Fire insurance developed somewhat later than marine insurance.† The first company, the Philadelphia Contributionship for the Insuring of Houses from Losses by Fire, opened in 1752. After only one year of operation, it had $108,360 of insurance in force. Other fire insurance companies organized during the latter part of the eighteenth century were

* The company chose marine insurance because it was an "established line of business" Marquis James, *Biography of a Business*, p. 18. By the end of the eighteenth century, marine insurance covered a wide variety of risks:

'Perils of the seas, men of war, fire, enemies, pirates, rovers, thieves, jettisons, letters of mart, and countermart, surprizals, takings at sea, arrests, restraints, and detainments of all kings, princes, or people of what nation, condition, or quality soever . . . and all other losses, perils or misfortunes, that have or shall come to the hurt, detriment or damage of the said vessel or any part thereof." P. Henry Woodward, *Insurance in Connecticut*, p. 131.

Fire insurance offered less opportunity for profits, since 2 already established and prosperous Philadelphia companies cornered the market. As to life insurance, it was a "new and undeveloped thing of which the public was skeptical." James, *Biography*, p. 18.

† Fire insurance companies were, however, probably incorporated before marine companies. Since the insurance of ships and cargoes were done for specific voyages there was less pressing need for a permanent capital fund. Edwin Merrick Dodd, *American Business Corporations until 1860*, p. 218.

similarly successful. The Insurance Company of North America decided to expand into fire insurance, and after a mediocre first year its premiums increased fivefold to $10,600 in 1796, only two years after its founding.[9]

The differences between the adoption of life insurance and other types of insurance were not simply a matter of timetables, but extended to the more significant issue of the form of their diffusion. Fire and marine insurance companies were established in response to public demand for their services. Life insurance companies, on the other hand, forced their product upon an unwilling clientele. It is indicative that while life insurance was first recommended by legislative committees, it was "the desire of a number of inhabitants . . . to have their estates insured from loss of fire"[10] that led to the formation of fire insurance companies. While fire and marine protection was for the most part sought by the public on their own, "a great effort has to be put forth, before men can be prevailed upon to insure their lives."[11] The *American Life Assurance Magazine* presented the differences clearly:

> As a general thing parties having property to insure on land or water required little solicitation on the part of agents to induce them to attend to their individual interests—merchants, manufacturers or storekeepers, did not require to be hunted up, repeatedly visited, or earnestly importuned. . . . But it was not so with the Life Assurance business. . . . In too many instances the Life insurance agent had months and years of unremunerative toil to perform, before he could prevail upon the father of a family to insure his life.[12]

The role of the various insurance agents reflects the difference in public response. While active solicitation by its agents is considered among the crucial factors that led to the adoption of life insurance, fire agents and marine brokers played relatively minor roles. A history of Connecticut insurance recalls how "persons desiring [fire] insurance solicited it as a privilege from the officers of the company."[13] Although fire insurance companies widely advertised during the eighteenth and early nineteenth centuries, their organizers felt that there was "no need to urge prospective clients."* Actual fires were more convincing than efficient salesmen. It has been suggested that demand for fire insurance first emerged as a result of the fires in Boston, Philadelphia, and major cities in North Carolina during the late seventeenth and early eighteenth centuries. In 1835, many property-owners "who had given little thought to fire insurance"

* Daniel Hawthorne, *The Hartford of Hartford*, p. 28. Fire insurance companies were using several hundred lines per insertion in newspapers when the common practice was half a dozen lines. Frank Presbrey, *The History and Development of Advertising*, p. 417.

were persuaded by the devastating New York fire of that year.[14] In marine insurance, the agent was comparatively rare. Unlike life agents, marine brokers do not have an agency contract with a specific insurance company but work with several companies. Although paid by the underwriter, he is legally the agent of the merchant or vessel owners whom he represents. Moreover, the contact between underwriters and clients is often worked out directly by personal interview and occasionally through the mail.[15]

Life insurance companies could not rely on passive marketing techniques. Unlike fire and marine insurance, they had to overcome powerful cultural resistance to their product. This explains the primary role of the agent, since energetic salesmanship became indispensable in breaking through client reluctance to deal objectively with the economics of death.

Well aware of their distinctiveness, life insurance men even now consider all other agents as "order takers and not salesmen."[16] The *sui generis* ideological qualities of life insurance were partly responsible for the failure of some of the early companies that attempted to combine it with fire and marine insurance. This "unwise and imprudent . . . union of things dissimilar,"[17] as it was labeled, received almost no public support.

Contemporary observers, perplexed by a public that was eager to buy fire and marine protection but staunchly resisted insuring their lives, asked: "Where is the moral distinction between insuring a ship for a voyage with a hundred souls on board and insuring the life of an individual?"[18] They marveled at how "readily men admit the force [of insurance] by insuring their houses, their stores and their merchandise against fire . . . by insuring their ships against danger," but would not insure their own lives.[19] The *Insurance Journal* discussed in its pages the "vast amount of difference in the patronage given to the two kinds of insurance, fire and life,"[20] and insurance booklets complained of the curious discrimination. In *Father's Life Boat*, a popular treatise on life insurance published in 1871, the writer comments: "There are some men who insure their property against loss by fire who seem to be opposed to life insurance. As if a man's house or his store could be worth more to his family than his life."[21] The preference for fire and marine insurance was often attributed to the selfishness of people. To its advocates, life insurance was the "pure, ripe fruit of absolute unselfishness," while "selfishness alone prompts men to resort to fire and marine insurance."[22] Prejudice against life insurance was justified by the ungrounded contention that fire and marine companies had greater financial stability and better scientific grounding. The *Journal of Commerce* conveyed this feeling: "Public opinion favors the notion that fire and marine insurance are both based upon broad and settled principles and that there is a certainty about them that life insurance does not and cannot possess."[23] Nichols has also commented on the "universal" public confidence in fire insurance, particularly during the first part of the nineteenth century.[24] The perception of life insurance as unscientific and unreliable was guided more by prejudice than by fact. In reality, both fire and marine insurance were laggard in knowledge as well as safety, but that backwardness did not stand in the way of their progress.

Insurance historians agree that at the beginning of the nineteenth century there had been no attempt to generalize the laws underlying fire insurance; the business remained, therefore, a matter of "pure chance."[25] As a result, premiums were often grossly inadequate and it was not unusual for a company to issue single policies for sums exceeding their annual income. Scientific understanding of marine insurance was equally limited. In 1839, marine underwriters, impressed with the "total lack of data on which to write marine risks and the losses which they had experienced," finally began collecting systematic information for their business.[26]

Life insurance became defensive in the face of constant accusations of unreliability. The *Insurance Monitor* explained: "The facts upon which life insurance is based are ascertained with an accuracy and are susceptible of mathematical calculation to a degree to which fire and marine insurance can furnish no parallel." The *Insurance Journal* asserted that the average chance of a person's death is "more certain and better known than is the average change of his property being destroyed by fire."[27]

Indeed, the actuarial foundations for an extensive life insurance business had already been developed by the early part of the nineteenth century. As to the economic reliability of life insurance companies, it has already been indicated that there were no failures until 1850. In sharp contrast, the history of fire insurance during the first part of the nineteenth century was filled with "vicissitudes, surprises and disasters." Fire insurance company losses between 1831 and 1850 were so great that all their premiums in the United States plus many additional millions of capital were needed to meet them.[28] Great fires ruined the companies. The New York fire of 1835 brought losses estimated at $15 million, and bankrupted all but three insurance companies in the city. Similarly, the history of marine insurance until 1830 was one of "periodical prosperity and depression." Although the volume of business was large, losses connected with the Napoleonic wars and the captures, detentions, and litigations involving American vessels made it a "highly speculative" business.[29]

Since the supposedly superior reliability of fire and marine insurance is unsubstantiated by fact, one must look elsewhere for an explanation of the prejudice against life insurance. The fact was that life insurance was considered by many as morally inferior to other types of insurance. Some were outspoken about their moral preferences. Prominent leaders in the business community considered it "unjust" and irresponsible not to insure property, but opposed life insurance because "providence intends that we take care of the future by taking care of the present" and life insurance "paralyzes a man's efforts."[30] Similarly, a *New York Times* editorial stated:

> In its application to fire and marine risks [insurance] is generally safe enough, because those are contingencies which none will court and against which insurance will make men in general none the less careful. But very much of the current talk about life assurance as the grand panacea for all possible evil and as the main reliance of all men who live on salaries or fixed incomes is calculated to encourage reliance upon something besides economy and industry and to lead accordingly to the relaxation and decay of those cardinal virtues of society.[31]

Insuring against a burning home or a sinking ship created fewer doubts in most people's minds than insuring their own lives.* Although they

*Fire and marine insurance have also been occasionally attacked as ungodly arrangements, but the opposition was not significant enough to affect their development. Ibsen in his play, *Ghosts* (New York: Bantam Books, 1971, pp. 81–82) offers a version of religious bias against fire insurance in Norway. One of the characters in this play, Manders, a pastor in the parish, argues that insuring an orphanage would "scandalize the community" for it would symbolize a lack of "proper reliance on divine protection." Earlier forms of marine insurance such as the medieval maritime loans were considered equally sinful, but for different reasons. Maritime loans, already practiced by ancient Greeks and Romans, were ordinary loans joined to a contract of insurance; the insurance premium being covered by a high rate of interest on the loans. This was regarded as a violation of the prohibition against usury, and maritime insurance was condemned by Christian and Jewish religious leaders in the Middle Ages. The objection, however, was against usury and not the insurance principle per se. Aleatory contracts of insurance without loans involved were apparently acceptable in Jewish Law. Indeed, after the sixteenth century when maritime loans were replaced by independent contracts of premium insurance, rabbinic law no longer objected to insurance. The legality of property insurance was upheld by canon lawyers and moralists as early as the fifteenth century. Stephen M. Passamaneck, *Insurance in Rabbinic Law*.

sought to justify their dislike in less subjective terms, it was largely the incompatibility of the idea of life insurance with other deep-seated values that led people to resist its development.

Comparative data from other societies further attest to the powerful effect of values on the development of life insurance. Morally condemned and often legally banned, life insurance did not develop in most countries until the mid-or late nineteenth century. During the sixteenth and seventeenth centuries, most European nations considered life insurance "unfit and improper."[32] *L'Ordonnance des Pays Bas* declared life insurance illegal in 1570; it was followed by *L'Ordonnance d'Amsterdam* in 1598, the Code of Middelbourg in 1600, *L'Ordonnance de Rotterdam* in 1604, the Swedish code of 1666, and the French *Ordonnace sur la Marine* of 1681.[33] To this day, life insurance is still not legally recognized in Saudi Arabia and Libya, where Islamic law prohibits all speculation on human life.[34]

Life insurance made no significant inroads in Europe until the 1860s. Up to the mid-nineteenth century there were no companies in Denmark, Norway, Sweden, Spain, Italy, Austria, Hungary, or Switzerland.[35] Although one company was organized in Belgium in 1824, life insurance received legal recognition there only in 1874. Germany, which later became a leading insurance center, had no life companies until 1827; 9 were organized between 1827 and 1852 with only disappointing results.[36] In 1860, Germans still considered life insurance a "doubtful novelty."[37] Similarly, Canada had no life insurance companies until 1847. In Japan, the first company was started only in 1881, and even then with only lukewarm public response.[38]

Meanwhile, fire and marine insurance were well established in most of these countries by the end of the eighteenth century and prospered with relative ease. For instance, by 1789, Denmark, Germany, Norway, Spain, and Sweden all had fire and marine insurance companies. Of Belgium's 31 insurance companies in 1857, only 2 sold life policies.[39] The acceptance of life insurance was not greater in countries where its principles were well known or its statistics better developed. Population statistics and actuarial knowledge progressed in France and in Sweden without stimulating the growth of life insurance. Dissatisfied with most explanations of the slow growth of life insurance, some observers have turned to subjective factors, suggesting for instance that national character was possibly a determinant of life insurance acceptance. One recent cross-national comparison concluded that "use of insurance among several nations is not completely explained by the respective levels of national income" and that it partially depends on the "ethics and morality of the society."[40] The different levels of life insurance purchases in England and America in the 1850s were attributed to national character, as were differences between Germany and England at that time.[41] To the French, the success of life insurance in England was a result of their love for gambling, "so natural to the English character."[42] To the English, it was Frenchmen who could "understand lotteries, tontines, speculation but not life insurance."[43] They suggested that life insurance was discouraged in France by the "light hearted inconsideration"[44] of the people and "the great infirmity of their public morals."[45] The concept of national character was also used as an explanation by the *Insurance Monitor*:

> A martial people, such as the French, who delight in the heroism of the battle field preferring the conquest of their eagles to the more peaceful conquests of individuality are not likely to encourage a benevolent system based upon the care of life for the sake of future generations.[46]

Unfortunately, national character is a concept too broad and too vague to afford serious explanatory power. To understand the development and the sources of resistance to life insurance, its growth will be traced in two countries which represent the two extremes of life insurance development: England, where its validity and legality were never questioned and it early became an important institution, and France, where opposition to life insurance reached its greatest peak.

ENGLAND

Continental observers were baffled by the easy development of life insurance in England.[47] The British example was used in America to goad an unenthusiastic public. Company publications asked: "Where is the evidence that an American loves his family less . . . than an Englishman?"[48] At a time when most European nations were banning life insurance, Queen Elizabeth in 1574 granted one Richard Chandler the right to issue any type of insurance policy. Legal and governmental support continued; in 1721 the British legislature called life insurance "advantageous and useful,"[49] and in 1852 Parliament described policyholders as the "best and most deserving class of society."[50] The Amicable Society, England's first life insurance company, started in 1706 and had obtained a full membership of 2,000 by its second year, despite its expensive premiums and uncertain actuarial foundations.[51] By 1800, there were 6 life insurance offices in England.[52] The Equitable, founded in 1762, had by then 5,129 policies outstanding amounting to £3,900,000 of insurance.[53] By the 1820s life insurance was as much an "acknowledged part of the London business scene" as were fire and marine insurance companies. Companies multiplied rapidly: between 1803 and 1808, 8 new companies were formed; between 1815 and 1830, 29 additional ones. Another 56 offices were successfully established between 1830 and 1844, so that by the early 1850s there were at least 150 life insurance offices in England.[54] In all of Europe at that time there were no more than 44 life companies.[55] The annual premiums collected by British life companies in 1859 were an estimated $30 million, compared to $7 million in the United States.[56]

Given this astonishing comparative success, it is puzzling that some insurance historians still ask, "Why was British life assurance so slow in developing?" Their contention is that British life insurance did not develop significantly until 1800, forty years after the founding of the Equitable and almost a century after the organization of their first life insurance company. The interpretation of this delay between inception and adoption is significant: the lack of respectability of the idea of life insurance is considered as a major obstacle.[57] Supple also suggests that among the primary reasons for the relatively slow development of life insurance was "the slowness with which the habit of insurance spread among potential policyholders."[58] The English case indicates that even where it developed most easily, resistance to the idea of life insurance interfered with its growth.

FRANCE

If life insurance had to fight only minor skirmishes in England, it fought its fiercest battle in France, where many considered it "repugnant to French sensitivity."[59] As late as 1861, France was the "only civilized country in which life insurance has not been fully understood,"[60] and in 1869 Sheppard Homans wrote about how incongenial life insurance was with French soil.[61] The Compagnie Royale, the first French life insurance company, was organized in 1787. "Its statutes were wise, its prospectus marked by a deep knowledge of life insurance," but the company failed within a few years despite solid financial backing and expert actuarial advice.[62] Such was also the fate of other companies formed at the beginning of the nineteenth century. The *Edinburgh Review* of 1827 spoke of their "very active, persevering and unsuccessful efforts":

> They have distributed booklets in great quantities as well as prospectuses and reports; but all in vain. They have been forced to withdraw their agents from many large cities as a result of their total lack of success. Even in Paris, there is total indifference towards this subject.[63]

Life insurance remained an "abandoned field."[64] In 1850, while England boasted $583 million worth of life insurance, France had $33 million. The business of all French companies in 1854 represented about one-quarter the amount done in 1800 by the Equitable of London alone. In 1869, American companies issued as much life insurance as French companies did in the fifty-eight years between 1819 and 1877.[65]

French antipathy was directed only toward life policies. Fire and marine insurance were accepted by the people and encouraged by the law. In 1807, at a time when life insurance had become illegal, the French Counsellors of State declared marine insurance an "excellent contract, a noble product of human genius."[66] Fire insurance likewise remained uncensured and expanded with ease and speed. One writer wondered why the Frenchman, "understands the need of insuring his house and his farm . . . [but] he cannot grasp the need to protect himself against the risk of death."[67] Several studies conclude that widespread popular prejudice and hostility were the most important obstacles for the development of life insurance in France. Meuron, for instance, writes:

> From whence this reluctance? What are the causes for the slow reception of an institution which has produced such positive results in other countries? We believe that it is mostly the result of the prejudice that still exists against life insurance.[68]

It is indeed hard to pin down more objective arguments. As one writer commented:

> From the closest study of life insurance . . . I have arrived at the conviction that there exists nothing in their organization, no radical defect, no important imperfection which can explain the prejudice against them in France.[69]

Insufficient actuarial knowledge was not a reason. In 1825, Juvigny wrote:

> It is doubly surprising if one considers that the mathematics that are the basis of insurance shine most brightly [in France] and that probability theory essential to insurance, was not only started here but is today better developed than among the English who are claimed the authors of such institutions.

In 1806, Duvillard had already produced a mortality table which was considered "a more exact and complete table than those published in all other countries."[70] Economic considerations did not create the resistance toward purchasing life insurance. Premiums were not exorbitant: "In France . . . though premiums are moderate, more so than in England, and the companies are in good credit, they have met with little encouragement to their strenuous exertions to spread the practice."[71] Nor was it an issue of meager family budgets. Money was available, but the French chose to spend it in other ways. Tontines, for instance, became a very popular investment. In contrast to life insurance, one did not have to "die to win": instead, the benefits were collected by the last survivor of a group insured. Between 1819 and 1821, with only 1 life insurance company in business, 9 tontines were authorized by the government. Twenty additional tontines were organized between 1841 and 1846. Only 8 life insurance companies emerged during those years, 4 of which quickly dissolved and sought authorization to become tontine associations. By mid-century, some 18 tontines were still running, with 395,446 'policies' representing subscriptions of nearly $80 million.[72]

Annuities were another popular investment among the French. An annuity contract is a promise to pay a fixed amount of money periodically during the lifetime of the annuitant. The payment yielded from the money invested in an annuity is larger than that of a regular investment. The most severe critics of life insurance gave their full support to annuity contracts.[73]

The partiality for tontines and annuities has been interpreted as a sign of French selfishness and their "decided preference for the insurance of sums payable during the lifetime of the assured."[74] But the sources of French prejudice against life insurance go far deeper than mere selfishness. The repudiation of all contracts dealing with the economic consequences of someone's death constitutes an integral part of French civil law. One of the major recommendations of the group commissioned by Napoleon Bonaparte to draft the French Civil Code was article 1130: "Future events may be the object of a contract. One may not, however, forgo a succession before its inception nor enter into any contract related to that succession."[75] That is, French law allowed contracts on future events such as the harvest of fruits or animals to be born. It excluded, however, successorial contracts which speculated with future events dependent on a man's death. Relinquishing an inheritance before the death of the grantor was held equally offensive to morality as a contract of sale on that inheritance.[76] There was precedent for this aversion to successorial contracts in Roman Law. French jurists, however, tightened the rule. While Roman law had approved of successorial contracts with the consent of the individual whose succession was the object of the contract, French law refused to recognize even such cases. Trusts were also illegal in France. In a trust, the person arranges for his money to be administered after his or her death by an individual or an institutional trustee. The major legal argument against contracts of succession and against life insurance was the danger of *votum mortis;* the notion that contracting for events dependent on someone's death could evoke the desire to accomplish that death in one of the parties to such a contract.[77]

Legal history is the most revealing source for understanding the development of life insurance in France. As early as 1589 *Le Guidon de La Mer,* a treatise on mercantile law, defined life insurance as "contrary to good morals" and condemned it. Its decision was reinforced by the *Ordonnance de la Marine* in 1681. The prohibition was unanimously supported by the most prominent French jurists of the eighteenth century. In a commentary on the 1681 decision, Valin spoke of the immorality of putting a monetary price on human life. Emerignon wrote: "A human life cannot be the object of commerce and it is disgraceful that death should become the source of commercial speculation."[78] Pothier likewise suggested: "The life of a freeman not being susceptible of appraisal it therefore cannot be the subject of an insurance contract: liberum corpus aestimationem non recipit."[79] Insurance of blacks was acceptable: as chattels, their monetary value could be estimated without an ethical breach. In 1793, the French revolutionary government made illegal all life insurance companies, on the grounds that: "Insurance replaces the service of humanity by the service of money and undermines the sense of compassion which should form the basis of society."[80] Nineteenth-century jurists continued to oppose life insurance. In 1804, the authors of the French Civil Code made no mention of life insurance, except for one commentary by Portalis that "these deals regarding the death or life of a man are hateful and dangerous."[81] In 1807, the Commercial Code also ignored life insurance. The prevalent feeling was, as expressed by one jurist Boulay-Patty, that life insurance should be left "to our English neighbours."[82]

Life insurance was given no legal recognition in France until 1850, when it was indirectly included under a general insurance tax. As late as 1861, a judge denounced the immorality and illegality of life insurance in a famous trial of a man accused of killing a woman to collect insurance money. By the end of the nineteenth century, the status of life insurance had significantly improved, as did its sales. Between 1819 and 1859, 40,258 policies had been written for 354 million francs, while in 1889 alone almost 38,000 policies were issued for a total of 393 million francs. Progress was also reflected in the changed attitude of the new generation of jurists, with whom life insurance became a legitimate and popular dissertation topic.[83] Like the enemies of life insurance in the past, the new supporters of life insurance focused more on morality than on economics. They sought to "loudly proclaim the morality of insurance."[84] One writer suggested: "Life insurance is not opposed to morality. On the contrary, the idea of insurance is an excellent touchstone to detect moral men; it can only be adopted by the moral elite."[85]

The task of comparative analysis in sociology is testing hypothesis about relationships between variables in different settings within a society or in more than one society. Significant variability between types of insurance in the United States underscores the unique ideological characteristics of life insurance. The differences between property insurance and life insurance do not lie within the organizational or economic framework of the insurance companies but in differential public response. Americans readily insured homes, stores, and vessels because the economic rationality of their investment was not disturbed by cultural considerations. Instead, insuring life was staunchly resisted as a challenge to powerful cultural and religious values.

Cross-cultural and across-time comparisons confirm the inhibiting effect of noneconomic factors. As early as the sixteenth and seventeenth centuries, European nations condemned and banned life insurance on cultural grounds. Even in England where the compatibility of life insurance with other values was greater, the business was checked by cultural opposition. Ideological antagonism to life insurance remains unabated in a few non-Western nations; Saudi Arabia and Libya to this day deny legal recognition to the industry. Variability between kinds of insurance is constant cross-culturally; most countries opposed to life insurance developed fire and marine insurance companies early and without significant opposition.

Chapter 4
The Impact of Values and Ideologies on the Adoption of Social Innovations:
Life Insurance and Death

> We especially protest against insurance being included in the category of dry subjects. Of course, we at once admit, that a volume of insurance tables is not calculated to beguile the general reader. . . . But behind the scenes of every office a dozen little dramas are enacted daily. . . . As to the prospect of death [life insurance] is necessarily associated with this topic. Indeed, next to affection and religion itself insurance has done more to smooth the pillow of the dying than any other agency in the world.[1]

Many diffusion studies claim that economic factors can adequately explain the adoption of innovations. Davis and North argue that the primary push for new institutional arrangements lies mainly in the possibility of profits that cannot be obtained within existing structures.[2] But the role of values and ideologies should not be underestimated. Barber is critical of the view that ideology is always the dependent variable in processes of social change. He suggests: "In systems of whatever degree of comprehensiveness ranging from the low extreme of a specialized dyad to the high extreme of a self-sufficient society, ideological systems may be either independent or dependent variables."[3] A comprehensive cross-cultural analysis of the diffusion of innovations lists the value compatibility of an innovation among the five most significant characteristics that determine its adoption or rejection.* The adoption of an incompati-

This chapter appeared in slightly different form in "Human Values and the Market: The Case of Life Insurance and Death in 19th-Century America," (November 1978), *American Journal of Sociology* 84:591–610. University of Chicago Press.

* The other four are: (*a*) *relative advantage* of the innovation over the preceding system, (*b*) *complexity* of the innovation, (*c*) *triability* or the possibility of trying the innovation on a limited basis, and (*d*) *observability* of the results of the innovation. Rogers and Shoemaker, *Communication*, ch. 4. Marketing studies have also shown that the beliefs of customers often have a greater role in determining purchases than the objective qualities of the product. See "The Analysis of Consumer Actions," by Arthur Kornhauser and Paul F. Lazarsfeld, in Paul F. Lazarsfeld and Morris Rosenberg, eds., *The Language of Social Research* (New York: Free Press, 1955), p. 399.

ble innovation often requires the prior adoption of a new set of values. Upgrading the role of cultural legitimation does not mean excluding interest factors, but rather incorporating both profitability and compatibility in a multivariable explanatory model.*

Unfortunately, most research has concentrated on technical innovations, producing as a result extensive data on the spread of drugs and fertilizers but little on the diffusion of social innovations.[4] Life insurance offers a unique possibility of examining the relationship between values and the adoption of a social innovation. The next two chapters will be concerned with some of the specific ideological issues involved in the legitimation of life insurance. The analysis turns by necessity first to death because of its intimate connection with life insurance.[5]

We will touch on the impact of cultural values regarding death on the development of life insurance and then examine some ways in which the novel institution influenced prevailing values. Opposition to life insurance resulted from the cultural prescription condemning financial evaluation of human lives. On the other hand, life insurance was made acceptable by another set of values that legitimized the symbolic association between money and death. Magical beliefs and superstitions regarding death and dying also stood against life insurance, while the ideological affinity between life insurance and an emerging "active" orientation toward death and disease constituted a source of cultural support for the institution.

PROFANE MONEY

In the mostly agricultural society of eighteenth-century America, the need for institutionalized systems to deal with the economic consequences of death was less urgent than it later became. Widows and orphans were able to stay on the land and provide for themselves. Voluntary associations supplied the only source of formalized assistance. These associations serviced particular national groups, such as the English, Scots, Irish and Germans. Although they were built on unsound actuarial principles and offered meager benefits to their members, their or-

*Bernard Barber refers to the erroneous prejudice that "Theories which state that values are one set of determining variables *really* mean that values is the determining variable." Barber, "The Limits of Equality: Social Stratification in Complex Societies," p. 7.

ganizational form is a precedent for later life insurance companies.[6] The nineteenth century ushered in a series of financial institutions specializing in the economic management of death, the most important being trust companies and life insurance. While voluntary associations were non-profit organizations and served other functions aside from financial aid,* the sole business of the new institutions was economic provision for death.

Trust companies, like life insurance companies, replaced more informal systems with professional management. White indicates: "In offering to accept money or securities in trust the company had moved into a field which historically had been occupied by private parties rather than by a specialized financial institution."[7] Traditionally, trustees had been the close friends or relatives of the man who placed his property in trust.

Another "family and neighborhood" affair that became a business was the funeral. The appearance of professional funeral undertaking is also traced to the beginning of the nineteenth century. Previously, the physical care and disposal of the dead had been mostly provided by neighbors and relatives, but in the nineteenth century it became a financially rewarded occupational specialty.[8] This process of formalization extended to the drafting of wills. The largely informal, generalized provisions drafted by a man shortly before his death turned into a highly structured system of estate planning in the nineteenth century.[9]

Thus, life insurance was part of a general movement to rationalize and formalize the management of death. The new institutions were primarily concerned with death as a major financial episode. Their business was to make people plan and discuss their death in monetary terms. Life insurance defined itself as: "The capitalization of affection. . . . Tears are nothing but salt water, to preserve a fresh grief, we suppose. Insurance is business, genuine, old-fashioned sixteen-ounce precaution."[10] Its avowed goal was to encourage men to "make their own death the basis of commercial action."[11] This was no simple enterprise. Putting death on the market offended a system of values that upheld the sanctity of human life and its incommensurability. It defied a powerful normative pattern: the division between the marketable and the nonmarketable, or the sacred and the profane. Durkheim has written: "The mind irresistibly refuses to

* They had institutionalized certain forms of emotional support for the family at the time of death. For example, all members were expected to attend a fellow member's funeral and console the bereaved. Absentees were fined. On other functions of voluntary associations see Roy Lubove, *The Struggle for Social Security*, pp. 1–2.

allow the two [sacred and profane] to be confounded or even to merely be put into contact with each other."[12] Sacred things are distinguished by the fact that men will not treat them in a calculating, utilitarian manner. The sacrosanct nature of human life is deeply ingrained in Western culture. Simmel traces the transition from a belief system that condoned the monetary evaluation of life, to the Judeo-Christian conception of the absolute value of man; a conception that sets life beyond financial considerations. The early utilitarian criterion was reflected in social arrangements such as slavery, marriage by purchase, and the wergild or blood money.[13] For Simmel, the rise of individualism was the determining factor in the transition: "The tendency of money to strive after ever-growing indifference and mere quantitative significance coincides with the ever-growing differentiation of men . . . and thus money becomes less and less adequate to personal values."[14] Considered "sub specie pecuniae," the uniqueness and dignity of human life vanished. Cultural resistance against treating life and death as commercial items is reflected in legal attempts to safeguard them from economic life. Roman law had early established the doctrine: Liberum corpus nullam recipit aestimationem (the life of a freeman can have no monetary estimate).* Successorial contracts were considered "stipulationes odiosae" and "contra bonos mores," because they surrounded death with financial considerations.[15] Roman tradition was perpetuated in many countries, particularly in France, whose Civil Code ruled that "only things belonging to commerce can be the subject of a contract."[16] Declaring that a man's life "cannot be the subject of commercial speculation," French jurists made illegal any contract on the lives of persons, such as life insurance, trusts, and successorial contracts. Wills, sufficiently surrounded by religious symbolism to remain untainted by commercial aspirations, remained the only legitimate vehicle to dispose of property after death.[17]

In the United States, the utilitarian treatment of human lives posed similar problems. Merely counting people was at one point considered sacrilegious. God-fearing churchgoers in the eighteenth century opposed census taking, recalling the disastrous plague which befell Israelites when King David, ignoring ancient taboos, ordered a census. Some suggest

* This explains why even countries that forbade life insurance in principle allowed the insurance of slaves. Their presumed lack of human value justified economic equivalences without presenting serious moral difficulties. See Edmund Reboul, "Du Droit des Enfants Bénéficiaires d'une Assurance sur la Vie Contractée par Leur Père," p. 23. Another early form of acceptable life insurance was that of pregnant women by their own husbands. René Goupil, "De La Consideration de la Mort des Personnes Dans Les Actes Juridiques," p. 17.

that censuses were rejected as illicit attempts to discover the secrets of God.* American law protects human life from commerce, declaring that the human body is not property and may not be "bargained for, bartered or sold." [18] Many social arrangements, regardless of their economic efficiency, have been condemned as offensive to the sacred qualities of life. The commercialization of blood donations has been attacked on such grounds.[19] The marketing of human organs presents a similar moral dilemma, and while organ donations have become more common, organ sales are still rare. A recent study explains why: "[The] kin and friends of the deceased after living, loving and laughing with the departed cannot bear to see his corpse treated as a piece of saleable merchandise." [20] Parsons, Fox and Lidz note: "Regardless of how scientific the setting in which this transaction occurs may be, or how secularized the beliefs of those who take part in it, deep religious elements . . . are at least latently present in the transplant situation." [21] Likewise, even after the repeal of most prohibitions against the sale of corpses, the majority of medical schools still obtain corpses and cadavers through individual donations and unclaimed bodies from the morgue. People refuse to sell the body for "ethical, religious or sentimental reasons." The law itself remains ambivalent. While the Uniform Anatomical Gift Act permits the gift of one's body or organs after death, "the state of the law on anatomical sales remains in a flux." [22]

Life insurance was felt to be sacrilegious because its ultimate function was to compensate the loss of a father and a husband with a check to his widow and orphans.† Critics objected that this turned man's sacred life into an "article of merchandise." [23] They asked: "Has a man the right to make the continuance of his life the basis of a bargain? Is it not turning a

* George A. Buttrick, ed., *The Interpreter's Bible*, p. 1172. In 1726, Governor Burnett of New Jersey was dissuaded from ordering a census of the population because it would "make the people uneasy, they being religious enthusiasts." As late as the Constitutional Convention of 1787 religious opposition was cited to national censuses; see James H. Cassedy, *Demography in Early America*, pp. 69–70. Probably, the enumeration of men was also considered degrading and dehumanizing. Statistics on marriage, crime, and suicide, for instance, were opposed by Europeans in the mid-nineteenth century as "true materialism; an attempt to degrade man, without considering his moral and intellectual faculties, into a machine." Adolphe Jacques Quételet, "Sur la Statistique Morale," p. 1.

† The monetary evaluation of life also presented legal complications. When a house burns down, or when crops are harmed by storms, it is possible to reach some objective measurement of the losses involved. When a man dies however, no accurate measure of value is possible. Therefore, the principle of indemnity cannot be fully applied to life insurance and a life contract assigns the risk a fixed value. Alfred Mannes, "Principles and History of Insurance," p. 96; and Charles O. Hardy, *Risk and Risk Bearing*, p. 249.

very solemn thing into a mere commercial transaction?"[24] Nichols recalls the time when "an investment whose profitable character depended on the failure of a human life was looked on as a speculation repugnant to the laws of God and man."[25] Life insurance benefits, however profitable, became "dirty" money. Women were particularly sensitive to the problem:

> Some women say that life insurance seems to them too much like benefiting by the husband's death. Others feel that if the good man were to die, and the proceeds of a policy of life insurance should be paid to them, it would seem like accepting "blood money," and others say that they would not enter any such sordid calculation of his future expectation of life.[26]

Life insurance promoters camouflaged the materialistic implications of their enterprise by reassuring potential customers that their business would be unlike any other: "Here the operations touch human existence. A man may barter and banter where mere goods are concerned but what a degradation to bring life operations to this low level!"*

SACRED MONEY

Paradoxically, money that corrupts can also redeem. Brown criticizes traditional sociology for perpetuating a secular and rational image of money without paying due attention to its symbolic and sacred functions.[27] There is a dual relationship between money and death, actual or symbolic. While establishing an exact monetary equivalence for human life represents a profanation of the sacred, the symbolic, unrestrained use of money may contribute to the sanctification of death. Durkheim briefly dwells on the sacred qualities of money: "Economic value is a sort of power of efficacy and we know the religious origins of the idea of power. Also richness confers mana, therefore it has it. Hence, it is seen that the ideas of economic value and of religious value are not without connection."[28]

The widespread practice of spending large sums of money at times of

***Our Mutual Friend*, (September 1867), p. 3. Juvigny, a major spokesman for life insurance in France had likewise protested: "The most beautiful work of creation, which bears the imprint of the divine hand that formed it, can have no common measure with a coarse metal." J. B. Juvigny, *Coup d'Oeil sur les Assurances sur la Vie des Hommes*, p. 60.

death testifies to the existence of a powerful and legitimate symbolic association between money and death.* As late as 1942, in the United States, more money was spent on funerals and accessories than in all hospitals and sanitaria.[29] Expensive funerals are held without regard to the financial position of the deceased. Funeral undertakers explain that "the love and the respect of the family for its dead is shown to the world by the quality of the funeral in terms of money spent."[30] Life insurance textbooks also suggest that for the policyholder: "the larger the amount of his insurance the more love he has for his family."[31] An early sales pitch of the life insurance companies was:

> To many an uninsured man, professing great attachment to his wife and boundless love for his children, and calling upon heaven to witness how he would lay down his life for them . . . the questions could aptly be put: How much do you love them? Enough to make a personal sacrifice to assure their support and comfort after you are gone?[32]

Accusing fingers routinely point at the undertakers, blaming unreasonable expenses on their exorbitant prices. Historical evidence, however, shows that high expenditures at the time of death preceded the rise of the professional undertaker in the nineteenth century. Habenstein and Lamers describe the "wanton lavishness" of eighteenth-century funerals, when gloves, scarves, and all kinds of expensive gifts were distributed.[33]

The abhorrence of pauper burials is another indicator of the importance of money at the time of death. It explains, for instance, the adoption of industrial life insurance by the working class in the late nineteenth century. The poor willingly sacrificed their meager earnings for policies that covered nothing more than burial expenses. Hoffman points out: "Only those who are familiar with the life and the labor of the industrial masses can fairly grasp the deeper meaning of the abhorrence of a pauper burial of a member of the family in the potter's field."[34] The symbolic ties between money and death are also revealed by the norm that

* In diverse times and cultures, irrational expenses at the time of death remain a commonly accepted pattern. Morley tells of nineteenth-century English widows of army or navy officers who spent on their husband's funeral enough money to cover their children's entire education, and were then forced to seek charity; see John Morley, *Death, Heaven, and the Victorians*, p. 24. Habenstein and Lamers offer additional cross-cultural evidence of this pattern; see Robert W. Habenstein and William M. Lamers, *Funeral Customs the World Over*, (Milwaukee: Bulfin Printers, 1963), pp. 30, 126. In Russia, where the state adequately provides funeral expenses, the family will still lay out private monies; see Vanderlyn R. Pine and Derek L. Phillips, "The Cost of Dying," p. 138.

proscribes bargaining at times of death. Comparison shopping for funerals is strictly taboo, even though it reduces costs.[35] Similarly, in the case of life insurance: "To count our pennies is tempting the Gods to blast us."[36] When it comes to death, money transcends its exchange value and incorporates symbolic meanings. Parsons and Lidz suggest that spending large sums of money may be an attempt to affect "the ultimate well being, or even the salvation of the deceased soul."[37] A study of funeral expenditures also points to the ritualistic uses of money:

> If expenditures are viewed as a secular ritual then money spent for funerals is serving a far different need than one of mere exchange of cash between two agents. . . . Because people increasingly lack both the ceremonial and social mechanisms . . . to help them cope with death, monetary expenditures have taken on added importance as a means . . . to express sentiments for the deceased.[38]

This dual relationship between money and death—actual as well as symbolic—is essential to the understanding of the development of life insurance. Sacrilegious because it equated cash with life, life insurance became on the other hand a legitimate vehicle for the symbolic use of money at the time of death.

MAGIC, DEATH, AND LIFE INSURANCE

William Graham Sumner wrote: "The fact of the aleatory element in human life, the human interpretations of it and the efforts of men to deal with it constitute a large part of the history of culture."[39] Malinowski directed attention to the uses of magic to "master the elements of chance and luck."[40] Among Trobrianders, death and disease were often ascribed to magical sources. The time of one's death remains the most frightening *alea* of all. Wahl notes the "remarkable paradox of an almost universal recourse to magic and irrationality"[41] to handle death even among the most firm believers in science and the scientific method. But while examples of the relationship of magic to death in less developed cultures are easily found,[42] little is known about contemporary magic rituals. For instance, few people make plans for their own death largely due to magical fears that to do so will hasten it. A study of wills comments on the prevalent belief that "when one makes a will he is about to die."[43] Most wills are, in fact, drafted shortly before death. One set of commentators points out: "It is a matter of common knowledge to persons in the estate planning field that a man will devote a lifetime of energy to operating a business or an estate and spend no time at all or little time in arranging to pass along his estate at death."[44] Likewise, people rarely prearrange their own funerals despite the evidence that this reduces expenses considerably.*

Its intimacy with death made life insurance vulnerable to objections based on magical reasoning. A company newsletter referred to the "secret fear" many customers were reluctant to confess: "the mysterious connection between insuring life and losing life."[45] The *Insurance Monitor* had earlier protested against this sort of prejudice: "It is rather humiliating to the human mind to reflect how long the absurd prejudices of superstitious bigotry stood in the way of this noble institution."[46] Even individuals of "high standing and character"[47] held these unreasonable reservations. The irrational fear of precipitating death was listed among the most common objections to life insurance. The lists compiled by insurance companies in an effort to respond to criticism quoted their customers' apprehensions about insuring their lives: "I have a dread of it, a superstition that I may die the sooner."[48] Or, expressed differently: "I am almost ashamed to confess it, but I have a feeling, a prejudice that I may die sooner."[49] Responding to the popular suspicion that life insurance would "hasten the event about which it calculates," Jencks urged the necessity to "disabuse the public mind of such nonsense."[50] However, as late as the 1870s "the old feeling that by taking out an insurance policy we do somehow challenge an interview with the 'king of terrors' still reigns in full force in many circles."[51]

Insurance publications were forced to reply to these superstitious fears. They reassured their customers that "life insurance cannot affect the fact of one's death at an appointed time."[52] Sometimes they answered one magical fear with another suggesting that not to insure was "inviting the

*Simmons, "Funeral Practices and Public Awareness," p. 12; Mitford, *The American Way of Death*, p. 73. Cultural distaste for prearranging one's death is reflected in the following statement by a judge in the course of a trial against a burial insurance salesman who also sold discount certificates for graves and grave clothes:

"Only a rare and eccentric individual would in person, or through an agent, purchase for himself a coffin and grave clothes before he died. Human nature is such that an individual revolts at acquiring and possessing during his lifetime such gruesome tokens of his end." Quoted in Edwin W. Patterson, *Cases and Materials on the Law of Insurance*, p. 23.

vengeance of Providence."[53] On occasion they were ironical: "Does your house burn any sooner for having insured it? Do you shrink from attending a funeral, or looking at deaths in the funeral or owning a lot in the cemetery?"[54] The audience for much of this literature was women. It is one of the paradoxes in the history of life insurance that women, intended to be the chief beneficiaries of the new system, became instead its most stubborn enemies. Many felt it was "premonitory of early death,"[55] "the very fact that her husband has insured his life thrills the bosom of his wife with fearful apprehension."[56] An Equitable booklet quoted wives' most prevalent objections: "Every cent of it would seem to me to be the price of your life. . . . It would make me miserable to think that I were to receive money by your death. . . . It seems to me that if [you] were to take a policy [you] would be brought home dead the next day."[57] Opposition by wives was a frequent item in the lists of common objections to life insurance. Magazine articles and company pamphlets expressed bewilderment at this resistance. A popular booklet commented: "It is almost incredible that one of the obstacles to the universal practice of life insurance is found in the opposition of wives and mothers."[58] In *Word to Wives*, the author likewise noted: "Upon no class of society do the blessings of life insurance fall so sweetly as upon women. And yet [agents] have more difficulty in winning them to their cause than their husbands."[59] The *Insurance Monitor* admonished its female readers:

> To woman, who is in the main the special beneficiary of life insurance, we say, if you are solicitous for its increasing diffusion show it in your words and by your works. We are ashamed to confess that she who is most interested has hitherto done nothing. Nothing![60]

A collection of nineteenth-century sayings devoted a whole chapter to the "woman problem." Its title was, "Do women like insurance? Widows do."* Fables and short stories were published by the companies seeking to frighten women by dramatizing the disastrous economic consequences of their stubbornness. They asked:

> Do you happen to know that many a woman is now living a "hand to mouth" existence, in the direst poverty and afflicted by sickness and disease, simply

*James T. Phelps, *Life Insurance Sayings*, p. 24. The advantages of life insurance for women had been humorously advertised as early as 1712 by the first English life insurance schemes: "Come all ye generous husbands with your wives Insure round sums on your precarious lifes, That, to your comfort, when you're dead and rotten Your widows may be rich when you're forgotten." John Francis, *Annals, Anecdotes and Legends* (London: Longman, Brown, Green, and Longmans, 1853), p. 74.

because she had been prejudiced against allowing or encouraging her husband to insure his life?[61]

The "Fable of the Two Wives" made a parable out of insurance:

> There were two wives, the one wise, the other foolish. The wise wife demanded of her husband even before their marriage, that he should insure, so that, should she be left desolate, yet would she not be destitute also. . . . But the foolish wife did scoff at and revile the agent who pleaded with her husband and had already persuaded him to insure. . . . Soon after the husband was stricken with a fever and died and the foolish wife was fain to sell even her trinkets to buy bread for herself and the children who had been born unto her.[62]

Occasionally, the texts were condescending and mildly ironic:

> The same woman would not think it wrong to receive money desposited in a savings bank or an investment. Why, then, the discrimination against life insurance? Where, then is the difference? It would take a woman to tell![63]

Impatient with the qualms of women, insurance advocates often turned caustic: "Many women give way to absurd prejudices against life insurance, and in airing these prejudices they give utterance to ridiculous sentimentalities which they should heartily be ashamed of being influenced by."[64] "Patience is exhausted," they claimed, "in the case of a woman who is heedless as to postpone, discourage or give up insurance."[65]

Thus, as a result of its involvement with death, life insurance was forced to grapple with magic and superstition, issues supposedly remote from the kind of rational economic organization it represented.

LIFE INSURANCE AND THE CONTROL OF DEATH

Fatalism and innovation are hardly compatible. Rogers and Shoemaker found earlier adopters of innovations to be less fatalistic than later adopters. They point to the difficulties of introducing an innovation among clients who believe their future is determined by fate.[66] The adoption of life insurance in the nineteenth century was dependent on the emergence of a nonfatalistic attitude toward death. Rosenberg suggests that between 1832 and 1866, both death and disease became progressively perceived as the postponable or remedial consequences of inadequate sanitation and other technical deficiences controllable by men.[67]

Parsons and Lidz also point to the replacement of fatalistic conceptions of death by an orientation system which emphasized human control over the conditional elements of life.[68] Life insurance publications became vocal spokesmen of this newer belief system. The *Insurance Monitor* told its readers: "It is difficult . . . to understand why man should not learn to look at the despot in the face and availing himself of the means at his command, use them to the utmost of his powers to disarm the tyrant of his terrors."[69] A life policy offered the possibility of controlling the economic consequences of death. The ultimate responsibility for dependents was taken away from God and handed to man. Traditionalists objected: "With the spirit of the unbeliever they determine that the family shall not be dependent upon Providence . . . when the head is removed by death."[70]

The growing interest in controlling death and disease was reflected in the fascination with prolongevity that began in the nineteenth century.* *Nile's Weekly Register*, a prominent mercantile periodical announced in 1823: "By examining the obituary notices contained in the . . . newspapers we propose to attempt a monthly collection of persons dying who had reached the age of 100 years or upward."[71] Religion, occupation, and even political and economic factors were examined as possible determinants of longevity. For some, longevity was an outgrowth of "cheerfulness, clearness of conception and benevolence."[72] Life insurance became the natural ally of longevity. While some refused to buy a policy because they feared they would die sooner, others bought it as a way to "buy off death."† Serious life insurance writings disclaimed these insinuations, contending that a policy was not a magic charm nor a guarantee against death: it was "no attempt to baffle [death] or ward it off."[73] Reluctant to forgo all credit, however, they were nonetheless willing to concede

* Prolongevity is the significant extension of the length of life by human action; see Gerald J. Gruman, "A History of Ideas about the Prolongation of Life," p. 6. Additional reasons for the interest in longevity were: (a) the growth of interest in demography, (b) the creation of institutions dedicated to the pursuit of scientific investigation, (c) the continuing debate between Europeans and Americans on the effect of the New World environment, and (d) the need for accurate mortality data for medical and life insurance purposes. Maris Vinovskis, "The 1789 Table of Edward Wigglesworth," pp. 572–73.

† Wilbert E. Moore has suggested that even today life insurance symbolizes a certain degree of mastery over fate which is independent of its economic functions. Moore, "Time—The Ultimate Scarcity," p. 60. A 1950 survey found the feeling of controlling fate among the leading motivations of life insurance buyers, Leonard L. Berekson, "Birth Order, Anxiety, Affiliation, and the Purchase of Life Insurance," p. 95.

that the tranquillity and peace of mind that came from making adequate provision for one's family could indeed promote longevity:

> We are not trying to trench upon the province of the medical man; but we may just observe that it is sufficiently obvious that this "question of life" . . . is attributable to the ease of mind and consequent health of body, resulting from the absence of . . . anxiety. . . . How many a man goes down with sorrow to an untimely grave in consequence of the painful fact which stares him in the face—that his health is failing and his family unprovided for! Just the opposite is the case with a man who did his duty [and bought life insurance].[74]

The curative powers of a policy were humorously conveyed through *The Cholera Microbe*, a popular fable:

> A Cholera Microbe, meeting by chance with a Typhoid Fever Germ . . . inquired how business was with him. The Typhoid Fever Germ replied with a yawn, that it had been unusually active this fall, but that he had not had nearly as much fun out of it as usual, because so many of his victims carried life insurance, which imparted so much tranquillity to their minds that over three-fourths of them recovered. As he bade him adieu, he added sadly: If ever we get a chance at any of those life insurance agents, we must pool our issues and put them under.

In another story, a physician is forced to admit that "insurance and not medicine" saved his dying patient.[75]

The impact of life insurance on longevity was not confined for long to peace of mind or to its magical attributes. By the beginning of the twentieth century, life insurance companies saw that extending the life-span of their customers would significantly reduce the costs of their business. Longevity was rediscovered as "a rich and unexploited field for saving money," and life insurance companies became among the first organizations to adopt programs for the conservation of human life.[76]

Clearly the legitimation of life insurance was supported by a nonfatalistic ideology which encouraged human control over all aspects of death.

THE IMPACT OF LIFE INSURANCE ON VALUES REGARDING DEATH

As a major social innovation, life insurance made its own impact on values. We will examine four different ways in which life insurance penetrated values regarding death: (*a*) as a secular ritual, (*b*) as an additional requirement for a "good death," (*c*) as a form of immortality, and (*d*) by redefining the value of life.

LIFE INSURANCE AS RITUAL

It is claimed that the rational-utilitarian approach to death typified by life insurance has deritualized and secularized death. Vernon, for instance, contends:

> In the American society, the bereaved is provided little formalized emotional assistance. . . . In terms of practical assistance the impersonality of the system is shown in the development of such useful, but not very emotionally satisfying aids as life insurance and inheritance laws.[77]

Keener observers deny the hypothesis of de-ritualization and see instead the secularization of religious ritual.[78] This "metamorphosis of the sacred," using Norman Brown's apt term, does not exempt ritual, but changes its nature. The dead can be mourned in very different ways. Parsons and Lidz suggest that in contemporary American society the mourner's obligation is to do his "grief work" rapidly and efficiently, early resuming a normal life.[79] Our "funeral games," Gollin agrees, are: "the full schedule and the uninterrupted daily round."[80] Funeral expenditures have been defined as a secular ritual.[81] Our evidence suggests that life insurance became another one. Curiously, it is its critics who have been particularly sensitive to the ritualistic overtones of life insurance. Welsh claims that life insurance is a way of coming to terms with death not only financially but emotionally and religiously. Its appeal, he claims, is based on "the prayer that one's death may somehow be worth something to somebody, even in terms only of money."[82]

The view of life insurance as ritual can be substantiated with firmer evidence. From the 1830s to the 1870s life insurance companies explicitly justified their enterprise and based their sales appeal on the quasi-religious nature of their product. Far more than an investment, life insurance was a "protective shield" over the dying, and a consolation "next to that of religion itself."[83] A popular booklet, *In Life Prepare for Death* skipped over the economic functions of life insurance to focus on its capacity to ease "the struggle with disease and the conflict with the king of terrors." The noneconomic functions of a policy were extensive: "It can alleviate pangs of the bereaved, cheer the heart of the widow and dry the orphans' tears. Yes, it will shed the halo of glory around the memory of him who has been gathered to the bosom of his Father and God."[84] It eased the confrontation with death: "Death stands at every man's door, with a license to call whom and when he will and his calls are imperative . . . [but] life insurance like a provident angel comes in, comforting the bed of disease, smoothing the pillow of the dying."[85] Life insurance made even salvation more likely:

> The dying Christian, who has done his best to provide for those whom he leaves behind him, can look to heaven with far more assurance . . . than those who have neglected this important duty. He has used the means, and he can rationally, and in full faith supplicate the Divine blessing on those means.[86]

LIFE INSURANCE AND THE "GOOD DEATH"

Most societies have some conception of what constitutes an appropriate death, whether that means dying on a battlefield or while working at a desk. In the Middle Ages, for instance, the dying man lay in his bedchamber surrounded by priests, doctors, family, and neighbors. He took stock of his life, pardoned his enemies, blessed his survivors, repented his sins, and received final absolution from the priest.* A "triumphant" death in pre-Civil War America meant a holy death; it involved spiritual transportation and the "triumph" of the faith.[87] Religiosity and moral generosity alone, however, soon became dysfunctional to a changed social context. In the eighteenth and early nineteenth centuries, widows and orphans had generally inherited sufficient land to live on and support

* See Phillipe Ariès, *Western Attitudes Toward Death*, pp. 9–12, 34. Lebrun shows how social class influenced attitudes toward death and the dead in eighteenth-century Anjou, France. The noble wanted to die young, "sword in hand, serving the king." The bourgeosie did not uphold the ideal of an early, violent death honoring instead longevity. The lower class was fatalistic and largely indifferent to death. To them, notes Lebrun, "their cow is more important than their wife." The loss of a cow could ruin the farmer, while a new wife was easily found. Francois Lebrun, *Les Hommes et La Mort en Anjou Aux 17e Et 18e Siècles*, pp. 426–29.

themselves. Urbanization changed this, making families almost exclusively dependent on the father's wage. If he did not assume responsibility for the economic welfare of his wife and children after his death, society would have to support them. The principle of testamentary freedom in American law exempted men from any legal obligation to their children after death. Moral suasion, therefore, had to substitute for legal coercion. It was crucial to instill men with a norm of personal financial responsibility towards their families that did not stop with death. More and more a good death meant the wise and generous economic provision of dependents. A man was judged posthumously by his financial foresight as much as by his spiritual qualities. Only the careless father left "naught behind him but the memory of honest, earnest work and the hopeless wish that loved ones . . . might somehow find their needed shelter from poverty. . . ."[88] Diamond and Goody point out how attitudes toward death and the dead serve as efficient mechanisms for controlling the behavior of the living. Newspaper obituaries or clergymen's eulogies, for instance, remind the living what behaviour is sanctioned by a particular social system.* The public reformulation of social norms after a man's death reaffirms their value for the living. Life insurance writings referred to the new standards of dying in America:

> The necessity that exists for every head of family to make proper provision for the sustenance of those dear to him after his death, is freely acknowledged and there is no contingency whereby a man can stand excused from making such a provision.[89]

As an efficient mechanism to ensure the economic provision of dependents, life insurance was gradually counted among the duties of a good and responsible father. The man who died insured and "with soul sanctified by the deed, wings his way up to the realms of the just, and is gone where the good husbands and the good fathers go."[90] *The United States Insurance Gazette* commented: "Society is fast tending to regard the man who leaves his family destitute, when a Life Insurance Policy can so cheaply be purchased, as foolish and criminal in his neglect . . ."[91] In 1869, the New York Life Insurance Company almanac predicted: "Ten or twenty years hence, the man who neglects [life insurance] will not be jus-

* For instance, obituaries and eulogies praising the labor of late business leaders in the nineteenth century were not only "a hymn to the departed entrepreneur but a hallelujah to living enterprise." Sigmund Diamond, *The Reputation of the American Businessman*, p. 78. See also Jack Goody, *Death, Property, and the Ancestors*, pp. 29–30.

tifiable at the bar of public opinion while he lives and . . . [he] will be censured after death."[92] An uninsured man, maintained the *Insurance Journal* thirteen years later, has no claims to the "regretful memory" or the "sorrowing tears" of his destitute family.[93] In *The Ideal Protection*, Standen wrote:

> It is a very old saying that "we should speak well of the dead" but it is a very difficult injunction to obey if they have so emphasized their intense selfishness while living, as to leave helpless widows and destitute children to face alone the miseries of starvation.

Readers were warned:

> Don't give people the opportunity to disparage your memory, and to say contemptible things about you, when you are dead; and they certainly *will* vilify you, if you set yourself up as a model husband and father, and yet leave your wife and children to beggary after you are gone.[94]

Economic standards were endorsed by religious leaders such as Reverend Henry Ward Beecher, who pointed out: "Once the question was: can a Christian man rightfully seek Life Assurance? That day is passed. Now the question is: can a Christian man justify himself in neglecting such a duty?"[95] The new criteria for a "good death" emerge from this excerpt from a sermon delivered in the 1880s:

> I call to your attention Paul's comparison. Here is one man who through neglect fails to support his family while he lives or after he dies. Here is another who abhors the Scriptures and rejects God. . . . Paul says that a man who neglects to care for his household is more obnoxious than a man who rejects the Scriptures. . . . When men think of their death they are apt to think of it only in connection with their spiritual welfare. . . . It is meanly selfish for you to be so absorbed in heaven . . . that you forget what is to become of your wife and children after you are dead. . . . It is a mean thing for you to go up to Heaven while they go into the poorhouse.[96]

In a more philosophical vein, an article in the *Catholic World* conveyed a similar message by establishing life insurance as the ethical duty of a good father and "the modern method of fulfilling the duties that belong to that which is to be."[97]

LIFE INSURANCE AND ECONOMIC IMMORTALITY

Lifton and Olson categorize four major modes of attaining immortality: (*a*) theological immortality, or the belief in a personal afterlife; (*b*) creative immortality, or the continuation of life through one's professional achievements; (*c*) immortality through continuation with nature; and (*d*) biological immortality, in which the person lives on through his children.[98] Theological concern with personal immortality was overrun in the nineteenth century by a growing concern with posterity and the social forms of immortality. Carl Becker points out that as early as the eighteenth century European *philosophes* replaced the Christian promise of immortality in the afterworld with the belief that good men would live in the memory of future generations.[99] This shift was reflected in the changing nature of wills. Earlier wills were concerned primarily with the spiritual salvation of the dying. The testator regulated all the details of his burial; assuring his chances of salvation by donations to the poor who would pray for his soul and by funding hundreds of thousands of masses and religious services in his honor, often in perpetuity. After the mid-eighteenth century, wills were no longer concerned with matters of personal salvation; they became lay instruments for the distribution of property among descendants. Vovelle attributes the change in wills to the "de-Christianization" and de-ritualization of attitudes towards death in the mid-eighteenth century.[100] It is likely however, that the new format of wills was less the reflection of a loss of religious belief and more an indicator of a *new* set of ideas and beliefs on immortality.* Feifel describes the transition in America: "When we gave up the old ideas of personal immortality through an afterlife we created the idea of social immortality. It meant that I could not live on but I would live on in my children."[101] The Puritan concern with individual salvation was pushed aside by the new emphasis on posterity. Men became less preoccupied with their souls and

* Ariès' interpretation of Vovelle's data may have some bearing on this hypothesis. Ariès uses the rise of the family and of new family relationships based on feelings and affection in the mid-eighteenth century to explain the change in wills. The dying person no longer used legal means to regulate the rituals of his burial because he now trusted his family to remember him voluntarily. Ariès, *Western Attitudes Toward Death*, pp. 64–65. The growing importance of family ties may have encouraged religious belief in posterity and social forms of immortality.

more with leaving an estate for their heirs: "When we look abroad upon the busy action of the world . . . and mark the struggling of mankind . . . almost the sole object which we see them striving to attain is wealth that they may transmit it with their names to posterity."[102] The concern with social immortality interacted with structural pressures generated by new economic conditions and the process of urbanization. The multiplication of people with no more capital than their personal incomes made the economic future of their children painfully precarious. The premature death of the breadwinner spelled economic disaster to his widow and orphans. The new institutions that specialized in the economic consequences of death, such as life insurance and trusts, responded to that economic plight by serving the practical needs of dependents. However, they went beyond mere functionality by also symbolizing a form of economic immortality.*

The appeal of life insurance as a pathway to immortality was early recognized by the insurance companies, who used it very explicitly to attract their customers.[103] Life insurance was described as "the unseen hand of the provident father reaching forth from the grave and still nourishing his offspring and keeping together the group."[104] "When a woman receives the proceeds of a policy that was written upon her husband's life," explained an insurance writer, "his true and loyal love has reached beyond the grave."[105] A policy made the "dead still live in good works."[106] On the other hand, not insuring led to the "humiliation of one's posterity."[107]

The idea of rewards and punishments after death also served to reinforce the father's responsibility for his widow and orphans. Goody suggests that the belief in afterworld retribution, like other supernatural beliefs, reinforces the system of social control over the living by placing it beyond human questioning.[108] The uninsured could anticipate an uneasy afterlife:

> Perhaps you will laugh at me when I explain . . . my mother used to quote from the sacred text the "cloud of witnesses," and after I am dead I don't care

* After finding no convincing economic explanation for dynastic trusts—a form of trust which is perpetuated for extended periods—Friedman, attributed this arrangement to a "dynastic impulse" or desire for immortality. Lawrence M. Friedmann, "The Dynastic Trust," pp. 548–49. The overtones of immortality in economic forms of support that outlive the provider are discussed in Thomas L. Schaffer, *Death, Property, and Lawyers*, p. 82.

> to be a "witness" of my family's struggles with sheer poverty. . . . Now, if my view is right, a good many departed souls must regret the final negative answer given to a life insurance solicitor.[109]

The dead assumed also a more active role than in the past; there is a shift from "service to serving."* They were no longer the passive recipients of their survivors' prayers; it was soon recognized that "the desire to outlive life in active beneficence is the common motive to which [life insurance] appeals."[110] A life insurance agent recalled his days as a salesman of immortality:

> Now suppose—just suppose we had a way of coming back from the dead ourselves. . . . Suppose you could walk into little Charlie's room and stand by his bed . . . and suppose the ghost of you could run its hand into a pocket and take out the price of a new pair of shoes. . . . You say: "Why taunt me? Men do not return." . . . Ah! but little Charlie will have those shoes. . . . I have a touch of immortality for sale. Would you buy?[111]

This appeal survives and is still today the basis of some of the most effective stories used by life underwriters on potential customers. To take but one example:

> Several years after a valued client of his died the underwriter met the dead man's son on the street. In the course of their conversation, the son said: "I wish I had known my father better. You know, after eleven years he's still sending us money?"[112]

Many sales talks are opened by asking, "Would you pay a hundred dollars to live forever?"

Beyond altruism and emotional satisfaction, the attraction of economic forms of immortality lay in the chance to exercise a degree of power and social control over the living even after death. Sociologically, immortality is a mechanism for role extension. Blauner points out: "The prospect of total exclusion from the social world would be too anxiety laden for the living, aware of their own eventual fate . . . [so they] construct rituals that celebrate and insure a transition to a new social status."[113] Humorists have captured this point:

*G. & M. Vovelle found that in nineteenth-century Provence the souls in purgatory are no longer represented simply as recipients of the prayers of the living but serving as mediators with God. "La Mort et l'au-de-la d'après les autels des âmes du Purgatoire (XV–XX siècle)," *Annales E.S.C.* (1969), 24:1625; quoted in Goody, "Death and the Interpretation of Culture: A Bibliographic Overview," in Stannard, *Death in America*, p. 4.

> A man who had quarrelled with his spouse, did not insure because it would benefit the dame, but was informed that he could bequeath the amount assured as he pleased. "Faith, I'll be doing it, then," said he, "I only hope to aggravate her as long as I lived; but . . . to lose this money will aggravate her after I'm dead."[114]

Irony aside, in America, as in other common-law countries, the law guarantees the "dead hand" an important say in ruling the future. Under the principle of testamentary freedom, a man, after making certain provision for his wife, can dispose of his property at will. He has no legal obligations to his children whom he is free to totally disinherit. Likewise, through the use of trusts and future interests a man can delay the ultimate disposition of his estate for about eighty years and during this period he can attempt to control the personal lives of his descendants.[115] This is another instance of the role of the dead as agents of social control of the living; in this case via control of property. Goody shows that even among preliterate peoples, the process of property transmission is seldom completed; among the LoDagaa of West Africa, for instance, ancestral spirits hold perpetual claims upon the worldly property of their descendant group and are entitled to share in the gains that accrue to them. Ancestors remain authority figures through their extended control over property. They are expected to punish their descendants who do not follow the prescribed social norms of the group. The dead man also controls the sexual life of his widows for a prolonged period of time after which he still remains the social father to any of their children.[116] This power over the surviving widow appealed to nineteenth century men as well. An article in the *Fireside Companion* advised its readers:

> Widows, well provided for, are not ready to go off. . . . Husbands who contemplate leaving their wives widows, should bear this in mind, and make handsome provision for them, so as to remove the temptation to fill their vacant place. Every husband can do it by insuring his life. . . . When a man leaves his wife nothing but his old clothes and the furniture, what can she do? She has the choice between keeping boarders and getting married.[117]

LIFE INSURANCE AND THE MONEY VALUE OF MAN

Life insurance became the first large-scale enterprise to base its entire organization on the accurate estimate of the price of death.[118] It was necessary to know the cost of death in order to establish adequate policy benefits and determine premiums. The economic evaluation of human life was a delicate matter which met with stubborn resistance. Until the late nineteenth century, life insurance shunned economic terminology, surrounding itself with religious symbolism and advertising more its moral value than its monetary benefits. Life insurance was marketed as an altruistic, self-denying gift, rather than as a profitable investment. The issue of the money value of man was raised only exceptionally. In 1851, one lecturer suggested that life insurance abated the fear of death "by making a comfortable and gainful business transaction of dying."[119] An article in 1856 on "The Money or Commercial Value of a Man" also discussed his "great commercial importance."[120] However, most life insurance writers of this period denied the economic implications of their enterprise:

> The term life insurance is a misnomer . . . it implies a value put on human life. But that is not our province. We recognize that life is intrinsically sacred and immeasurable, that it stands socially, morally and religiously above all possible evaluation.[121]

Later in the nineteenth century, the economic value of human life finally became a less embarrassing topic in insurance circles. The *Insurance Gazette* could suggest: "The life of every man has a value; not merely a moral value as weighed in the scale of social affection and family ties but a value which may be measured in money."[122] The Reverend Henry Ward Beecher urged men to make their death "the basis of commercial action."[123] Life insurance advertising reflected the more candid approach: "Your good health has a money value in it which you may use if you see fit. . . . Is it not wise to turn to account this capital by insuring it?"* All

* Booklet published by Equitable Life Insurance Co., 1873. The greater acceptance of the economic value of a man's life did not, however, include women. The *Insurance Monitor*, among others, was outspoken against the insurance of wives for the benefit of husbands:

"Insurance against loss of property of any kind, houses, debts, horses, is legitimate, because to each of these a money value can be assigned. To these are added the highest and best insurance of all, the lives of men in their capacities as husbands . . . because man is the money-getting power upon which the woman is dependent. . . . The husband who can deliberately set a money value upon his wife, is so far destitute not only of affection for her, but of respect for himself, has so much greed and so little manhood. . . To him she is but a chattel . . . as such she is insured." "The Insurable Value of a Wife," *Insurance Monitor* (September 1870), 18:712d.

The insurance of women, although uncommon, was not unknown. See Owen J. Stalson, *Marketing Life Insurance*, pp. 77, 153, 192; Mildred F. Stone, *Since 1845*, pp. 20–23 The insurance of children was similarly opposed by many individuals and organizations who obeuphemism was finally put aside in the first World Insurance Congress held in San Francisco in 1915. One speaker unabashedly declared: "In this age of commercialism, it is fitting and proper that everything, including human life be reduced to a money equivalent."[124] The process of introducing the economic value of human life culminated in 1924 when the concept was formally presented at the annual convention of life underwriters:

> The most important new development in economic thought will be the recognition of the economic value of human life. . . . I confidently believe that the time is not far distant when . . . we shall apply to the economic organization, management and conservation of life values the same scientific treatment that we now use in connection with property.[125]

Two major consequences of legitimizing the economic evaluation of man were a new and frankly utilitarian approach to life values and a new definition of death. Similarities between life values and property values were investigated and publicized. The life value, for example, was to be subjected to the same principles governing depreciation of property. Approaching life as another economic asset also suggested the possibility of life wills. While property wills were restricted to the distribution of material possessions, life wills added a new type of inheritance: "the money value of the economic forces within us." Death was redefined by the new economic terminology:

> It is highly important to repeat that in the Human Life Value concept it is vital not to interpret death in the sense that lawyers, doctors or clergy are accustomed to use the expression. The concept deals with economics, and death therefore must be viewed from an economic standpoint.[126]

Accordingly, death meant "all events ending the human life earning capacity." It was neatly categorized into premature death, casket death, living death (disability) and economic death (retirement).[127] Disease, from this perspective, was the "depreciation of life values" and premature death an unnecessary waste of money. Annual medical checkups were encouraged on the basis of economic efficiency: "Why the human being

---

jected to the economic evaluation of a child's life. In the 1870s, industrial insurance companies began insuring the poor. For the first time children under ten years of age became insurable on a regular basis. There were at least seventy legislative attempts in various states to prohibit it as being against public policy and the public interest. The *Boston Evening Transcript* reflected their prevalent feeling that "no manly man and no womanly woman should be ready to say that their infants have pecuniary value" (March 14, 1895).

does not willingly take an expert inspection and inventory of himself periodically, as he does of his material property is difficult to see." [128] In 1930, Dublin and Lotka developed the first estimate of capital values of males as a function of their age. By establishing differential financial values for lives, they also set a new criterion for stratifying them. Exceptional lives were those that made the greatest contributions, while substandard lives burdened their communities with financial loss. Even the handicapped were similarly appraised:

> The money value of a handicapped person will range from a negative quantity representing the cost of maintenance of a person . . . incapable of self support to a very creditable figure for the most successful of the rehabilitated.[129]

Promoters of the human life value concept were aware of treading on delicate ground. Some attempted to deal with the conflict by making explicit distinctions between the sentimental and spiritual value of life and its worth as a productive asset, admitting that the former "escapes our powers of evaluation in figures." [130] Others more realistically recognized the need for a "whole new philosophy of values" [131] to make the public understand the economic approach to life and death.

The general relationship of values to the diffusion of innovations has been illustrated by the different ways in which values and ideologies regarding death interacted with the institution of life insurance. Life insurance was subjected to the antagonism of a value system that condemned its materialistic assessment of death, and to the power of magical beliefs and superstitions that viewed with apprehension any pacts dependent on death for their fulfillment. Using money to cope with death was not, however, always unseemly, and life insurance was supported by symbolic ties between death and money that made spending large sums of money a form of sanctification. Ideological harmony also existed between life insurance and another set of values that emphasized the controllability of death and disease at the beginning of the nineteenth century. Life insurance made it possible to control the economic consequences of a man's death. It even had conferred upon it the capacity to prolong the life of its customers, through its allegedly magical restorative powers.

Life insurance did more than simply respond and adjust to prevailing values regarding death. It influenced those values by introducing economic overtones into many traditional concepts. For instance, life insurance assumed the role of a secular ritual and introduced new notions of immortality that emphasized remembrance through money. A "good death" was no longer defined only on moral grounds; the inclusion of a life policy made financial foresight another prerequisite. Finally, life insurance redefined death as an economic episode and life as an economic asset.

Chapter 5
Life, Chance, and Destiny

> Gambling lures men from industry, frugality and accumulation, by hopes of gain through processes less slow than these and less self-denying and in this result, also life insurance assimilates to gambling. "Eat, Drink, and be Merry, for tomorrow we die" and a life insurance will provide for our family is the tendency of life insurance.[1]

Changing attitudes toward risk taking and gambling had a major impact on the legitimation of life insurance. During the first part of the nineteenth century, a traditional economic morality and a powerful religious ethos made gambling both socially and theologically suspect. Public opinion had also been adversely affected by recent unfortunate experiences with speculative ventures. Lotteries, of great popularity and acceptance in the late eighteenth century, had been corrupted by fraudulent practices. By 1840, twelve of the twenty-six states had made them illegal and the majority of the others only awaited the expiration of current contracts.[2] The socially unstabilizing effects of speculation had been impressed upon the American public by the disastrous consequences of the unbridled land ventures in the 1830s. These had generated fraud and corruption and led to the economic ruin of many.[3] Tontines were equally in "disrepute" at the beginning of the century.[4] Very popular in Europe, the tontine was an openly speculative form of life insurance.[5] Each subscriber contributed a certain amount of money which was invested for the benefit of all. Until his death, each participant received an annual income which then passed on to the survivors. The last to die was the "winner."

After the Civil War, as risk became a prominent feature of the more complex economic system, certain forms of risk-taking assumed important socioeconomic functions, transforming traditional conceptions of risk and gambling. The impact of changing attitudes toward risk on the development of life insurance will be analyzed. While the traditional perspective made the life insurance venture a religious and a social threat, a less deterministic religious outlook and the entrepreneurial economic ethos turned life insurance from a pariah into a leading economic institution.* First, the accusation that life insurance was a form of gambling must be accounted for. How could a system designed to reduce risk and provide security be confused with gambling?

LIFE INSURANCE AND THE STIGMA OF GAMBLING

Every list of *Popular Fallacies about Life Insurance* included its definition as a form of gambling. "I look upon it as gambling," was the response of many who refused to buy a policy.[6] An early treatise on life insurance reported: "To many . . . the very suggestion of a proposal to insure one's life appears . . . objectionable . . . on moral grounds that it looks like a wager, a bet or that appealing to the doctrine of chances, it partakes of the nature of gambling."[7] Elizur Wright, prominent in the history of life insurance, even justified life insurance for the poor as "gambling made useful." For the rich, however, it was "gambling which lacks justification perhaps as much as any other, if not more."[8] Standen recalled: "years ago it used to be said as an argument against life insurance that a man had to die in order to win." The response to such "foolish arguments" was clear: "The man who dies certainly wins nothing. . . . No one supposes that life insurance enables a man's family to win by his death. It is not the purpose and intent that the family should be a "winner."[9] In the minds of many, life insurance was simply a new speculative fund-raising device to substitute the floundering lotteries and the unsuccessful tontines. Its alleged lottery spirit became a major source of prejudice against it, forcing life insurance advocates to insist upon the differences between the two. The *Insurance Gazette* explained: "Life insurance contracts do not partake in the least of the nature of lotteries, or games of chance as some erroneously affirm, nor are they wager contracts."[10] The prejudice survived, and was heard as late as 1895 in the angry remarks of a Lutheran minister who accused life insurance of being

* While the traditional attitude was dominant earlier and the liberal one later in the century, the division is not absolute. Just as we find life insurance advocates even before 1840, traditionalists attack it as late as the 1890s. The effectiveness of the latter's criticism, however, was dissipated with the success of life insurance.

nothing but "money speculation": "One seeks for little money to obtain a great amount just like card playing and other games. It is a mean, low lottery game, yea, in fact worse than such for one places his life at stake." [11] The same dismal fate that had befallen lotteries was predicted for life insurance:

> In former days . . . lottery schemes were introduced as sanctified means to raise funds for charitable purposes and to rear up church edifices. . . . In our times, no one claiming piety would advocate such causes. Life insurance . . . will be in a quarter of a century hence as unpopular as lotteries now are.[12]

The history of life insurance reinforced the credibility of these accusations. Early forms of life insurance were outright bets on human lives. Huizinga traces the existence of these wagers to the end of the Middle Ages in Genoa and Antwerp when bets were placed on the life and death of persons, and on the birth of boys and girls.[13] Seventeenth-century traveling merchants gambled with their own lives by placing bets on their safe return. Another common speculation was on the death of rulers and the election of popes. In eighteenth-century England, insurance and wagering went hand in hand, and it has been alleged that no form of gambling became "so varied, so universal, so wasteful or so demoralising" as insurance.[14] An insurance mania led to the establishment of companies that would insure almost anything. Speculation with lives were the most popular:

> Policies were openly laid on the lives of all public men. When George II fought at Dettingen, 25 percent was paid against his safe return. When in 1745 the Pretender was defeated, thousands of pounds were laid upon his capture, his death, even his whereabouts. When Lord Nithsdale escaped from the tower . . . the wretches who had periled money on his life and to whom his impending execution would have been a profit, were noisy in their own complaints.[15]

Dying became such a common subject of insurance wagers that on one occasion London's *Public Advertiser* was forced to announce:

> We have the pleasure to assure the public . . . that the repeated accounts of her Royal Highness the Princess Dowager of Wales being very ill and her life in great danger are entirely false, such reports being only calculated to promote the shameful spirit of the gambling by insurance on lives.[16]

There were even cases of mass speculation on lives. When eight hundred German immigrants were brought into England by a speculator who then abandoned them without any food or shelter, wagers were immediately begun as to how many would die within a week.[17]

Life insurance speculation continued into the nineteenth century. As late as 1844, weekly insurance "auctions" were held at London's Royal Exchange where old men unable to pay their premiums sold their policies to the highest bidder. The buyer, who continued the payments, was betting on the speedy death of the insured.* Another form of gambling with life, known as "graveyard insurance," briefly flourished in the United States in the early 1880s with speculators insuring the lives of old people, preferably paupers who were likely to die soon.†

The kinship between gambling and insurance, which was a fact of history, was also sanctioned by law under the general rubric of aleatory contracts: *Actus quo fortuna praedominatur.*[18] In all aleatory contracts "the performance of that which is one of its objects depends on an uncertain event."[19] The parties involved in gambling "voluntarily engage to make the transfer of money or something else of value among themselves contingent upon the outcome of some future and uncertain event."[20]

Similarly with a life insurance contract: "One party agrees to pay another a certain sum of money upon the happening of a given contingency which happens to be the death of the insured."[21] Thus, the risk of a fortuitous event is at the core of both types of contracts.‡ The technical

* This practice resulted from the companies' refusal to buy back their policies. Public sales of policies by their owners also took place in the United States. J. A. Fowler, *History of Insurance in Philadelphia*, p. 796. A nonforfeiture law was finally passed in 1880 which granted a cash surrender value to every life policy after payment of two annual premiums.

† A letter from Uncle John to his nephew Richard on Speculative Insurance, a pamphlet published in 1880 and found in the New York Public Library, describes this "unclean" business:

"A common experience of a policyholder is this, to take out his papers on some simple old man likely to die soon, this brings him in contact with the officers or agent, and he hears the word death, death, death, until he is sure the old fellow must be bad, and it looks so far that he takes another heavy policy on him and looks out for another subject. . . . Bye and bye he gets a letter, finds it is an assessment. . . . "A B of your class is dead, pay up." In a few days he gets another. . . . He just here discovers that if the old man don't die till the last of the class there will not be a single man left to pay him, and quietly, minus his money, he steps down and out. Others . . . use all their money and all that can be borrowed, even to the mortgaging of farms" (p. 2).

The English *Spectator* reported in 1891 a similar arrangement; speculators insured "gassed lives," men doomed to early death because of their unhealthy occupations, *Spectator* (November 14, 1891), 67:673.

‡ Devereux points out how gambling developed out of magical and religious practices used by men to handle the problems of uncertainty. Edward C. Devereux, Jr., "Gambling," p. 53. Legally, a fortuitous event is defined as: "An event which is dependent on chance. It may be beyond the power of any human being to bring the event to pass, or may be within the control of a third person, so long as it is not the expectation that the promisor shall cause it to happen" Samuel Williston, *A Treatise on the Law of Contracts*, p. 572.

parallels between gambling and insurance still plague insurance experts. As late as 1964, the issue was raised by an article in the *Journal of Risk and Insurance* which asked: "Are insurance and gambling the same? . . . Are they at or near the polar extremes of morality?"[22] Many confess being "hard-pressed" to separate the two.[23] The difficulty lies mostly in the intangible qualities which distinguish insurance from gambling, such as purpose and morality. As Hardy points out: "Though the form is the same, the moral aspects of the questions . . . are exactly opposite."[24] The purpose of the contract and the motivation of the contracting parties, generally felt to be irrelevant to other contracts, become the clue to the legitimacy of aleatory contracts. While the purpose of gambling is to create artificial risk, the intent of insurance is to reduce risk by transferring it to specialists.

The concept of insurable interest developed to guarantee the legitimate contractual motivation of life insurance. It was first introduced in England in 1774 as a legal weapon against the widespread wagering in lives. The statute prohibited all insurance on lives "except in cases where the persons insuring shall have an interest in the life of the persons insured."[25] Defining insurable interest, however, has not been an easy task. American legal experts complained of the difficulty of taking the life insurance contract "out of the class of wager policies."[26] Most legal decisions on the subject were so confusing, that contracts of "doubtful legitimacy" were often tolerated.[27] The legal difficulty arose from the nature of the object being insured. While insurable interest in fire or marine policies was easily estimated in dollars and cents, financial considerations alone were inadequate to establish insurable interest in a human life. Pecuniary interest became one gauge, but equally serious consideration was given to degree of love and affection. In the estimation of one judge: "Natural affection in cases of this kind is considered as more powerful—as operating more efficaciously—to protect the life of the insured than any other consideration."* Such uncertain legal foundations increased the difficulty of separating life insurance from wager policies. Matters were further com-

* Warnock v. Davis, 104 U.S. 779. The definition of what constitutes insurable interest varies among countries. England, with few exceptions, requires pecuniary interest, while American courts have been particularly liberal in accepting affective factors. John F. Onion, "Insurable Interest in Life," *Minutes of the Proceedings of the Legal Section of the American Life Convention* (Chicago, September 16, 1918), p. 14. While English Law, for instance, disallowed the insurance of children by their parents for lack of pecuniary interest, a United States ruling upheld the right of parents to insure their children:

"The insured need not necessarily have any pecuniary interest in the life of cestui que vie. . . . If it appears that the relation, whether of consanguinity or affinity, was such beplicated by the doctrine of assignability, which holding that insurable interest was required only at the inception of the policy, meant that subsequent lack of interest would not annul the contract. This permitted an insured person to name a beneficiary without insurable interest in his life, thereby reopening the possibility of speculation. Elizur Wright observed that a policy "which was perfectly legitimate . . . at its inception, may be continued until it degenerates into a sheer bet."[28]

Thus, historical and legal factors combined to create the nexus between life insurance and gambling. The speculative origins of life insurance as a wager on human life cast a shadow of illegitimacy on even the best of life insurance ventures. The *Merchants' Magazine* complained that life insurance "has often incurred the odium which . . . should be applied to those wager policies, which like parasitic plants, have grown upon and deeply affected the parent trunk."[29] In addition, no forceful legal standards were adopted to extirpate all gambling features from life insurance contracts. The doctrine of insurable interest, upon which their legitimacy rested, offered only uncertain guidelines of distinction.

---

tween the person whose life was insured and the beneficiary . . . such interest will uphold the policy." Warnock v. Davis, 104 U.S. 775.

There are exceptions to this decision, and in some jurisdictions a parent must prove pecuniary interest in order to insure his child's life in his or her favor. 24 Couch 239 (2d ed., 1960).

In America, the strength of moral obligation and affection often overcame the lack of legal ties. A woman has an insurable interest in the life of a man with whom she has been living as his wife even without a marriage ceremony (24 Couch 237). Likewise, a woman who took a girl from an orphan asylum into her home without being formally appointed her guardian was considered to have an insurable interest in the girl's life solely on the basis of the latter's moral obligation (24 Couch 240). However, difficulty of determining what degree of affection would suffice to preclude ulterior mercenary motivations led some to advocate the definition of insurable interest strictly in pecuniary terms:

"If persons could insure the lives of their relations or friends merely on the ground of friendship or the sorrow experienced on their loss it would tend to all the evils of wager policies, and be the more dangerous because persons, united by those ties, are naturally thrown off their guard and much more exposed to the fraudulent designs of those who are inclined to take advantage of such a situation." *Hunt's Merchants' Magazine* (October 1855), 33:502.

THE RELIGIOUS THREAT

Religion provided a strong source of cultural opposition to life insurance particularly, although not exclusively, during the first half of the nineteenth century.* As Standen recalls: "Thousands of persons of religious influence turned their backs upon life insurance, as an impious institution that they dared not countenance for fear of perpetrating some unpardonable sin." Speculating with the solemn event of death seemed to many a degrading sacrilegious wager, which God would "resent and punish as crime." By insuring his life a man was not only "betting against his God,"[30] but, even worse, usurping His divine functions of protection. Life insurance misled men into taking "future consequences or results in their hands, which is God's prerogative." Satan could have found no better ally: "We believe Satan never fitted so keen and sharp pointed an instrument to pierce the soul of a saint as Life Insurance, to induce him to loosen his hold on his heavenly father."[31] The concept of insurance itself was not new. As Sumner points out:

> Insurance is a grand device and is now a highly technical process but its roots go farther back than one would think. . . . Man on earth having always had an eye to the avoidance of ill luck has tried in all ages somehow to insure himself-to take out a "policy" of some sort on which he has paid regular premiums in some sort of self-denial or sacrifice.[32]

Sumner suggests that religion developed primarily to cope with the aleatory element in human life.† From a traditional deterministic perspec-

* According to G. A. MacClean, religious antagonism to life insurance existed as early as the medieval period, and led to the destruction of life insurance records for fear of ecclesiastical reprisals. *Insurance Up Through the Ages*, p. 35. In other periods, life insurance was considered an illicit exchange of funds which violated the canonical prohibition of usury. Terence O'Donnell, *History of Life Insurance in Its Formative Years*, p. 91; P. J. Richard, *Histoire des Institutions d'Assurance en France*, p. 12.

† William Graham Sumner, *Folkways*, p. 21. Magic is another traditional mechanism to handle uncertainty; see Bronislaw Malinowski, *Magic, Science, and Religion*, p. 8. With some exceptions, there has been little systematic study of the role of chance in social affairs. Vilhem Aubert analyzes the role of chance in "Chance in Social Affairs"; Thomas Mathiesen studies social reactions to the unanticipated in "The Unanticipated Event and Astonishment," *Inquiry* (1960), 3:1–17; Robert K. Merton deals with the sources of the unanticipated social event in "The Unanticipated Consequences of Purposive Social Action," p. 894–904. My study analyzes life insurance as a social mechanism to cope with the uncertainty of the time of an individual's death.

tive, trust in the wisdom and goodness of God was sufficient hedge against the uncertainty of death. Widows were counseled to "dwell on the power of God," as He was particularly concerned with their welfare:

> It has grown into a kind of current adage "that whomsoever may seem to be overlooked by Providence, God takes special care of widows and orphans." Who could not mention the names of some whom he has seen extraordinarily provided for in their necessities and seemingly helpless, hopeless widowhood!

God replaced the lost husband: "Your maker is your husband. . . . He who removes the arm of flesh that sustained the wife, lends his own arm of spirit and power to sustain the widow."[33] Religious fundamentalists objected to the rationalization of holy protection through life insurance. This secular intruder destroyed the credibility of a divinely regulated religious order in which the economic consequences of a man's untimely death to his widow and orphans were borne by God. Life insurance was God's rival: "It militates against the dearest invitations of God to his children to trust their personal and family temporal interest in the hands of their saviour."[34] Insurance companies refuted these "absurd notions," vigorously denying that life insurance was an "impious attempt to prevent or control His will."[35]

Paradoxically, religious sensitivities were not equally offended by other types of insurance, and it was common for opponents of life insurance to purchase fire or marine policies. One particularly acerbic religious censor of life insurance found only words of praise for property insurance "as a principle emanating from the Gospel concentrated into a system by the providence of God. . . ."* Life insurance spokesmen tried to impress upon the public the unfairness of this double standard. As an article on *The Morality of Life Insurance* pointed out:

> Many persons have doubted the propriety of insuring their life through a mistaken notion that life insurance is distrusting God or his protecting care. But no one doubts the propriety of investing funds in safe and undoubted securities that the heirs may derive benefit from them. Yet what is the difference of the

* George Albree, *The Evils of Life Insurance*, p. 17. The sanctity of human life remained the core of this distinction between types of insurance. Albree asked: "Is not man better than sheep? . . . Man was made in the image of God. For these reasons we do not want man . . . endowed with a conscience to be made an article of merchandise" (*ibid.*, p. 18). The *Insurance Monitor* exposed Albree's inconsistency claiming that "if Mr. Albree would be entirely consistent, he must denounce the man who buys a homestead with a view of making his family independent and comfortable in case of his own death, or who "lays up" a store of food or fuel, or clothing against the winter." *Insurance Monitor* (March 1871), 19:206.

two in respect to the government and providential arrangements of our heavenly benefactor?[36]

Others indicated that a man was no less interfering with Providence when he bought an overcoat to protect himself against cold weather, or when he secured his house with lightning rods. One popular tale, *Converting a Deacon,* told the story of a minister who infuriated his deacon by insuring his life. A few days after the deacon had irately accused him of tempting Providence, the minister found him calmly installing lightning rods on his house. He showed the deacon how that type of protection could also suggest distrust in God. The deacon learned his lesson and bought a policy.[37]

Protestant clergymen played an active role in molding public attitudes towards life insurance. While many became its fierce opponents, another group turned into the champions of the novel institution.* Theologically, the conflict was set between the fundamentalist supporters of a deterministic ethos that held Providence responsible for a man's family after his death, and spokesmen for a developing voluntaristic religious outlook to whom "Providence helps he who helps himself." The Scriptures—occasionally the very same passage—were quoted by both groups to substantiate their opposing views.[38] They struggled over the interpretation of Jer. 49:11: "Leave thy fatherless children to me, and I will preserve them alive, and let the widows trust in me."

The reinterpretation of biblical texts has been a popular and powerful tool of theologians trying to accommodate traditional religious doctrine to scientific, economic, or social progress. In this case, biblical exegesis was used by liberal theologians to include life insurance within the providential design. The debate over life insurance was but one expression of a long-lasting dispute concerning the role of Providence in public affairs, the historical origins of which Viner traces back to the earliest stages of Christian and non-Christian theology. Providential doctrines were initially

* Henry E. May points out that in the period 1828–61 the churches, although they had lost most of their claim to political control, continued supervising the morals of the country. May, *Protestant Churches and Industrial America,* p. 3. Sympathetic clergymen contributed more than theological support. The first two American organizations for life insurance were for Presbyterian and Episcopalian ministers. Clergymen also sought insurance in non-denominational companies. A report of the Mutual Benefit Life Insurance Company's first nine months of operation in 1846 showed clergymen as the second largest group of insured, after "merchants and traders" Mildred F. Stone, *A History of the Mutual Benefit Life Insurance Company* (New Brunswick, N.J.: Rutgers University Press, 1957), p. 19.

concerned with the relations of Providence to the physical order of the universe. Sixteenth- and seventeenth-century scientific progress, with the Copernican revolution in astronomy and geological discoveries, posed the first challenge to orthodox theology and its biblical account of the mode of operation of the physical universe. Providential doctrine extended to the economic order; from the seventeenth through the nineteenth century, for example, it became a commonplace notion that commerce between nations had been designed by Providence as a unifier of mankind. Providence determined the social order as well. Unequal social stratification systems were accepted as another expression of Divine wisdom, intentionally designed to maintain social order and civil peace in human society.[39] The idea that social inequality was determined by a benign Providence prevailed in eighteenth-century America, and served to justify existing social conditions. The misery of the poor was defined as a natural and just part of the divine plan. Optimistic orthodox theology upheld that deprivation was morally uplifting. The poor were also more likely to be happier and even healthier than the rich. The suffering of the bereaved widows and orphans was no less rewarding: "In God's government, the loss of the head of a family may be blessed to many of the members, may force them into habits of industry and economy, and may induce them to give up practices which were injurious to spirit, soul and body."[40]

In the nineteenth century, the goodness and necessity of poverty were questioned and effective action was sought to modify the social order: "God's will no longer seemed a satisfactory explanation for differences in social condition."[41] This tampering with the social order was frightening to many. Life insurance was perceived as an instrument of that undesirable change and a challenge to deeply rooted convictions that the existing social order was to be regulated by Providence.* To its enemies, life insurance was an "irreligious scheme,"[42] a social "ulcer" which "induces the Christian to rest on an arm of flesh rather than on the promises and power of the Lord."[43] Elder Swan, a famed revivalist of the 1840s, used his sermons to "crush the pernicious novelty:"

* The introduction of moral statistics in Europe in 1835 triggered a similar confrontation between deterministic and voluntaristic ideologies. Moral statistics, which provided the basis for predicting rates of marriage, crime, and suicide through fairly immutable social laws, were decried as a form of religious determinism. See Adolphe Jacques Quételet, "Sur la Statistique Morale," pp. 1–111; J. Lottin, "La Statistique Morale et le Determinisme," pp. 21–24; Aristide Gabelli, *Gli Scettici della Statistica;* August Meitzen, *History, Theory and Techniques of Statistics,* pp. 73–87.

> Suppose that Jesus, on His way to the Jordan, had met John among the foothills and to the question, "Wither goest thou?" John had answered: "Behold, all these years I have trusted in the God of Israel and have been sorely pressed by many troubles. Wist thou not that I go up to Jerusalem to get my life insured? Would the church, my hearers, have outlived the few and feeble days of infancy had treachery so foul been permitted to occur and to pass unrebuked? If lack of faith was a sin then, it is a sin now. Avoid the snares of a perverse generation, and say to the tempter "Get thee behind me, Satan."[44]

A German Lutheran pastor from Hartford, Connecticut, warned his congregation: "While I am a pastor in this church, none of my parishioners shall carry life insurance."[45] A Reverend Bishop of the Protestant Episcopal Church was quoted as saying: "Believing the system of chance distributions of gains, in all forms, from the polite 'art union' down to the policy of insurance, to be fraught with evil to the community I have deemed it my duty uniformly to refuse it my sanction."[46] Mennonites went to the extreme of excommunicating any member who insured his life.[47] Although weakened by the success of life insurance, the traditionalist rhetoric persisted. As late as 1899 a conference of Lutheran ministers condemned life insurance as "antagonistic to Bible teachings."[48]

Liberal theological support for life insurance was no less vigorous than the fundamentalist opposition.* Its spokesmen were clergymen who rep-

* Although I located no sources on Jewish-American attitudes towards life insurance, an interesting study of traditional Jewish opinions reveals vigorous enthusiasm and theological support. In the past seventy years, almost without exception, rabbinic halachic decisions have endorsed the insurance of lives. On a religious level, the rabbis insistingly refute the notion that life insurance symbolizes distrust of God's providence or lack of faith, suggesting instead that it is God's will that man shall provide for his death. In response to popular superstitions and prejudice, the rabbis also deny all magical objections, namely the fear that insuring one's life is "opening your mouth to Satan." According to the Talmud, one should not stir up judgments against oneself in Heaven, by suggesting the possibility of one's death. In 1925, one Hungarian rabbi, invoking earlier halachic sources, responded that according to Jewish law a healthy man can prepare in advance his grave and shrouds. Similarly, the drafting of a will is permissible, while none of these practices are thought to tempt the Devil. Far from attracting the evil decree or being a sin, it is suggested by the rabbis that since death is inevitable, early preparation for it instills a sense of seriousness in life and may stimulate repentance. On that basis, life insurance would not only be considered acceptable but theologically meritorious. To counter magical fears with more practical arguments, it is also suggested that if indeed life insurance attracted the evil decree, all companies would be rapidly bankrupt by the ill-timed death of their customers. Finally, besides religious legitimation, the rabbis found group justification for the insurance of lives, particularly if a policy is bought from a Talmud *chacham* (student). It is a contribution to the Jewish people to subsidize its scholars in this way. This information is from M. Slae, "The Relationship of Halacha to Insurance." *Noam* (Jerusalem 1978), vol. 20. See also M. Slae, "Insurance in

resented an emerging religious view which allowed for the active participation of man in the management of death. They upheld life insurance as a "Christian duty"[49] and dismissed the idea of tempting Providence as outdated superstition. Total reliance on God and Providence was no longer laudable piety, but selfish carelessness:

> Let him not have the folly or the hypocrisy to say, as is sometimes said by those who neglect this precaution [life insurance], that they trust to Providence. What right has any man to trust Providence to do for him, directly or through the mediation of others what it has enabled him to do for himself? . . . The wisdom and goodness of Providence appear in giving him this power and placing him in circumstance in which he can exercise it.*

Henry Ward Beecher, who was particularly vehement in his support of life insurance, insisted: "We have no right to trust God for anything which he has enabled us to obtain by our own skill and industry."[50]

Life insurance companies found an effective technique to silence religious hostility by recruiting sympathetic clergymen as their "pamphleteers." Some clergymen even extended their canvassing to their pulpits.

---

the Literature of Halacha," in *Rabbi David Cohen Memorial Book, Nazir Ehav* (Jerusalem: Nezer David Assoc., 1977), 3:292–327. Both articles are in Hebrew.

* Rev. Dr. Cook, "Life Insurance," pp. 381–82. The dire economic situation of many clergymen was another persuasive element in their support of life insurance. Nineteenth-century ministers were sometimes "forced to fight for their small incomes." Jackson Turner Main, *The Social Structure of Revolutionary America* (New Jersey: Princeton University Press, 1965), p. 207. According to one report, the average annual salary of a clergyman in 1859 was $500. The estimate of an adequate salary for a professional family in that period was $2,000. *American Life Assurance* (October 1859), 1:123. In 1873, the average annual income of clergymen rose to a meager $600, about one-half the salaries of mechanics "Life Insurance among Clergymen," *Insurance Monitor* (Feb. 1, 1873), 19:129. Congregations were urged to insure their clergymen as a way to relieve the misery of their widows and orphans:

"The insurance of the lives of clergymen by their people is a subject demanding earnest attention. It should be the uniform and settled policy of every congregation . . . when they have installed over them a minister, to insure his life for the benefit of his family. The cost is but little, and should be cheerfully borne by the people." George Cardwell, *A Month in a Country Parish*, p. 55.

From the congregational standpoint the payment of a life insurance premium was far more economical than to raise the minister's salary. A moderate policy of $2,000 cost $47.80 annually. From an 1824 policy from the Massachusetts Hospital Life Insurance Company, quoted by Owen J. Stalson in *Marketing Life Insurance*, p. 75. In 1873, a $5,000 policy could be obtained for $50 or $60 per year. Some congregations formed an association for "promoting life insurance among clergymen." "Life Insurance among Clergymen," p. 129.

A Reverend C. H. Spurgeon, after basing his sermon on the text, "Take no thought for the morrow what ye shall eat, or what ye shall drink," announced in his service that he had insured his life for $5,000 and "have thus been able to carry out the injunction of the text and not be overanxious for the morrow."[51] By the late nineteenth century, refutations of the fear of offending Providence became tinged with condescending irony. The following story reflects the new levity:

> "Ah! John," said a loving young wife, "it seems like tempting Providence to get your life insured; almost as if you were preparing for death, you know," and she wept a little. . . . "Don't be foolish, little one," he gently remonstrated; "if I should be called suddenly, you would have ten thousand dollars." "Ten thousand dollars, John!" she said. "I thought you were getting insured for twenty-five!"[52]

THE SOCIAL THREAT

For many, life insurance not only offended religious sensitivities, but weakened the very fiber of society by institutionalizing gambling and encouraging murder for money. "Does a man shorten his life by insuring it?" inquired the *Merchants' Magazine* in 1856, and explained: "The crime of arson is familiar to insurers against fire and upon the same principle it need surprise no one to learn that the crime of murder is sometimes committed to secure the premium on a life insurance policy."[53] An inquiry was conducted that same year in England into the "number of suspicious deaths occurring with life insurance offices." The report, widely publicized in the United States, found numerous cases of rich men speculating with the lives of paupers.[54] A similar type of speculation was later carried on in the United States. The dangers were clear:

> When a man is continually harboring in his mind the idea that as soon as the subject dies he will be possessed of largely increased riches, it is not in the human nature to suppress the desire. . . . What a desire he has that the Lord would call the old man off. . . . What this spirit may lead him to do God only knows.[55]

The only restraint to even wider speculation was the difficulty of circumventing the requirement of insurable interest, which minimized the possibilities of insuring the lives of strangers:

> If an entire stranger to me were permitted to take out a policy on my life, his sole interest . . . would be in my speedy death. The law therefore wisely takes from him the temptation to bring about the event by forbidding such contract.[56]

To its detractors, even the most legitimate use of life insurance introduced an interest factor that polluted "domestic purity." The story was circulated of a well-known New Yorker whose policy became renewable as he lay gravely ill in bed, without any money left to pay the required premium:

> His wife knows the contingency. . . . The policy would expire on the morrow and though his recovery was possible, the support of his family depended on his speedy death. Conjugal duty and pecuniary interest were in demoralizing conflict. . . . Was the wife to attempt a prolongation of his life under the hazard of a widowhood of penury? . . . He died before the hour at which his policy was to expire.*

There was more concern, however, for the social hazards of life insurance than for its physical dangers. Without insurable interest, life insurance was no more than a "mere wager, a bet on my life, a gambling contract" and as such, "opposed to good morals and sound public policy."[57] As one writer points out: "Rather strange to relate . . . the objection to life insurance as inciting murder has been less dwelt upon and its evils less pointed out . . . than the one relating to wagering contracts."[58] American courts were particularly concerned with the harmful social and economic effects of all wagering contracts. While English common law had no general prohibition against the enforcement of wagering contracts, almost every American state adopted some statutory or constitutional provision making wagers illegal to some degree. A prominent jurist explains why:

> In this country, by legislation and judicial decision the hostility to wagers of every nature has been marked. Wagers are inconsistent with the established interests of society, are in conflict with the morals of the age and as such are void as against public policy.[59]

*A. B. Johnson, "The Relative Merits of Life Insurance and Savings Banks," p. 673. Short of murder, another fraudulent use of life insurance was the substitution of a healthy person for a sick one in the medical checkup required to authorize a policy. The *Insurance Monitor* foresaw this as the new "Jewish crime:"

"The indictments handed down by the Grand Jury in this city last month show the Jew in a new role. . . . In fire insurance he has become so notorious that change of name has become an almost necessary part of the programme. . . . [The Jew] . . . has been quick to learn from the Gentiles the trick of substituting a healthy life for the medical examination." "Life Bugs," *Insurance Monitor* (August 1895), 43:326.

Objections to wagering in England did not have a similar moral underpinning. The legal enforcement of wagers was simply held to be a nuisance and an unnecessary waste of legal time and effort. Accordingly, wagers on human lives were dismissed as a "mischievous kind of gaming" and not as immoral contracts.[60]

From the American perspective, gambling and speculation threatened an especially cherished bulwark of the social order; individual motivation to work in socially productive employment. As early as 1806, a Massachusetts court declared: "The practice of gaming . . . withdraws the exertions of men from useful pursuits. . . . By pointing out a speedy, though hazardous mode of accumulating wealth it produces a contempt for the moderate, but certain profits of sober industry." * Similarly, the rationale of American statutory provisions against wagering was that it "destroys . . . all desire to engage in legitimate employment or business."[61] The law reflected the traditional Puritan religious precepts which condemned all occupation without social purpose. Under similar influence, secular business authorities urged the young to select socially useful occupations.[62]

Paradoxically, using social utility as a parameter of morality condoned certain forms of gambling. Eighteenth century lotteries, for instance, had been justified by their economic contributions to the general society; they served to finance extensive civic and state projects. Religious opposition was minimal, as the churches adopted lotteries as their major fund-raising device.[63] Society's ambivalence towards gambling has discouraged the establishment of universal rules to distinguish legitimate from illegitimate forms. As a result existing criteria are arbitrary and highly variable.† The only path to respectable wealth was through the sober and gradual ac-

* Amory V. Gilman, 2 Mass. 1, 10–11 (1806). Devereux indicates the socioeconomic sources for this antagonism to gambling: "Since its rewards are distributed on the basis of chance, gambling would appear to make a mockery of the legitimate economy with its stress on rationality . . . and hard work, and its assumed correlations of effort, merit, and reward." "Gambling," p. 56.

† Herbert A. Bloch, "The Sociology of Gambling," p. 216. At times, certain chance devices were even asserted to be divinely justified as the means to uncover the will of God. Devereux, "Gambling," p. 58; Aubert, "Chance in Social Affairs," p. 7; Gillian Lindt Gollin, *Moravians in Two Worlds*, p. 58. In Norway, the use of lots was legally justified as the only impartial mechanism for jury selection. American emphasis on the principle of social utility is still reflected in contemporary insurance law. In Connecticut and Oregon, one can insure the life of another person in which he has no interest, provided the beneficiary is a charitable, educational, or religious institution. Richard H. Hollenberg, "Is a Uniform Statute on Insurable Interest Desirable?" p. 77.

cumulation of money. Weiss explains: "Money tied to work and gradually accumulated by the sweat of one's brow was deserved but money amassed without commensurate labor was not." Shortcuts to wealth were "contrary to God's law,"[64] leading inevitably to fraud and failure. *Hunt's Merchants' Magazine* warned its readers: "Do not make too much haste to be rich. By this means nineteen-twentieths of our merchants fail. . . . Caution, prudence, sagacity and deliberation are all necessary to success."[65] Freeman Hunt, the prominent business publicist, explained most frauds by "the attempt to grow rich rapidly by financiering rather than by diligence in business." He advised young men:

> Let speculators make their thousands in a year or a day. . . . Let your business be some one which is useful to the community. . . . Do not be in a hurry to be rich. Gradual gains are the only natural gains.[66]

This moral perspective made the sudden creation of wealth by a life insurance policy immediately suspect. Its benefits were deemed as corrupting and socially disruptive as any other speculative gain:

> The elements which go to make up an independent working man are not to be sought in this direction at all. The less he has to do with gambling in any shape or guise the better for him. True "independence" is not to be secured by paying tribute year after year to any self-constituted irresponsible company under the promise of large repayment upon some remote contingency.[67]

Life insurance would not only "paralyze a man's efforts,"[68] but jeopardize the very principle of self-help: "It is calculated to encourage reliance upon something beside economy and industry and to lead accordingly to the relaxation and decay of those cardinal virtues of society."[69] For many, life insurance was nothing more than a "scheme by which lazy men could shift the burdens of their own responsibilities upon the shoulders of other people."[70] Other forms of insurance, as we have seen, were exempt from moral condemnation, and the very critics of life insurance, oblivious to the contradiction, considered it "unjust" and even "criminal" to leave property uninsured.[71]

Those who attacked life insurance hailed savings banks as the institutional hallmark of two cardinal virtues: gradual accumulation of wealth and self-help. The savings bank, claimed the *New York Times*, in 1853, "is as good an insurance company as any man needs."[72] The payoff was not limited to money: "A man's self-respect and the respect of his wife and children will increase continually as his savings augment."[73] Life insurance and savings banks were pitched against each other in a moral dispute, with each front claiming for itself the highest social virtues. To its advocates, only savings banks could successfully awaken the "appetite for accumulation:"

> A boy who makes snowballs will throw them away as fast as he makes them, but should he chance to roll up one of more than ordinary size it will excite in him an ambition to enlarge it, instead of throwing it away. The principle applies to money. Should (a man) deposit any of his earnings in a savings bank an appetite for accumulation is immediately produced by the unusual possession of a surplus.[74]

By replacing gradual accumulation by instant wealth, life insurance was not only morally nefarious but dangerously inefficient. A. Johnson, president of a savings bank, warned the public in 1851 that life insurance counteracted the design of Providence to keep men active through the "pressure of wants" and not the "anodyne of security." "Easy" money could only be carelessly squandered or naively lost. It was pointed out that the heirs of rich men "rarely exhibit self-denial in expenditures or energy in business."[75] A writer in the *Merchants' Magazine* concluded:

> One of the worst mistakes men make is in leaving gifts . . . to be dispensed after their death. . . . To this error can be traced the ruin of so many young men whom the death of a father leaves rolling in wealth.*

Neither could inexpert and vulnerable widows be expected to handle properly the sudden wealth created by insurance benefits:

> This money comes into her possession when she is without experience in money matters, and totally unacquainted with any way of investing her funds. . . . How great would be the danger of a widow's losing all she might thus come into possession of. Her position, too . . . is one in which she might easily be imposed upon by injudicious and designing persons, and be thus deprived of the benefits of the insurance.†

* The case of a McDonough estate in New Orleans was presented as an illustration of the misuse of inherited wealth:

"Not one dollar of charity has ever been received from the estate, not one negro been sent to Liberia, nor the tears and sorrows of one poor orphan boy ever been assuaged. . . . The last will and testament of John McDonough has been frustrated and thwarted." "Dead Men's Shoes," *Hunt's Merchants' Magazine* (October 1860), 48:522–23.

† "Life Insurance," *Hunt's Merchants' Magazine*, (May 1862), 46:490. Stories had begun circulating earlier in the century on the unstable nature of "easy wealth" obtained through lottery winnings. John Samuel Ezell, *Fortune's Merry Wheel: The Lottery in America*, p. 82. The dangers of easy wealth remained a favorite argument against life insurance. In 1912 a savings bank historian commented:

"Every savings bank man can tell tales of money suddenly acquired going as quickly as it

Savings banks were upheld as safeguards against these dangers. Widows and orphans would be better prepared to preserve the slowly accumulated savings of a deceased father than the sudden wealth of a life insurance policy.

Life insurance spokesmen responded to this barrage of criticisms with equally forceful and vocal arguments. Self-dependence was presented as a major contribution of life insurance, and the reason for its moral superiority over other institutions such as hospitals, orphan schools, and almshouses, which "tend to the infusion of a dangerous leaven of carelessness as to the future."[76] The *Insurance Monitor* denied that life insurance reduced motivation to work or made men "careless and negligent of their pecuniary affairs:"

> The same argument would equally apply to all endeavors to emancipate ourselves from the risks to which human life is subject. . . . But far from this being true . . . [life insurance] promotes economy, industry and a habit of forethought and care.[77]

It also protected against the "zeal to get rich fast." Accusations of gambling were silenced by highlighting the speculative potential of savings banks:

> If I had so much money in the bank, I might be tempted to use it in some inviting speculation and hazard every dollar. . . . I must confess I have been sorely tempted to get a living in some easier mode than working our rocky soil, and often wished I had a few hundred dollars to try my hand at some speculation. Now, with this Policy of Insurance, the craving speculative demon is kept down.[78]

The insurance world pointed to the underlying philosophy of savings banks as evidence of moral weakness. Savings banks operated on the principle that "we shall take care of the future by taking care of the present and take care of our descendants by taking care of ourselves."[79] This made them "earthly" institutions, while life insurance came "from above, pure, heavenly and divine."[80] Particularly during the first half of the nineteenth century and into the 1860s, life insurance prided itself for upholding the virtues of altruism and self-denial over selfishness and acquisitiveness:

came. . . . The widow who "invested" her two thousand of life insurance money at Sheepshead Bay when the races were on, only to come back broke . . . another who invested her portfolio in jewelry . . . are but types of thousands to whom money has been a curse through the spendthrift habit urged along by the fact that it was easy money and therefore of little value." William H. Kniffin, Jr., *The Savings Bank and its Practical Work*, pp. 32–33.

> Actions having self for their object and end, exercise and strengthen selfishness. . . . In life insurance, present good is sacrificed to purchase a future advantage for others—an advantage the insured cannot share—and which is only realized after death. . . .

The insured, claimed the *Merchants' Magazine*, were a moral elite, "the very best class of the community."*

The dispute between savings banks and life insurance reflected a deeper conflict between a traditional economic morality and the emerging entrepreneurial ethos. McConnell notes that in the 1860s economic conduct "overflowed the traditional boundaries,"[81] transforming the meaning of economic virtues such as self-help, thrift, and honesty. The proliferation of business risks in the increasingly complex commercial system made its mark on traditional attitudes toward risk and speculation. In the first place, the individual assumption of risk crucial to an earlier definition of self-help was replaced by a new collective approach and the expansion of risk-bearing institutions such as insurance companies.† While savings banks had symbolized an earlier definition of individualistic self-

* "Benefits of Life Insurance," *Hunt's Merchants' Magazine* (September, 1865), 53:390. The dispute was not exclusively ideological; each of the parties also claimed superior economic benefits for its position. The following story presents in a capsule the arguments of life insurance advocates:

"A Savings Bank Account and a Life Insurance policy, both the children of a prudent businessman, met after his death to see what they could do for the aid of his family. With the statement "I am ready cash," the Bank Account paid the funeral expenses and lifted up its voice and said: "I contribute every dollar deposited plus a snug sum of compound interest." The Insurance Policy said: "I contribute every dollar deposited and a snug sum of compound interest and the prepaid fortune for this case made and provided." And it lifted the mortgage from the home and the whole family from poverty to comparative independence." "A Trial of Strength," in James T. Phelps, *Life Insurance Sayings*, p. 85.

Life insurance took much of the business away from savings banks. Goldsmith's study shows how the spread of private life insurance reduced the amount of savings in individual households. R. W. Goldsmith, *A Study of Savings in the United States*, p. 18.

† It was no longer feasible to follow the policy of the early trust companies that limited their services to the dependent class. White explains their rationale:

"They held this attitude not because they believed it was beyond the ability of the company to take care of more funds, but because their New England Puritan heritage put an emphasis on indivdual responsibility. They did not wish their institution to serve individuals who ought to be able to serve themselves." Gerald T. White, *A History of the Massachusetts Hospital Life Insurance Company*, p. 77.

Another expression of the new flexibility of the notion of self-help was that many successful businessmen no longer depended on their individual savings to get started, but relied on the financial assistance of others. Donald McConnell, *Economic Virtues in the United States*, p. 149.

help, insurance companies were at the vanguard of the new collective form, assuming risks for the entire population. Tishler discusses this shift:

> In the light of the conventional faith in the penny savings bank, the newer collective form represented a further step in the direction of redefining self-reliance when economic dysfunctions had rendered the purely individualistic efforts useless—except in the moral sense.*

The morality of the new cooperative approach was brought forth in life insurance writings:

> A life insurance company is a combination of intelligent men who join hands in the effort to alleviate the sum of human misery and want, and who are wise enough to listen to the command: "Bear ye one another's burden."[82]

Secondly, as risk increasingly became an integral part of the American economic system, certain forms of risk taking and speculation assumed new respectability. Rational speculation that dealt with already existent risks was differentiated from pure gambling which created artificial risk.† By the end of the nineteenth century, speculation was being defended as serving "an important economic function."[83] The new legitimacy of the

*Hace Sorel Tishler, *Self-Reliance and Social Security 1870–1917*, p. 24. For Tishler, social security was the next stage in redefining self-reliance. Ironically, the objections to social security expressed by life insurance advocates in the 1870s were almost identical to those used fifty years earlier against their own industry. The ultimate justification for the defense of voluntary institutions did not hinge on issues of economic efficiency, but once again morality was at stake. Roy Lubove, *The Struggle for Social Security*, p. 10. It was contended that social security would be unable to fulfill a number of indispensable educational, social, and moral ends. Above all, it would undermine the principles of thrift and self-help.

†Certain speculative ventures were legitimated as mechanisms to absorb the perils of existing risks. In the commodity market, futures trading in provisions and commodities was formally organized after the Civil War to protect merchants against their growing vulnerability to unexpected price changes. Through futures contracts, or hedging, the risk was shifted to a specialized group of speculators. These were differentiated from gamblers and renamed risk specialists. Occupational specialization was an important prerequisite to the acceptability of speculation as the only means to avoid "the moral evil of reckless participation." Cedric B. Cowing, *Populists, Plungers, and Progressives*, p. 49. Supporters of the earlier traditional economic morality saw in futures trading only "gambling dens full of parasitic speculators." Richard J. Teweley, Charles U. Hanlow, and Herbert L. Stone, *The Commodity Futures Game*, p. 11. Their attempts, however, to restrict or abolish futures trading invariably failed. On the development of other risk-bearing mechanisms, and on differences between gambling and "legitimate" speculation, see Charles O. Hardy, *Risk and Risk-Bearing*, pp. 66, 128.

speculative appeal was reflected in the development of life insurance. The instant creation of wealth through the benefits of a life policy, initially rebuked as speculation by a traditional economic morality, eventually became an advantage to be boasted over the slower process of the savings bank. "Life insurance secures a fortune instantly," advertised the prospectus for Equitable in 1885, which went on to describe the reasons for its popularity:

> It furnishes the only known method of creating capital instantly. There are other methods of accumulating fortunes: The poor man may after years of frugality realize some interest upon his small deposit in the savings bank. . . . But the investor in life assurance has no sooner made a payment of a moderate sum, than he finds from one thousand to one hundred thousand dollars to his credit.[84]

Similarly, while for the greater part of the early nineteenth century life insurance companies had protested and denied all speculative connections, in the 1860s their business thrived on an openly speculative policy.

Tontines, rejected by the public at the beginning of the century, were reintroduced in 1867 so successfully as to become the leading factor in the fantastic growth of life insurance during that period. All except three life insurance companies—The Connecticut Mutual Life Insurance Company, the Mutual Benefit, and the Provident Life and Trust—adopted its system. Tontines "took like wild fire" and there was no question that the attraction of speculation was responsible for their impact.* Agents sold tontine policies as "possible prizes in a great insurance lottery" where you did not have to die to win.[85] Hendrick later recalled: "Thousands willingly staked their own chances of living and paying with the similar chances of their fellow insurers and risked all their own life insurance for a possibility of getting a part of that of their less fortunate associates."[86] Opponents were in the minority, their voices barely audible when they

* Burton Hendrick, "The Story of Life Insurance," pp. 411–412. The appeal of tontines was closely related to a changed definition of the purpose of life insurance. While for the first part of the nineteenth century life insurance was designed for the protection of dependents, its investment potential was gradually uncovered. Henry H. Hyde of Equitable, responsible for introducing tontines, was quite candid on this subject: "The Tontine principle is precisely the reverse of that upon which Life Assurance is based. In the former case the motive is essentially selfish." Quoted by Hendrick, "Story of Life Insurance," p. 402. Traditionalists saw tontines as a "complete perversion" of the true nature of life insurance. From a letter by Jacob L. Greene, President of the Connecticut Mutual Life Insurance Co., *New York Tribune*, Jan. 4, 1886, p. 5, quoted by Stalson, *Marketing Life Insurance*, p. 493. Changes in the definition of life insurance will be traced in the following chapter.

denounced tontine policies as "pure gambling" and as "life insurance cannibalism." *

Life insurance was caught between two ideologies of necessary risk and gambling. The traditional deterministic view which prevailed during the earlier half of the nineteenth century feared the disruptive potential of wagering on an orderly social and religious world. Life insurance was attacked as ungodly gambling and an unacceptable challenge to the role of Providence in human affairs. It was accused of undermining social principles as well. By holding out the promise of instant wealth, it discouraged the gradual accumulation of money and weakened individual motivation to seek useful employment. By assuming others' risks, it undermined self-reliance.

A different, more entrepreneurial ideology of risk emerged from the growing complexity of the economic system and the proliferation of business risks, particularly after the Civil War. Strictly individualistic conceptions of self-help dwindled, replaced by more efficient cooperative risk-bearing techniques. In addition, the indispensability of efficient risk management legitimized and upgraded certain speculative ventures as risk-bearing enterprises, clearly differentiated from purposeless gambling.

From the religious viewpoint, voluntaristic theological conceptions rejected the role of God as an all-purpose insurance policy and upheld the duty of man to provide for the economic contingencies of his death to his

*Greene, quoted by William Cahn, *A Matter of Life and Death* (New York: Random House, 1970), p. 109; Elizur Wright, 1882, quoted by R. Carlyle Buley in *The Equitable Life Assurance Society of the United States*, p. 99. Tontines were outlawed in 1905 as a result of the Armstrong investigations, a series of legislative hearings which resulted in stricter governmental regulation of life insurance companies. Stalson indicates that after 1905: "The speculative appeal gave way to the conservative, and protection, not profits became the theme of life insurance marketing." Stalson, *Marketing Life Insurance*, p. 547. In 1939, the "Colgrove plan" attempted to revive tontine policies but was declared invalid by the courts as a wagering contract because of lack of insurable interest in the lives of other policyholders: "The very basis of the scheme is a wager for personal profit, an opportunity to speculate on one's chances of outliving the other members." Knott v. State, 136 Fla. 184, p. 200. Life insurance companies have recently attempted to revive the speculative appeal by introducing "variable life insurance," in which policyholders' premiums are invested in the stock market, making the cash value of the policy fluctuate accordingly. *New York Times*, Business section, November 26, 1972, p. 1. There has been little interest in this policy, among other reasons, because the public feels it is "too risky, too much of a gamble" and it is "gambling, a prostitution of life insurance." *The Map Report–1973 Survey*, pp. 90–93.

family.* Life insurance emerged as the most efficient secular risk-bearing institution to handle the economic hazards of death through cooperative self-help. The new legitimacy of speculation was revealed by the success of the tontines that began in 1867. After years of disguising its speculative potential behind careful rhetoric and vigorous denials, life insurance finally succeeded through the unabashed exploitation of its most speculative features.

*To the pragmatists of the late nineteenth century, the belief in God became itself another risk they were willing to assume as an insurance policy against eternal damnation in case He did exist. William James, *Essays in Pragmatism* (New York: Hafner Publishing Co., 1948), pp. 91, 106.

Chapter 6
Marketing Life:
Moral Persuasion and Business Enterprise

> Insurance replaces the service of humanity by service of money and undermines the sense of compassion which should form the basis of society.[1]

In the eighteenth century, the widow and her orphans were assisted by their neighbors and relatives, as well as by mutual aid groups that ministered to the economic hardships of the bereaved. In the nineteenth century, the financial protection of American families became a purchasable commodity. Life insurance companies offered a policy in lieu of kin and friends, and by 1851 over $100 million of security were being bought. The shift from mutual assistance to the marketplace signaled a drastic departure from a system of gift relationships to a new economic type of exchange. While status prescribes reciprocal types of exchange, market relationships are regulated by contract and not obligation. In a gift-exchange system, men are bound by trust and community solidarity, but in the impersonal economic market they come together as buyers and sellers of commodities. The shift from voluntary aid to paid aid has been analyzed by Titmuss in the context of blood donations. Titmuss contends that commercialization destroys crucial social bonds by discouraging altruism and voluntary giving among men.[2] The informal type of mutual aid given by a community to widows and orphans was replaced by a formal contractual agreement to a commercial institution and the payment of yearly premiums. Spontaneous help was bureaucratized by systematic and rational risk-bearing techniques. But although life insurance provided an efficient financial alternative to cooperative methods of support, it did not qualify as their moral substitute. Systems of voluntary mutual aid were deemed morally and socially superior to paid protection, which obliterated "spontaneous love and duty."[3] Groups like the Mennonites which had encouraged the formation of mutual aid groups among their members objected vehemently to commercial life insurance because it was "contrary to the spirit of genuine mutual aid and brotherhood."[4]

Resistance to the shift from "cooperativism" to contract was not unique to white middle-income groups for which ordinary life insurance was primarily intended.* It was similarly experienced by other socio-ethnic groups later in the nineteenth century. In the 1870s commercial life insurance lured by the vast untapped lower-class market, began selling industrial insurance to the poor.† It competed with nonprofit fraternal

*The urban middle class, businessmen in particular, became the foremost purchasers of life insurance. The very rich had other financial protection to offer their families, while the poor could not afford the high premiums of regular life insurance. For example, the monthly report of the New York Life Insurance and Trust Company for August 1839, showed that of 18 persons insured, 7 were merchants or brokers, and 3 manufacturers. *Hunt's Merchants' Magazine* (October 1839), 1:368. Of 796 life policies issued by the Mutual Life Insurance Company of New York between February 1843 and August 1844, 396 were to merchants, clerks, and agents, 37 to brokers, and 25 to manufacturers. *Hunt's Merchants' Magazine* (October 1844), 11:340. Similarly, in 1845, merchants, traders, and manufacturers constituted the largest groups insured in the State Mutual Life Insurance Company. H. Ladd, *A Heritage of Integrity* (New York: Newcomen Society of North America, 1954), p. 11. A summary of the Mutual Benefit Life Insurance Company's first nine months of operation in 1846 showed "merchants and traders" once again as the largest group to become insured: 412 out of a total of 936. Mildred F. Stone, *Since 1845*, p. 18. The first report of the New England Mutual Life Insurance Company in 1846 presents similar evidence. The largest proportion of policies were bought by merchants, traders, and brokers. *Hunt's Merchants' Magazine* (April 1846), 14:389. Currie explained the attraction of life insurance for middle-class businessmen in the nineteenth century:

"To the merchant, or man of business, the system of Life Assurance has many things to recommend it to his favourable notice; the very property which he calls his own to-day may become another's tomorrow. . . . While he is . . . congratulating himself upon his favourable position, circumstances, unknown and unforeseen, may be taking place around him, which . . . are calculated ere long utterly to blast his hopes . . . with bitter misfortune." Gilbert E. Currie, *The Insurance Agent's Assistant*, p. 123.

Currie's book was issued in America that same year receiving widespread attention. The fear of failure and the threat of downward mobility permeate business periodicals of the nineteenth century. Life insurance companies capitalized on the pervasive anxiety of the middle-class, becoming its safeguard against unexpected reversals of fortunes that could leave a family destitute at the father's death. For other evidence on the fear of failure among nineteenth-century businessmen, see Michael B. Katz, *The People of Hamilton, Canada West* (Cambridge: Harvard University Press, 1975), pp. 188–89. The relationship between the adoption of life insurance and issues of social mobility and stratification is a subject for further research.

†Regular life insurance that catered to business, professional, and white-collar markets was "class insurance," too expensive for the poor; while industrial insurance was "mass in-

societies organized in the same period by the growing mass of urban industrial workers, which along with death payments offered its members important social benefits. The difference between both organizations was clear: "Life insurance as carried on by corporations or companies is solely a matter of contract, while all forms of organizations such as Fraternal Orders are either wholly or largely operated on the ancient basis of status."[5] Despite the undisputed technical superiority of industrial insurance companies, whose security and efficiency remained unmatched by fraternal societies, by 1895 the insurance in force of fraternal orders still surpassed that of regular life insurance companies.* Sponsors of commercial insurance complained against the unreasonable popular preference for the "magic" word cooperation over financial solvency, and against the generalized resistance "to establish a company solely on business principles, offering insurance as a matter of contract without any pretense of pseudo-philanthropy."[6]

Commercial life insurance companies for blacks met with similar prejudices. In 1898, DuBois lamented the rise of secular business institutions that replaced the earlier black mutual benefit associations. While admitting the greater efficiency of the former, DuBois feared the corrosion "of the spirit of cooperation with the ethics of capitalism."† Thus, the change

---

surance." Frederick L. Hoffman, *History of the Prudential Insurance Company of America*, p. 3. A few ordinary life insurance companies had offered low-priced policies since 1840 but without success. The Prudential, America's first industrial insurance company, began its operations in 1875. While the middle-class bought life insurance as family protection, lower-class life insurance was burial insurance, purchased to avoid the degradation of a pauper funeral.

* On the higher degree of efficiency and reliability of industrial insurance, see John F. Dryden, *Addresses and Papers on Life Insurance and Other Subjects*, p. 56; Hoffman, *History of the Prudential*, p. 33; Morton Keller, *The Life Insurance Enterprise*, p. 11. The assessment plan adopted by fraternal societies was their major technical deficiency. Unlike level premium life insurance which charges policyholders a relatively higher premium in earlier years to build up a reserve for later years when the risk of death increases, fraternal members were assessed only to pay current expenses and death losses. As the membership grew older and their death rate increased, assessments became larger and increasingly frequent, dissuading younger members from joining. Lester W. Zartman, "History of Life Insurance in the United States," pp. 91–92; Richard de Raismes Kip, *Fraternal Life Insurance in America*, p. 94.

† W. E. B. Du Bois, "Some Efforts of Negroes for Their Own Social Betterment," Atlanta University Publications no. 3 (Atlanta: Atlanta University Press, 1898), pp. 17–21; cited by Walter B. Weare, *Black Business in the New South*, p. 17. Du Bois introduced racial overtones to the issue, hoping that "the American zeal to profiteer would not overtake the African impulse to cooperate" (*ibid.*). Black mutual aid groups had assisted their members in

from mutual aid to a commercial system of economic provision for widows and orphans was, for most groups, no mere organizational innovation but a complex cultural transformation as well, from an ideology of altruistic exchange to a market ideology. The market as ideology represents certain value elements such as efficiency, equity, and freedom to make markets possible. The ideology of altruism endorses a different set of values such as trust, community solidarity, and community feeling. From this ideological perspective, freedom represents freedom *from* the market and market relationships.*

How did the life insurance industry respond to the strain of marketing life and protection? There were two major stages, the first extending from the early nineteenth century to the 1870s. During this time, life insurance companies appealed to the ethics and not the pocketbooks of their customers, using moral persuasion to convince a skeptical public of the legitimacy of their enterprise. They were so effective that by the 1870s the marketing of life insurance had become big business. A second stage then began during which life insurance discarded its moralistic approach for sober business methods. The shift from moral persuasion to business enterprise can be traced in three contexts: the industry's self-image, the functions of the life insurance policy, and the buyers' motivation.

THE INDUSTRY: FROM BENEFICENCE TO BUSINESS

The life insurance business had to establish its legitimacy by convincing the public that paid protection for widows and orphans was not merely technically efficient but a morally superior system. Institutionalized charity and bureaucratized altruism were depicted as the necessary and positive

---

sickness and death since the eighteenth century. An earlier effort to commercialize black life insurance in 1810 had quickly failed. Industrial insurance companies excluded blacks with the rationale that their excessive mortality rates resulted in unfair higher premiums for white policyholders. The companies fought a losing battle against legal efforts to end such discrimination and after 1894 most states passed laws compelling life insurance companies to consider black applicants. See Hoffman, *History of the Prudential*, p. 137.

*On the market as ideology versus the ideology of altruistic exchange, see Barnard Barber, "The Absolutization of the Market," pp. 3–4. On the different definitions of freedom, see *ibid.*, pp. 17–18.

developments of a higher stage of mankind: "Perhaps in no instance is the value of mutual aid better exemplified than in its use and appliance to the principle and practice of life assurance in civilized communities." [7] Life insurance rose "a step farther in the scale of a refined charity," [8] replacing mutual aid associations which belonged to a "previous stage of civilization." [9] It assured the survival of altruism in modern society by transforming the transient "sentiments and emotions of charity and benevolence" [10] into factual deeds. A life insurance company, explained the *United States Insurance Gazette* "gives to charity a serener face and a more attractive countenance, in fact, raises the entire level of society . . . and confers new dignity upon the human race." [11]

Earlier modes of assistance were all declared equally unreliable and inadequate.* Voluntary arrangements were dismissed as honorable but impractical:

> If it were practicable, no system of assurance would be so complete as a common brotherhood. But that which seems to our moral nature so desirable a consummation is surely never to be realized on earth. What gives life assurance its greatest claim to confidence is the fact that it is entirely practical. [12]

Life insurance writings warned particularly against dependence on the "capricious and stinted" aid of friends and neighbors, [13] asking readers: "Can a man expect the world to do for his family what he has refused to do for it himself?" [14] All illusions concerning the warmth and generosity of spontaneous, mutual forms of support for the bereaved were destined to be shattered by a cruel, pitiless reality: "Hard . . . is the lot of those who are cast upon the cold charity of the world. . . . If the head of the family wishes to protect his wife and children from the worst ills and misfortunes of life, he must not trust the world." [15] The community would always be "unwilling" to provide aid, the kindness of the family was "cold," and the charity of the friend "reluctant." [16] Friends, warned Knapp, "pity, but do not relieve; advise, but give not wherewith to put their excellent plans into execution." [17] Although eager to instill a charitable image of life insur-

* Barber notes the mixture of positive and negative elements in ideologies; indicating how "where one value or norm preference is being justified, its opposites or alternatives have to be criticized to strengthen the positive justification." Bernard Barber, "Function, Variability and Change in Ideological Systems," p. 247. As one way to establish its own legitimacy, the emerging market ideology of protection had to discredit previous altruistic modes of assistance. Similarly, industrial insurance advocates later in the nineteenth century disparaged fraternal societies as a "complete perversion of the principle of association." Hoffman, *History of the Prudential*, p. 19.

ance, its sponsors were careful to distinguish it from traditional forms of charity:

> Some persons look upon insurance as another word for charity, whereas the two things are as widely different as possible. The one creates a feeling of self-respect and independence, whereas the other destroys both, and often pauperizes that which is intended to benefit.[18]

Life insurance intended to place its beneficiaries "above the need of public charity,"[19] sparing the widow all unnecessary humiliation:

> Perhaps the mother may have a scanty pittance doled out to her by some charitably disposed individual, but . . . given in a manner—with that pitiful patronizing air which with some persons takes the place of sympathy . . . which stings the poor recipient to the quick and probes the wound it pretends to heal.[20]

The only respectable substitute for the "willing and unwearying hands" of the lost husband was life insurance, "an association that is legally as well as morally bound to impart the necessary aid in the days of trouble."[21]

The "heaven-born" beneficence of life insurance justified its commanding place among the "human and benevolent institutions of the day."[22] A speaker at the first convention of life insurance underwriters conveyed the prevalent doctrine of life insurance as an instrument of social benevolence: "Among all the charitable and philanthropic institutions which embellish and adorn the age in which we live, there are few, if any, which more emphatically commend themselves to our feelings and our judgement than life insurance."[23] Far from being an agent of materialism, life insurance was destined to become a force of spirituality: "[Life insurance] is destined to achieve an emancipation of the mind from the worship of the 'almighty dollar' and cure that eating cancer of the soul, the overreaching desire and passion for acquiring riches and to substitute in place the contented mind."[24] The great success of the mutual companies in the mid-1840s was largely the result of an operating structure that enhanced the morally beneficent features of life insurance while effectively minimizing its commercial aspects. Mutuals were described as "a brotherhood of provident husbands and fathers. . . . They have formed themselves into a mutual association, the great object of which is to protect their families against want."[25] Although mutual companies had the same corporate structure as the earlier stock companies, their operations were not for profit and any surplus was returned to the policyholder as a dividend. This fit well with the notion that profits tarnished an essentially Provident institution. In addition, policyholders rather than stockholders held theoretical voting control of mutual companies creating an "illusion of depositor ownership" attractive to many who mistrusted a profit-making institution.* The benevolent purposes and nature of mutual companies were repeatedly stressed in their early advertising. The moral satisfactions of its leaders were dramatized, effectively outstaging all commercial motivations. Insurance organizers sought no better reward than "the blessings of many a widow and many an orphan."[26]

In the struggle to legitimate the marketing of life values, the life insurance business summoned the aid of religion. Heiner was forthright: "If life insurance is morally wrong, then society itself will have to be reconstructed. . . . The principles of life insurance are sanctioned by the spirit of Christianity." The origins of life insurance were traced to the early Christians who "sold off their individual possessions and held everything in common." To follow the example of the first Christians was, therefore, the guarantee of the industry's theological respectability:

> No one will doubt . . . that the principle . . . adopted by the early followers of our Lord, received the sanction of the Divine approbation. . . . If the early Christians felt called upon to make provision for poor widows in the Church indiscriminately, why should it be thought out of place for a husband . . . to lay up a few hundred dollars in a life insurance office . . . for the benefit of his own poor wife and children.[27]

The Christian roots were particularly tangible in America, where the pioneering life insurance corporations had been designed for the benefit of clergymen's widows and orphans. The organizers of these funds defined their task as a "pious charity," and the logical extension of the "sacred oracles of God" to help all widows and orphans.† Religious legi-

* Douglass C. North and Lance E. Davis, *Institutional Change and American Economic Growth*, p. 120. Actual control of the companies, however, was never with the policyholders but rested in the organizations' top officials. Spencer L. Kimball, *Insurance and Public Policy*, pp. 48–49; Keller, *The Life Insurance Enterprise*, p. 41.

† Religiosity pervaded the enterprise; meetings were held in church and preambled by sermons. The administration of the Fund was gratuitous, "without the least bias to lead it away from perfect benevolence to the objects of relief." See John William Wallace, *Historical Sketch of the Corporation for the Relief of the Widows and Orphans of Clergymen in the Communion of the Protestant Church*, pp. 12, 19, 21. The same was true for the Presbyterian Fund. See Alexander Mackie, *Facile Princeps: The Story of the Beginning of Life Insurance in America*, p. 130.

timation was extended from the form and purpose of life insurance to its technical principles. Even actuarial laws were felt to be divinely inspired:

> Life assurance, rests on Divine law, as its only true basis, and the assured in so doing at once places himself under the protection of this law. Hence it banishes speculation from society and brings all things in subjection to Divine government and will.*

Secular terminology was avoided, and the expectation of human life was euphemistically referred to by some insurance writers as the Scriptural "appointed day."[28]

Life insurance was hailed by its supporters as a "national blessing"[29] and lauded as "God-like" and an "auxiliary to the cause of religion:"[30]

> Hitherto the religious portion of the community have looked upon life insurance rather askance . . . yet the destitution, and poverty, and wretchedness and misery and vice and ignorance and crime that must be exiled by it, should make it the handmaid of religion, and a frequent theme from the pulpit. Millions upon millions of dollars . . . are now laid up in deposit in this Widows' and Orphans' Bank, to be paid out at the order of God.[31]

Only those unburdened with financial anxieties were free to concentrate on religious matters and achieve that "equanimity of temperament which is essential to the gradual development of the religious life."[32] The religious influence of life insurance permeated a man's entire being: "A few thousand dollars, contracted for under a sense of moral duty, as a provision for the family, shall work an inward state of mind prompting to a correct life. . . . Life insurance has a manifest religious tendency on the mind of man."[33] Insurance writers contended that irreligiosity was much more likely to develop among the uninsured whose miseries suggested "the most hard and unworthy thoughts of God himself and his eternal Providence."[34]

Once life insurance was packaged as a religious item, there could be no better salesmen than the clergy. Knapp reported on the enthusiasm of many ministers:

**Mutual Life Insurance Company* booklet (New York: 1855). Heiner similarly silenced religious objections by pointing out that the regularity in mortality rates indispensable to life insurance was "an institution of Divine Wisdom." Elias Heiner, "An Examination and Defense of Life Insurance," p. 152. Religious precedent was also found for the chance distribution of gains in life insurance: "The prophet Jonah was cast into the sea by lottery and a miracle attested the divine approbation. And was not the Apostolic office imposed on Matthias by lottery also?" Moses L. Knapp, *Lectures on the Science of Life Insurance*, p. 208.

> Many of the clergy in the United States have manifested deep and abiding interest in the progress of Life Insurance. . . . It is not transcending the truth to say that the most enlightened portion of the clergy of all denominations warmly espouse . . . life insurance, some even taking it upon them to act as local agents for companies . . . and urge the practice upon their flocks.[35]

We have already indicated that life insurance companies actively recruited these religious agents, to sell policies and to write company booklets. Sympathetic statements by prominent clergymen were eagerly reprinted by insurance publications.* If selling life insurance was a religious enterprise, then the purchase of a policy was a religious duty and its omission a religious sin:

> How wickedly do even otherwise religious people procrastinate! . . . Yet are you not by neglecting to make provision for your family, placing them in the way of temptation? . . . Answer that question, religious reader and then see if your conscience will . . . allow you to omit the neglect of life assurance from the list of sins for which you daily seek forgiveness.[36]

Life insurance had to be assumed as a "responsibility to God and the family:"[37] "It is an imperative religious duty on me to provide for my own especially those of my own household lest I "deny the faith and show myself worse than the infidel."[38] Rev. Dr. Cook similarly urged upon his audience the religious urgency to insure:

* The testimony of clergymen who themselves were insured, or who advocated the insurance of other clergymen was a particularly valuable proof of the religious status of life insurance. For instance, a Reverend Andrew Manship was quoted:

"In my critical state, in view of my domestic affairs, next to the grace of God and the sympathy of my friends, I found my mind relieved by having, when well, taken out a Life Assurance policy. . . . I desire to call the attention, particularly of my brethren in the ministry to this subject." On file at the New York College of Insurance, 1868.

For similar statement by other clergymen, see *The Life Agent's Vade Mecum or Practical Guide to Success* (New York: Wynkoop & Hallenbeck, 1870). Companies also used the religious press to promote their industry, paying for adequate coverage of life insurance in the leading religious journals. R. Carlyle Buley, *The Equitable Life Assurance Society of the United States*, pp. 1:162–63. Their favorable comments were then reprinted in insurance journals; see for example, "Life Assurance a Benevolent Provision," *American Life Assurance Magazine* (October 1859), 1:122–28. Albree bemoaned the "fanatical spirit" that influenced Christians to become agents and the excessive patronage of the religious press, claiming that "scarcely a paper will admit into its columns any article . . . calling into question the principles of life insurance." George Albree, *The Evils of Life Insurance*, p. 23. On the commercial morality of some of the religious press in the nineteenth century, see Henry Farnham May, *Protestant Churches and Industrial America*, p. 55.

> Can anything be more atrocious than to neglect carelessly or still more to neglect selfishly, the means in his power of rescuing them? [his family] I look to the moral danger and degradation . . . when I say it is the lesson of natural affection, of moral principle and of religious duty, to take every competent means to prevent such a consummation.*

Although the major thrust was on religious legitimation, life insurance also invoked its socially redeeming powers which made it "the commissariship of subsistence of millions that would otherwise be left powerless and penniless, to constitute the scum of society. . . ."[39] At a time when the corrupting influences of poverty were being exposed, life insurance could also claim to combat crime by reducing the number of impoverished dependents.† Legal authorities were often cited by insurance advocates to substantiate the links between poverty and crime: "My experience as a Magistrate . . . has made me familiar with the causes of crime and poverty . . . or rather poverty and crime, for in nine out of ten cases, crime follows poverty."[40] Beyond its moral impact this reduction of pauperism and crime would advance "national prosperity"[41] and lower taxation more effectively than "the legislation of our wisest statesmen."[42] Life insurance fulfilled still another crucial social function as a "life-saving

* Cook, "Life Insurance," p. 377. Black life insurance organizers in the late nineteenth century provided similar moral and religious legitimation for their business. The 1899 charter of the North Carolina Mutual Life Insurance Company, whose motto was "Merciful to All," established that a certain percent of the proceeds would be donated to the Colored Asylum at Oxford, North Carolina. Charles Clinton Spaulding, its general manager, felt he directed "a church as well as a business." He attributed the success of the company to its divine origins. Black ministers were also instrumental in securing new customers from among their congregants, and "Insurance Sundays" were arranged at some churches at which ministers preached on insurance. See Weare, *Black Business in the New South*, pp. 31, 184, 185. Weare suggests that for lower-class black customers the relationship of life insurance to death imbued the industry with particular religious significance making it more than a profane social arrangement. Black insurance companies found an additional powerful legitimation for their profitable venture in the theme of racial uplift and racial cooperation. More than an economic institution, the North Carolina Mutual became "an expression of Afro-American thought centering on the doctrine of self-help and racial solidarity." The company was expected to "cure economic and social ills, enhance racial pride, improve race relations; in short it could solve the "Negro problem." *Ibid.*, pp. 95–96. Its other motto, "The Company with a Soul and a Service," expressed the effective fusion of altruism with capitalism, by which the commercialism of life insurance was amply justified by its contributions to the black race.

† Rothman points out how the differences between dependency and deviancy narrowed in the nineteenth century, with the poor becoming "potential criminals." David J. Rothman, *The Discovery of the Asylum*, p. 164.

household cement, that . . . shall hold the broken family fragments together." While preventing family dissolution on the one hand, it also performed the more joyful task of encouraging the unions of "young and unsophisticated hearts": "A young man . . . need not postpone his marriage till he is half worn out with toil, in trying to accumulate something to start with but enter upon life young . . . if he will but be considerate enough to insure his life."[43] The moral and social contributions of the life insurance business made its acceptance a social responsibility. To the question, "Why should I insure my life?", life insurance companies responded: "Because it is a social duty. Every man uninsured is inflicting a great injury upon society. . . . He is running the risk of burdening it with the support of those whom he is at any moment liable to leave without resources."[44]

LIFE INSURANCE REDEFINED

Thus, the life insurance business during its early years fought ideological resistance with moral and theological weapons. No arguments were spared to convince a reluctant and often hostile clientele of the privileged religious and social standing of the industry. The rhetoric was convincing, and between 1840 and 1860 life insurance became successfully established as a morally beneficent institution. Paradoxically, this prosperity destroyed the eleemosynary image so carefully constructed.* The inordinate expansion of the life insurance industry after the Civil War transformed the major companies into powerful corporate institutions.† Its

* The transformation is an example of the "unanticipated consequences of purposive social action," a phenomenon contributing to much social change; see Robert K. Merton, "The Unanticipated Consequences of Purposive Social Action," pp. 894–904.

† For North, the period between the end of the war and the early years of the twentieth century was the "coming of age" of life insurance. In the thirty-five years after 1870, life insurance in force for all reporting companies increased by 577 percent. Douglass C. North, "Capital Accumulation in Life Insurance Between the Civil War and the Investigation of 1905," p. 238. At the core of this expansion were the three titans of the industry: the Mutual, Equitable, and New York Life, all New York corporations organized before the Civil War. Competition between them was intense and often unscrupulous; agent stealing was fairly common as were premium reductions. Keller, *The Life Insurance Enterprise*, p. 70; North, "Capital Accumulation in Life Insurance," p. 248.

new leaders found their traditional moral weaponry rusty and useless in a battle that no longer sought ideological victory but unlimited economic expansion. Standen comments: "The strict methods of business enterprise; the keen incentives of financial gain; the skill and intelligence that money only can buy, were necessary to place the growing institution in a position of assured success." * The moralistic emphasis of earlier years became not only incongruous and cumbersome but almost suspicious: "A business that puts on the garb of charity is justly suspected of having something to conceal; of being unable to stand the tests of honest trade."[45] More appropriate mundane appeals replaced moral persuasion and company booklets began advertising their success in accumulating surplus, reduced rates, and large dividends. One insurance spokesman described the shift in emphasis:

> We have heretofore thought almost exclusively of [life insurance's] moral and beneficent side, hereafter we shall think more of what we may call its physical side, of the enormous force which it will be compelled . . . hereafter to exercise in the affairs of men.[46]

The protection and welfare of policyholders became secondary to the industry's overriding concern with acquisitive accumulation and economic growth. By the 1870s, the great beneficent institution of the forties had become big business.† The profitability of life insurance, however, was

* William T. Standen, *The Ideal Protection*, p. 71. North points out how adherence to earlier methods would have blocked any further expansion of life insurance, and attributes the continued growth of the industry in the late nineteenth century to the innovative marketing techniques of the large companies. North, "Capital Accumulation in Life Insurance," p. 252. Indeed, those that resisted the changes, as did the Connecticut Mutual Life Insurance Company, lost most of their business. White similarly attributes the failure of the Massachusetts Hospital Life Insurance Company to its philanthropic charitable background that discouraged aggressive salesmanship. Gerald T. White, *A History of the Massachusetts Hospital Life Insurance Company*, pp. 22, 56.

† The development of the Massachusetts Hospital Life Insurance Company illustrates the shift. During its first half century the company was viewed as a charitable organization destined primarily to support Boston's first hospital. After 1878, "the charitable aspect is evident only historically" (White, *A History of the Massachusetts Hospital Life Insurance Company*, p. 105; and the company had become one of Boston's leading financial institutions. Traditionalists were appalled at the transformation of life insurance into a ruthless moneymaking venture. Colonel Greene, president of the Connecticut Mutual Life Insurance Company, staunchly resisted the trend, remaining the epitome of "the entrepreneur of the conservative firm who conscientiously performed the manifest functions of life insurance . . . providing family protection." North, "Capital Accumulation in Life Insurance," p. 240.

During his entire term of office, 1878–1905, Greene engaged in a much publicized bitter

no sudden revelation. Despite charters and prospectuses that read as if they were charitable institutions, the early companies had already been money-making undertakings.* Mutuals were no less part of the market economy than stock companies had been. North and Davis argue that mutuality was adopted only because of its proven sales value, not out of benevolence or philanthropy.‡ The elimination of commercial self-interest by the mutuals, therefore, had been more illusory than real. Although their surplus, unlike that of stock companies, was indeed distributed among policyholders, the enterprise was still highly profitable to its

---

struggle with Henry B. Hyde, president of Equitable and chief promoter of tontines. Their antagonism stands as a symbolic struggle between the changing definitions of life insurance. Hyde refused to consider life insurance "a great cooperative scheme for relieving human distress." To Greene, it was a religion:

"He viewed it in its broad social and moral aspects. . . . It was a monument to family affection . . . an institution engaged not in money-making or in promoting the private interests of its trustees, but in disseminating public benefits." Burton Hendrick, *The Story of Life Insurance*, pp. 242, 547.

Greene held on to his principles to the economic detriment of his company. When he began his term as president in 1878, the Connecticut Mutual was the second largest company in the country. By 1905, the New York Life sold as much insurance in six months as the Connecticut Mutual had totally in force. North, "Capital Accumulation in Life Insurance," p. 240.

*Credit, for instance, had always been a primary activity of the industry. See Karen Orren, *Corporate Power and Social Change* (Baltimore: Johns Hopkins University Press, 1974), p. 15; James G. Smith, *The Development of Trust Companies in the United States*, p. 230. Even organizers of the early religious funds were not loath to borrow from their corporations to finance personal business ventures or investments in real estate. Alexander Mackie, *Facile Princeps*, pp. 144–45.

†The mutual principles had already proven successful in the organization of savings banks and fire and marine insurance companies. See North and Davis, *Institutional Change and American Growth*, pp. 120–21; Walter S. Nichols, *Insurance Blue Book, 1876–1877*, p. 38. Stalson leaves little doubt that "personal business selfishness" and not mutuality inspired insurance promoters. Owen J. Stalson, *Marketing Life Insurance*, p. 124. The management of large funds and the promise of very high salaries and considerable prestige lured organizers, although the major attraction of mutuality was that it required a minimum initial capital investment. See Orren, *Corporate Power and Social Change*, p. 15; Stalson, *Marketing Life Insurance*, p. 108; Kimball, *Insurance*, p. 49; Shepard B. Clough, *A Century of American Life Insurance*, p. 111. Company histories characteristically dwell only on their founders' altruistic motives. According to Stone, for instance, the objectives of the Mutual Benefit Life Insurance Company were exclusively to "help people together do something for themselves and their families which no one could accomplish by himself. Their association was not a money-making enterprise, but a service." Mildred F. Stone, *Since 1845*, p. 2.

organizers and executives in the form of large salaries and considerable power.

If the commercialism of life insurance after the seventies was no revelation, the willingness to admit it broke all precedents. Profits were no longer embarrassing and became the legitimate aim of the industry. The image of life insurance companies as "benevolently philanthropic institutions" was disparaged by insurance writers: "They give a certain service for a certain price. . . . They transact business on a business basis, and the sooner they strip away the philanthropic veneer the better."[47] *Hunt's Merchants' Magazine* discouraged all appeals to "the feelings or the fears" of customers, urging instead the primacy of "the practical features of life insurance as a business:"

> All considerations grounded on its beneficial character must be laid aside. Men do not enter upon the trade of writing risks upon lives out of benevolent motives. . . . In its relation to the individual citizen who is asked to invest his money . . . it challenges discussion on straight business principles . . . as any other financial trust.[48]

The *Insurance Journal* was similarly outspoken: "We do not claim that life insurance is a charity or a benevolent institution, it is a business as much as banking or farming."[49] Standen's article, "Life Insurance as a Practical Business versus Life Insurance as an Impractical Sentiment," provides an unequivocal statement of the new urgency to secularize life insurance and dismantle its traditional religious and charitable aura:

> It is to the best interest of all policyholders that they shall be taught to regard life insurance as a practical business institution—managed on purely business principles, and to be judged only by rules of recognized business procedure. The sooner they learn to sever it from all connection with impractical sentiment, the better it will be for them.[50]

After years of requesting public acceptance as beneficent institutions, life insurance companies now demanded to be judged strictly on business terms.

Company practices dispelled any remaining illusions of their philanthropy. The extravagant salaries of top officials were hardly justifiable for leaders of supposedly eleemosynary insitutions, and the amount of profits derived from forfeitures was clear evidence that the companies did not always operate for the betterment of individual policyholders.* As their

* Pure tontines had no surrender value and the modified deferred dividend policies that replaced them offered only a meager cash surrender value. It is estimated that ap-

self-image changed, the nature of public criticism against life insurance companies also shifted from ideological censure to economic indictment.[51] There was a growing demand for legislative protection against the companies' business methods:

> The public has intrusted to the companies a money interest that is far too great for the honesty, ability and prudence that have been brought to its management. The public has intrusted this money to the companies in the absence of legal safeguards. . . . These are slowly and painfully . . . being raised around this great trust.[52]

THE POLICY: FROM PROTECTION TO INVESTMENT

The transition from ideology to commercialism can also be seen in the varying ways the life insurance policy was characterized at earlier and later times. What was earlier described as family protection now was lauded as family investment.

The moral legitimation of life insurance, accomplished during the first stage of its development, was buttressed by the exclusively noble purpose of its product at the time. The policy was "a saving mercy in the presence of disaster,"[53] serving no other interest than family protection and devoid of all commercial value. Companies restricted their sales appeals to the need for protection:

> The duty to provide for their families, should induce every person to give this subject a careful consideration remembering the injunctions of the Scriptures, that "if any provide not for his own, and especially for them of his own house, he has denied the faith and is worse than an infidel."[54]

Insurance journals similarly described life insurance in terms of its protective functions as a "resource which common prudence and foresight impel everyone, with a due sense of his responsibility to those dependent on him for their subsistence, to avail himself of."[55] To dramatize their impact, life insurance publications did not hesitate in using death as their "solicitor," invoking the brevity of life to hesitant customers:

---

proximately 60 percent of all policyholders died or lapsed receiving no dividends. An 1887 investigation found that only one in ten terminated policies matured by death, while the others were forfeited. North, "Capital Accumulation in Life Insurance," pp. 241–42.

What a mighty procession has been marching toward the grave the past year . . . since the first of January, 1853 more than 31,500,000 of the world's population has gone down to the earth again. . . . Only think of it:

Life is short and time is fleeting
And our hearts, though strong and brave
Still, like muffled drums are beating
Funeral marches to the grave.[56]

Readers were mercilessly confronted with the inescapability of death: "Death never pauses. . . . Every second of time . . . some "human soul takes wing."[57] Until the 1870s sentimentality kept life insurance undefiled by materialistic concerns and the investment potential of a policy remained untapped. However, as life insurance moved from beneficent institution to big business, the prosaic commercial possibilities of a policy acquired new prominence.* Insurance writers discovered that "even this almost sacred thing has a secular value": "Should death be long deferred, the annual premiums paid on the policy are making it . . . a more valuable collateral upon which money can be raised. Not a few men . . . have escaped adversity and poverty by the hypothecation of a life policy."[58] The introduction of nonforfeiture laws which bequeathed the policy with monetary value, was largely instrumental in redefining its functions from purely protective to a form of savings and investment for the policyholder.† Tontines, expressly designed to benefit the surviving premium payer, marked the climax of the development towards investment insurance. Tontine policies were commonly referred to as "bonds" or "consols" rather than insurance.[59]

Life insurance advertising after the 1870s reflected the new emphasis

*Supple points to a similar process in England, after the 1870s. Barry Supple, *The Royal Exchange Assurance*, p. 218. Rogers and Shoemaker's study of innovations found how as diffusion proceeds very often "changes occur in the meaning of an innovation and even in the use to which it is put." Everett M. Rogers with F. Floyd Shoemaker, *Communication of Innovations*, p. 169.

†In 1860, Elizur Wright, then chairman of the board of the Massachusetts Insurance Commissioners, secured the passage of the first nonforfeiture law, which provided for single-premium term insurance instead of forfeiture; finally in 1880, cash surrender value was instituted after payment of two premiums. The promise of dividends by mutual companies, absent from the earlier stock companies, can be considered a prior triggering factor in the discovery of the investment potential of life insurance. Already in 1852, Norton observed how the desire for "pecuniary profit" persuaded some men to buy life insurance, "as one of the best investments that a man can possibly make of his money." Charles B. Norton, *Life Insurance: Its Nature, Origin and Progress*, p. 251. On life insurance as savings, see Sheppard Homans, "The Banking Element in Life Insurance," pp. 49–52.

on investment by adopting an unemotional rational approach to its product. Traditional sales appeals were criticized: "What has thus far been urged of life insurance is an argument that it saves our homes from the claims of creditors, leaves a support for wives and children. But all these plans place enjoyment in the distance." There were better reasons to buy a policy: "One, because you can instantly create disposable property. . . . Second, because you can provide future wealth for yourself. . . . Third, because it is an advantageous investment."[60] Discussions on family affections, thrift and prudence were displaced by booklets such as *The Business Worth of Life Insurance* or *A Fortune for Everybody: How it Pays or the Best Investment for Business Men.*[61] Company publications briefly skimmed over the protective functions of a policy to concentrate on policyholder moneymaking:

> Recently Life Assurance has been attracting considerable attention merely in the light of a profitable investment of funds. Shrewd businessmen who have examined its merits are coming to regard it as one of the best investments of funds that can possibly be made.[62]

While agents had once been advised that it was "more important to move the feelings than to convince the reason,"[63] they were now encouraged to remember that the purchase of life insurance was "just plain common sense from a business standpoint."[64] Agents' manuals disparaged the old "sentimental" approach: "There are a thousand ways to interest the customer . . . without calling upon Death to act as your solicitor." Life insurance was to sell as a "business necessity"[65] and agents were to instruct their clients on the "value of investment" without much "discourse . . . upon death."[66] This pragmatism imposed new demands on life insurance salesmen who could no longer rely on their personal attributes but needed specialized knowledge:

> In the cases of persons insuring for the benefit of their families . . . "on the undying love theory" and not for investment . . . no doubt these [moral] qualities impress and win the insured. . . . In the case of insurers for investment, an intimate knowledge of investments and an ability to demonstrate the superior character of the various forms of life insurance as investments are the first essentials.[67]

By the end of the century, interest in the investment features of life insurance overrode all other considerations. In the excitement about savings banks, investments, guaranteed incomes, five percent Consols and gold bonds, complained one critic, "you will find the life insurance feature of their contracts only incidentally mentioned."[68] The impersonal, business-like approach to life insurance was intensified in the early decades of the twentieth century by the industry's leading ideologist or spokesman, S. S. Huebner, who defined life insurance as "corporation finance applied to human values:"

> Every business which owns a valuable machine appraises its value, charges depreciation against earnings as the machine wears out, accumulates a depreciation fund to provide for its ultimate replacement, and obtains protection against its damage or destruction. These same principles can be applied through life insurance . . . by an individual in the financial management of his personal and family affairs.[69]

The changed functions of the life insurance policy found legal expression in the expanding definition of insurable interest. When men insured their lives only to protect their families, affection was the major proof of insurable interest, and few beyond the family circle held insurable interest in a man's life.* The emerging pragmatic and commercial approach to life insurance in the 1870s encouraged the insurance of lives for strictly business purposes, extending the existence of insurable interest between strangers linked by nothing but economic interests. For instance, each member of a business partnership was declared to hold insurable interest in the life of his partners, and a corporation in the lives of its officers, key employees, and principal stockholders, "whose services and qualifications are of such a nature that the corporation would suffer substantial pecuniary loss by their death."†

* The insurable interest held by a creditor in the life of his debtor was the only exception. In the earlier years, friends apparently held insurable interest in each other's lives, although at present, "a mere friend, as such has no insurable interest under a regular life policy." III *Couch Encyclopedia of Insurance Law* 24:144; T. R. Jencks, "Life Insurance in the United States," p. 124.

† I *Couch on Insurance* 261. Employers have similar insurable interest in executives and important employees, although none in minor employees. Bertram Harnett, *Taxation of Life Insurance* (Englewood Cliffs, N.J.: Prentice-Hall, 1957), p. 55. Insurance by employer-corporations on the lives of valuable executives increased after a 1920 amendment to the federal income tax law which made the proceeds of these policies nontaxable. Edwin W. Patterson, *Cases and Materials on the Law of Insurance*, p. 342. The concept of "key-man" insurance finds its unexpected precedent in one of the earliest forms of insurance—on the lives of slaves. Slave-owners paid large premiums to insure the lives of competent servants or skilled workers.

THE CUSTOMER: FROM ALTRUISM TO SELF-INTEREST

The "vocabulary of motives" used to describe the purchaser also shifted over time, from values to interests.[70] In its first step of development as a beneficent institution with purely protective functions, life insurance appealed to the altruism and generosity of its customers. The morally redeeming force of the enterprise was confirmed in its encouragement of moral virtues above economic self-interest: "All of our institutions provide for our present wants, this one for the necessities of those that come after us. It is the least selfish of all modes of investing our earnings."[71] Fowler characterized the industry similarly:

> In its aspects of beneficence it was like the introduction of a standard of honor, integrity and virtue beyond the capabilities of a community. It asked, in its highest purpose something of self-denial, something of repression of the lower elements of selfishness.[72]

The purchase of a policy became a spartan moral apprenticeship for the insured:

> When he insures his life it is for the benefit, not of himself, but of others. . . . On the contrary, he must subject himself, perhaps to severer efforts and greater self-denials. He parts with little comforts he formerly enjoyed and lives more sparingly in all things. . . . The man . . . has acquired no small mastery over the selfish workings of his nature, and is in a fair way to possess . . . the benevolent principles and spirit of the gospel. . . . [He] is becoming assimilated to the angels.[73]

The moral influence of life insurance was a popular theme among insurance writers who felt the insured man took "a step forward in morality."[74] *Hunt's Merchants' Magazine* unequivocally declared that only life insurance could "elevate the tone of a man's moral being, refine his nature and render him more beneficent to men."* The selflessness of premium-payers was particularly praised. It took many forms; a man could eliminate "an unnecessary journey or an idle amusement," or he could

* "Benefits of Life Insurance," *Hunt's Merchants' Magazine* (November 1865), 80:390. Company seals reinforced this image. The insignia of the Mutual Benefit Life Insurance Company, for instance, was the "pelican in her piety" with its motto "Merui-Je Meurs Pour Ceaux que j'Aime," an ancient symbol of self-sacrifice in religious heraldry based on a legend that in case of famine a mother pelican will pierce her own breast to feed her babies with her blood. See Charles Corcoran, *Search for a Sign*, p. 15; Stone, *Mutual Benefit Life Insurance Company*, p. 4.

cut down on "tobacco, cigars, liquor, billiards, bowling, oyster-suppers, convivial meetings, theater-goings." Touching stories circulated about poor men willing to sacrifice a meager cigar stipend to pay life insurance premiums.[75]

The altruism of a life insurance purchase was upheld as a mark of its superiority over "selfish" forms of insurance: "The insurance of property is only a selfish insurance . . . the insurance of a life is the exact opposite of a selfish insurance."[76] There was however, one way in which the policyholder found personal reward: "We gain from the moment the insurance is effected the satisfaction of thinking that a provision has been . . . made for those dear to us. . . . We are freed from a load of anxiety, which cannot but be depressing."[77] Thus, appeals to the moral self-interest of buyers took the place of economic enticements. Insurance money bought spiritual well-being, a "feeling of security"[78] and "peace and contentment."[79] Only life insurance could assuage the anxieties of the dying. Moral payoffs were attractively presented as well worth the money invested in a premium: "An insured man . . . enjoys during his life a solid satisfaction which may be safely reckoned worth the sacrifice he makes in paying the premiums."[80]

Moral persuasion was not only instrumental in reinforcing the moral claims of the life insurance business, but it was almost indispensable in overcoming the intangibility of a policy, particularly in its earlier years when life insurance was little more than an uncertain promise.[81] Worse still, the benefits of a policy were tied up to the death of its buyer and few were eager to spend money "when they knew that no direct use could be made of it till the nails were put in their coffin."[82] Rogers and Shoemaker found that observability of an innovation or the degree to which its results are visible to the adopter is one of the major determinants of the rate of adoption. This helps to explain the particularly low rate of adoption of insurance and other preventive innovations such as birth control methods or inoculations against disease.[83] The promise of moral rewards offered prospective insurance buyers at least some concrete and positive payoff for their purchase of life insurance. Moral persuasion soon drifted into techniques of moral intimidation. It was well to praise the virtues and rewards of the insured, but it was equally urgent to demonstrate the depravity of those who shirked their duty.[84] The *United States Insurance Gazette* warned that "a neglect of this sort must soon taint the character of an individual,"[85] and its prognosis found confirmation in the endless lists and commentaries on the obnoxious personalities of the uninsured.

They were negligent, "deficient in judgment and honor,"[86] invariably "mean, selfish, spendthrift, idle, shiftless."[87] For some, a man who refused to insure was simply foolish, while others found him irremediably wicked: "He died without even a policy of insurance on his life." "Stupid, wasn't it?" "No. We would not call it stupidity. We think the very much harsher term 'wickedness' fits the case a great deal better."[88] Insurance advocates forecast that eventually no family man would be "held as honest or in any way good" who left his family unprotected:[89] "It will soon be considered a positive dereliction of duty, and an evidence of indifference on the part of a father to the safety and welfare of his family, to omit or delay so important a safeguard."[90] The depth of a man's affection was judged by the possession of a policy, and the uninsured were accused of feeling nothing but a "very vaporing love"[91] or "vacillating sentiments of fancied affection"[92] towards their families. They were also castigated as sinful religious derelicts: "If he provide not for his own, especially his own house, he is scripturally reckoned among those who deny the faith and are worse than infidels."[93] The process of moral, religious, and social stigmatization was completed by labeling the refusal to insure a social crime: "The man who dies uninsured, commits a social crime hardly distinguishable . . . as to guilt, from the crime of one who dies a defaulter in a public office and leaves his friends and neighbors to pay."[94]

After the 1870s, as the life insurance industry adopted sober business tactics and the investment features of a policy were advertised more loudly than its protective functions, moralistic appeals dwindled.* The altruism of potential customers became less crucial, and insurance writings acknowledged and encouraged the right of policyholders to seek personal economic advantages from their purchase. Phelps advised:

> Don't groan when you pay life insurance premiums. It is not an expense, and you are not paying something for nothing. You are saving money and insurance is taking care of it for you. . . . This is business done in a business-like manner. Each one pays his share and does so because it is for his interest to do so.†

* It was essentially a change in emphasis, so that techniques of moral persuasion were never entirely discarded. Moral intimidation in particular was still commonly used by insurance spokesmen into the late nineteenth century. It is still used in contemporary advertising.

† James T. Phelps, *Life Insurance Sayings*, p. 11. The image of man as rational and eminently self-interested was also dominant in general business advertising between 1890 and 1910. Merle Curti, "The Changing Concept of 'Human Nature' in the Literature of

The cash-in value of a policy gave additional impetus to this trend by granting life insurance a new degree of material tangibility.[95] While old-style insurance men bemoaned the appeal to customers' "cupidity,"[96] early twentieth-century insurance manuals insisted that a policy was "just as utilitarian for self-advancement and personal gain as any other economic act."[97] Huebner found it regrettable that life insurance had been for so long regarded as an "intangible and altruistic service . . . for the protection of widows and orphans and related only remotely . . . to the insured's personal advancement and happiness."[98]

MARKET OR MORALS: THE UNRESOLVED DILEMMA

Life insurance, observed Moses Knapp in 1853, is mixed "with the exceeding selfishness or money grasping power of commerce, and the holiest sympathies of philanthropy, . . . founded on self-interest, yet being trained to benevolence."[99] Years later, the president of a prominent New York life insurance company similarly recognized the "semi-religious and semi-business" character of the industry: "We have then in this business . . . an unprecedented combination of the moral and the material, of conviction and reason, of preaching and mathematics, of the zeal of the fanatic and the dispassion of a business contract."[100]

The dual nature of life insurance found acclaim at the first World Insurance Congress in 1915 where it was stated that no other activity "comes nearer combining the altruistic and commercial instincts of man."[101] This polarity, however commendable to its observers, led to endless tension within the industry. If, as commercial ventures, the primary goal of life insurance companies was profit making, as beneficent organizations protecting widows and orphans they were expected to rise above sordid pecuniary concerns. Contradictory normative expectations created a structural source of institutional ambivalence that was never fully re-

American Advertising," 41:340. Commager traces the growth of self-interest in savings patterns from the nineteenth to the twentieth century: "Where an earlier generation had saved in order to leave an estate, the new generation was inclined to save for more immediate and personal purposes." Henry S. Commager, *The American Mind*, p. 423.

solved.* When beneficence was stressed, there were accusations of inefficiency or economic naiveté, but emphasis on a wholly rational impersonal economic approach to life insurance was found morally objectionable. Thus, the shift from beneficence to business after the 1870s was never fully accomplished. Standen noted and deplored the difficulty of dissociating life insurance from emotional appeals: "Men persistently refuse to regard life insurance as a legitimate business enterprise, preferring to treat it as a sentimental institution."[102] Late nineteenth-century insurance writers still referred to life insurance as "hope to the desponding, cheer to the weary, strength to the weak."[103] Many refused to deal with it simply as "a question of pure profit and loss," recalling the "very large moral side it has apart from any business considerations."[104]

* The uncomfortable blend of business and altruism was already evident in the first religious life insurance corporations which supplemented members' payments with "benefactions as might be given by charitable and well disposed persons." *Fundamental By-Laws and Tables of Rates for the Corporation for the Relief of the Widows and Children of Clergymen in the Communion of the Protestant Episcopal Church*, with preface by Hon. Horace Binney, p. 5; Mackie, *Facile Princeps*, p. 92. Trustees of the Episcopalian Fund recognized their enterprise as a "mixed design of contract, and of bounty not contracted for," and determined its by-laws "in the spirit of charity, as well as of contract," anticipating the dividend policy of later mutuals by the distribution of any surplus income among its members as a charitable "bounty." The constraints of running a business, however, set limits to their beneficence so that for instance "however charitably disposed to families other than those of deceased contributors," they only supported the latter. In addition, participating clergymen resisted any unbusinesslike policies objecting particularly to the fact that "bounties held forth to their widows and children are to be administered as charity and are not demandable by the legal contract." *Fundamental By-Laws*, pp. 6, 11, 15, 29, 37.

The ambivalent status of life insurance is further revealed in the controversial issue of its taxation. Tax exemption was demanded on the basis of the beneficent mission of life insurance: "It is just as sensible to tax asylums and hospitals as to seek to gain a revenue from the deposits which foresight and affection have set apart for the protection of thousands of helpless citizens." "Philosophy of Life Insurance," *United States Insurance Gazette* (May 1868), 26:3.

Moral appeals focused on the injustice of penalizing the premium payer, suggesting that "the effort of the thoughtful, the unselfish and the diligent . . . should not go unrewarded." Meanwhile, the large liquid assets of insurance companies were early regarded by legislators as a source of revenue to be tapped by taxation, and from the mid-nineteenth century insurance taxation became an important source of income for the typical American state. See Nichols, *Insurance Blue Book*, p. 18; Kimball, *Insurance*, pp. 250–51; Clough, *A Century of American Life Insurance*, p. 27. Tax advocates regarded life insurance as a particularly profitable business, and were skeptical of its humanitarian pleas and its claims of "eleemosynary service." Philip L. Gamble, *Taxation of Insurance Companies*, p. 62.

Even some of the most hard-bitten business leaders of the industry slipped into sentimentalism in speaking of life insurance as "a conviction first and then a business." [105] Social values and sentiments are expressed symbolically and strengthened by physical places or objects. The cathedrallike architectural design of many late nineteenth-century insurance buildings also kept religious symbolism alive, perpetuating the notion that "life insurance is built on a little lower level than a church."

> I pointed out to the architectural arrangement of the office of one of the largest companies while in conversation with a chief officer and called him a priest. The outline of the building preserves the ecclesiological forms. The very murmuring of the many at work . . . suggests worship.[106]

There was a surge of hostility against those who forgot too easily the "ultimate exalted purpose" of life insurance, seeking only "to reap a present advantageous effect from it":[107]

> Many persons make the speculative investment idea of Life Insurance the chief inducement for taking a policy. They look at Life Insurance as at oil wells and mining stock always having an eye to dividends. They make it mercenary instead of prudential; they make it selfish instead of benevolent.[108]

The *Insurance Times* denounced the "craven idea and common delusion" that life insurance was an investment, reminding its readers that its true mission was to rescue the world from the sorrows and troubles of untimely death.[109] Lowering it to the plane of "ordinary transactions in profit and loss," degraded and prostituted the purity of life insurance.[110] The buyers' greedy pursuit of dividends was criticized, while companies were urged to "stick to life insurance and leave dividends to the banks." [111] Agents who forgot their "mission," selling policies primarily as profitable investments were denounced as "zealots . . . who appeal to the low and venal motives that influence action." *

The success of fraternalism after the 1870s can be understood as an-

* "Solid Facts," *The Insurance Times* (May and June 1868), 1:202. See also Philip Sayle, *Practical Aids for Life Assurance Agents*. Putting ideological considerations aside, the promotion of life insurance as investment was misleading in practical terms, the contract remaining essentially one of protection. Cash surrender values resulted from the level premium plan which charged more than the cost of pure risk in earlier years, thereby building up a reserve against rising risk in later years. Unwisely glamorized as a major savings device, they were no more than an auxiliary contractual right that protected the policyholder who discontinued his contract. The fact that it was no independent savings account was underscored by the loss of insurance coverage once the cash value of a policy was withdrawn. Robert I. Mehr, "Development of Life Insurance in the Past Two Years in the United

other reaction to the dominant commercialism. It was a formal attempt to recapture the spirit of mutual aid by returning life insurance to its beneficent and protective functions. Fraternal societies were welcomed as nonprofit organizations in which "there are no salaried officers, no great buildings, no real estate and no great amount of money to tempt one to forfeit God's grace."* All investment features were omitted from their policies, while the impersonal contract that bound life insurance companies to policyholders was replaced by an informal certificate of membership. The rejection of commercialism extended to a complete disregard for the principles and techniques of ordinary life insurance. Mortality tables, compound interest calculations, and legal premium reserves were abandoned by fraternal organizers as undesirable "implements of darkness, designed to separate the trusting citizen from his money and place it at the disposal of stock manipulators."[112] Commercial security was replaced by fraternal bonds.†

Before long, the pendulum swung back in the other direction, abandoning mutuality once more for the market. The emotionalism that made fraternals so attractive also was found to obscure "the judgement of reality and hard mathematical facts," becoming dangerously inconsistent "with the necessary cold-blooded calculation and business direction

---

States," Pacific Insurance Conference, Aug. 26–31, 1973, pp. 2–4, cited in *The Nature of the Whole Life Contract*, p. 18.

*From *The Irish Catholic Benevolent Journal* (November 1878), quoted in Sister J. H. Donohue, *The Irish Catholic Benevolent Union*, p. 7. As benevolent organizations fraternal societies were exempt from federal income tax as well as all state, county, district, municipal, and school taxes. Kip, *Fraternal Life Insurance*, pp. 152–53. Fraternal societies attracted not only the working-class population but professional groups as well. Although fraternal policies were far less expensive than regular life insurance, a better price was not the clue to their appeal. Commercial assessment companies that were organized during the same period tried to capitalize on the success of fraternal societies by offering equally cheap insurance coverage but, without matching their emotional appeal, promptly failed. Nichols, "Fraternal Life Insurance," in Lester Zartman, ed., *Personal Insurance*, p. 374; Miles M. Dawson, "Fraternal Life Insurance," in *Insurance* (Philadelphia: American Academy of Political and Social Science, 1905), p. 129. Marcel Mauss saw the emergence of fraternal societies along with social security systems as indicators of the resurrection in contemporary society of the theme of the gift, and of purer sentiments such as "charity, social service, and solidarity." Marcel Mauss, *The Gift* (New York: Norton, 1967), pp. 64–66.

†Nichols points out that "in truly benevolent organizations this fraternal feeling has proved a valuable aid in sustaining societies that were financially embarrassed." Nichols, "Fraternal Life Insurance," p. 373. Fraternal policies had no cash-in value or loan privileges. Only family members could be designated as beneficiaries.

which assures the wise management of funds."[113] Many fraternals failed, while others were beset with serious financial problems. Those that survived did so at the expense of their basic principles, adopting at some point the methods of commercial life insurance.* In the end fraternal societies were hardly distinguishable from regular legal-reserve life insurance companies. Institutional ambivalence thus finds similar resolution to more personal forms of ambivalence. Merton and Barber examine the effects of inconsistent normative expectations for the occupants of a status in a particular social role, pointing out that the impossibility of simultaneously fulfilling contradictory demands often results in oscillation of behaviors.[114] The structural sources of ambivalence of the life insurance enterprise make it likely that swings in balance will repeat themselves in response to the enduring tension and contradictory demands of altruism and commercialism.

The informal economic assistance of bereaved dependents during the eighteenth century was rationalized and commercialized in the nineteenth century by the life insurance industry. The fulfillment of obligations to widows and orphans which had rested on noncontractual informal relationships turned into an efficient but impersonal economic transaction. In order to establish the legitimacy of its enterprise, life insurance had to justify the shift from trust to contract by securing convincing moral credentials. During the first stage of its development from the early nineteenth century to around 1870, the business based its sales appeals on moral persuasion, and the industry was defined as a beneficent religious and social institution more concerned with the welfare of its clients than with profits. The life insurance policy was conceived exclusively as a protective resource for the benefit of dependents while its purchase was the generous altruistic act of the family head, devoid of all selfish motivations. This religious and social legitimation was also true of American business in general at the time. Sanford refers to the "psychic" factor of moral justification which distinguished America's industrial pioneers from their European counterparts. American industry was not justified by profits alone but as an agency of moral and spiritual uplift. Business served God, character, and culture.[115] However, if profit alone was an unacceptable mo-

*For example, originally fraternal societies allowed no agents, and unpaid members solicited new ones among their friends. Then "deputies" or "field workers" were appointed with meager commissions, until finally the larger fraternal societies started calling them agents, adopting the terminology of commercial insurers. Kip, *Fraternal Life Insurance*, p. 155.

tivation for most commercial enterprises it was a particularly unseemly justification for a business that dealt with human life and death.

After the 1870s the extraordinary success of life insurance redirected the business. The great impact of moralistic appeals led ironically to their undoing. Its legitimacy now largely unquestioned, life insurance sought untrammeled business expansion and replaced moral persuasion with more adequate marketing techniques. Profits were no longer hushed in embarrassment but vaunted as a sign of success and the industry discarded its beneficent self-image to become big business. Life insurance as protection fell into the background, overpowered by the enthusiastic revelations of its investment potential. As the selfish economic interests of the premium payers were acknowledged and even encouraged, earlier appeals to their altruism were disregarded as unrealistic. The prospect of economic profit loomed larger than the promise of moral rewards.

Thus, after disguising its commercialism for almost three-quarters of a century, the life insurance industry became embarrassed by its former sentimentality and sought identification as a sober economic institution. The protection of widows and orphans however, could not be easily reduced to pure economic exchange, and those who upheld it as a distinctively moral enterprise criticized the new trends. The success of fraternals became a formal manifestation of discontent against the prevalent commercialism of life insurance, until their emotionalism was, in turn, tempered by the realistic demands of economic management. All this oscillation can be largely understood as the result of the structurally ambivalent status of life insurance determined by the marketing of products such as death and protection, culturally defined as beyond monetary evaluation. This created an inescapable dilemma: in order to survive as a business life insurance was compelled to maximize profits, but profits alone remained a justification too sordid for an institution of its kind. The contradictory trends in its historical development reflect the industry's inner tensions caused by the uneven demands of market and morals.

Chapter 7
The Life Insurance Agent: *Problems in Occupational Prestige and Professionalization*

> Few men are more ridiculed and maltreated; few after all, actually accomplish more good. We are annoyed at their persistence; but that very persistence has provided millions of helpless women and children with support.[1]

Pioneer American life insurance companies used no agents, limiting themselves to passive marketing tactics such as discreet announcement advertisements. Their business was transacted exclusively by mail or in person at the company's head office. In the 1840s, the mutuals revolutionized the traditional approach by introducing aggressive person-to-person solicitation by agents who went into the homes and offices of prospective customers.* An original group of part-time agents quickly expanded into a major corps of full-time workers, leading in the 1850s to the organization of the general agency system. Life insurance companies, through home-office management officials, appointed representatives in different areas of the country. These general agents hired salesmen in their districts and sent back to the home office a percentage of their income. The system progressed beyond all expectation, and by 1905 the

* The agency idea had its origins in late eighteenth-century England. However, the function of these early agents was not soliciting customers but selecting "good risks" among outside-of-London applicants. In the United States, the first agents were employed by the New York Life Insurance and Trust Company in 1830. They were primarily attorneys and bankers who acted as local loan representatives for the company, selling insurance as a minor sideline. Apparently, they did no active solicitation, simply offering life insurance to customers who came to their offices for other business. Person-to-person solicitation of risks was introduced in 1842 by the Mutual Life Insurance Company of New York. The best secondary source on the development of the agency system is J. Owen Stalson, *Marketing Life Insurance*. See also Robert Ketcham Bain, "The Process of Professionalization: Life Insurance Selling," p. 42, and Morton Keller, *The Life Insurance Enterprise*, p. 67.

three leading companies, Equitable, Mutual Life, and New York Life, employed between ten and fifteen thousand general and subagents apiece.

Most insurance historians point to the aggressive marketing system introduced in the 1840s as the single major explanatory variable for the diffusion of life insurance in the nineteenth century, comparing the failure of the earlier companies who would not push their wares to the overwhelming success of the mutuals after mid-century. Marketing systems, however, do not develop in a sociological vacuum. Their structure and characteristics are deeply interrelated with such other variables as customers' social and cultural backgrounds. In the case of life insurance, ideological resistance to commercializing death influenced not only its rate of diffusion and the marketing ideologies of life insurance companies described in earlier chapters, but the entire marketing structure. To analyze very concretely the impact of cultural values on the marketing system, we turn to the nineteenth-century life insurance agent, the most visible representative of the industry to the customer and the only one within the life insurance hierarchy to be exclusively involved with selling policies. This chapter will explore how the strains of marketing life affected the role of the agent within the company, his self-image, and his prestige within the community.

THE INDISPENSABLE AGENT

The early stock companies could afford dignified but inefficient space advertisement. They began business with a sizable capital stock and most of them relied on income from their successful trust departments to offset floundering life insurance sales. Unlike them, the mutuals in the 1840s had no initial operating capital or trust business, depending exclusively on policyholders' premiums. Struggling for survival, unable to wait any longer for customers to arrive, they devised an aggressive system of solicitation. The agent became the pivotal factor in the new marketing organization, and was soon recognized as the "great element of success in life insurance."[2] His efforts were more effective than "all the newspapers in the world."[3] Where extensive advertising failed, the agent succeeded:

> It is quite clear that the only method to be depended on for obtaining business is personal application to the parties. . . . The expensive and all but useless plan of advertising may be completely superseded. While one agent may be puffing his office in every newspaper in his neighborhood from year to year, the working agent is steadily, noiselessly and successfully accumulating a large and extensive business.[4]

Company leaflets were similarly unpersuasive; usually discarded "with hardly a passive glance."[5] Agents were advised against maintaining, "a costly office . . . elaborate furniture and huge gilt signs":

> Not one man in a hundred or thousand in this country ever comes into an office to get insured of his own accord. Some agent has presented the subject to him, has talked and argued with him, and finally persuaded him to make an application. . . . The gilt sign did not attract him.[6]

Hunt's Merchants' Magazine reported that "the universal testimony of experienced officers is that agents are indispensable in this business,"[7] while company presidents publicly acknowledged their dependence on the selling agent:

> I know that however extensively we might advertise, however carefully we might manage our companies, however faithfully we might apply the best of our talents to the production of plans of insurance, they would all fail unless the earnest and persistent agent took hold of them and compelled recognition by his persistence.[8]

The marketing structure of late nineteenth century industrial insurance companies became similarly centered on their agents who were "as necessary to the business of life insurance as fuel is to the locomotive. . . . Without agents there would be no insurance."[9] Hendrick, a severe critic of the agency system, nonetheless avowed: "Men do not insure of their own free will. They must be clubbed into it. The company that employs no agents does no business."[10] Indeed, unsolicited applicants were suspect and subjected to particularly rigid medical examinations under the premise that only someone anticipating early death would insure voluntarily.

Of course, there were some who decried the agency system as an economically inefficient and unnecessary parasite. *Hunt's Merchants' Magazine* noted in 1870 the "increasing complaint . . . made of the agency system by which a large proportion of all the sums invested in Life Assurance is paid to the middleman who negotiates the contract."[11] Critics insisted that life insurance would sell better without agents who characteristically persuaded people into "insurance that does not insure:" "Good wine needs no bush" and there will be no need to tease people into insurance."[12] In a letter to the editor of the *Insurance Monitor,* one actuary suggested the "practicability of dispensing altogether with the employment of soliciting agents," replacing them with advertising in newspapers and popular magazines. Pointing to the success of savings banks, the writer asked, "Why should a Life Insurance company not be able to give a similar voluntary patronage?"[13]

Historical evidence, however, attests to the failure of all experiments to sell life insurance directly. The most notable attempt to market life insurance without agents was made by the Equitable Society of London, founded in 1756. Applicants were expected to appear personally before the membership committee of the governing board. Although it survived and offered lower cost insurance than its competitors with agents, Equitable's business remained insignificant, issuing no more than a few hundred policies yearly.* In America, the major test case for agents came in 1907 when the Commonwealth of Massachusetts following the suggestions of Justice Louis D. Brandeis enacted the first legislation permitting savings banks to sell life insurance.† Brandeis declared the agent's work "eco-

* The London Life in 1806 and the London Metropolitan in 1835 made similarly unsuccessful attempts to sell life insurance directly. In 1904, London's Equitable wrote 258 policies, the London Life 252, and the London Metropolitan 174, while the London Prudential with agents wrote approximately 71,874 new ordinary policies and 675,000 new industrial policies in 1905. John F. Dryden, *Addresses and Papers on Life Insurance,* p. 106. See also L. G. Fouse, "The Organization and Management of the Agency System," p. 64.

† In England, the savings bank departments of the post offices were authorized in 1865 to write annuities and life insurance. There was no personal solicitation by agents. In 1904, after a trial of forty years and with more than 23,000 post offices serving as agencies there were only 12,875 policies of this type. The Pearl Life Assurance Co. of London, founded only a year earlier than the post office had in force 2,320,463 policies and the Refuge Assurance Company of the same age as the Pearl, had 2,628,650 policies in force. During that year, the post office wrote only 517 new policies while The Prudential of London wrote 71,700. In 1929, the English post-office system was discontinued. In the United States, Elizur Wright, first insurance commissioner of Massachusetts, obtained a charter from the legislature in 1876 to form "The Massachusetts Family Bank," a nonagency stock company that would sell life insurance over the counter. The family bank remained an ideal and was never put into operation. See Donald R. Johnson, *Savings Bank Life Insurance;* Philip Green Wright and Elizabeth G. Wright, *Elizur Wright* (Chicago: University of Chicago Press, 1937); and Charles R. Henderson, *Industrial Insurance in the United States.*

nomically unjustified," contending that "lavish payments for solicitors and agents' commissions. . . . common among the promoters of mining enterprises and of patents, have no place in the business of life insurance." [14] He became determined to prove that life insurance could sell at a lower cost and as effectively without an agency force. Despite lower prices, savings bank life insurance made very small inroads, never accounting for as much as 6 percent of the yearly new life insurance business of Massachusetts.* As the president of the New York Life Insurance Company anticipated in 1911, a company without agents was akin to a church without preachers: "Few people go directly to a church and ask to be enrolled. Few people will go to a life insurance company and ask membership. . . . The great companies are all akin in their methods to the aggressive churches." [15]

Even fraternal societies who initially discarded salaried agents along with other commercial features of life insurance companies were forced to rehire them to recapture a dwindling membership. As late as 1963, a study found that customers "still rarely . . . seek out the agent of the company," concluding that to this day "little life insurance would be sold without the actions of the salesmen."†

While the indispensability of the agent has become an accepted fact, it remains largely unexplained in the literature. The innovative marketing system of the mutuals is given unanimous historical credit for independently creating the first mass market for life insurance, but without sociological examination of the conditions that determined the need for aggressive person-to-person solicitation. In sharp contrast to life policies, fire and marine insurance sold with only minor participation of their agents. One agent explained:

> It needs no argument to persuade men to take out fire insurance. . . . Ordinary minds, male and female, even children to a greater or lesser degree

*Two other nonagency life insurance companies were chartered in Massachusetts in 1907 but neither completed its organization. New York in 1939 and Connecticut in 1941 authorized savings-bank life insurance with similar mediocre results as in Massachusetts. No other states followed suit. Johnson, *Savings Banks Life Insurance*, pp. 2–22, 134, 200–1.

†F. B. Evans, "Selling as a Dyadic Relationship," p. 77. In the 1930s, Sears, Roebuck & Co. organized Hercules Life Insurance Co., a mail-order concern. Few customers bought policies from their catalogue and four years later the project was abandoned. The high lapse rate and low voluntary conversion rate of low-cost government life insurance issued by the Bureau of War Risk Insurance to soldiers and sailors in World Wars I and II further attested to the need for agents. Bain, *The Process of Professionalization*, p. 187.

> succeed in soliciting fire or marine insurance . . . while one of the most difficult things to accomplish is to persuade men to adopt these absolutely necessary duties of life insurance.[16]

Customers who would not insure their lives unless pursued sought voluntarily the protection of their homes and ships. Differences were so great that "the agent who has been properly trained to carry on a fire insurance or a general insurance business has received a very unfortunate training if he afterwards adopts life insurance soliciting as a profession."[17] The distinctive role of the agent in life insurance was not simply an ingenious marketing device of the industry, but a response to powerful client resistance. As we have seen, the management of death could not be rationalized and bureaucratized as easily as the management of property. In the eighteenth century the economic consequences of death were resolved within the primary group; the widow was assisted by neighbors and friends. Nineteenth-century life insurance companies institutionalized the care of the bereaved. Death however, could not be transformed into a routine commercial transaction. The early stock companies overlooked the social and cultural uniqueness of the life insurance business, expecting customers to purchase their policies no differently from any other merchandise. Their newspaper advertisements and company booklets accurately portrayed the advantages of insuring life but persuaded few to buy a policy. In an analysis of the different roles of mass media and interpersonal channels in the diffusion of innovations, Rogers and Shoemaker point out how "mass media channels are often more important at creating awareness knowledge of a new idea, whereas interpersonal channels are more important in changing attitudes towards innovations."[18] Katz and Lazarsfeld similarly determined the superior impact of personal advice over mass media advertising in marketing.[19] Face-to-face interpersonal contact was needed to deal with the stress and the tragedy of death. Persuasive and persistent personal solicitation alone could break through the ideological and superstitious barriers against insuring life. The agency system introduced in the 1840s succeeded by replacing ineffective secondary reinforcements with the impact of personal influence. The impersonality of the remote life insurance company was offset by the presence of the life insurance agent in the home of his customer.

THE AGENT AS SALARIED MISSIONARY

The institutional ambivalence of the life insurance enterprise, torn between conflicting goals of business and altruism, was reflected at the individual level in the role ambivalence of its salesmen.* Life agents were aware that, "although working at a business the most beneficient, one that appeals to the sense of duty and the finer instincts of men, we are working for pay." [20] Agents, however, were expected to rise above sordid pecuniary concerns and engage in their vocation with the zeal of a priest and not the cupidity of the average salesman. One elderly agent recalled how solicitors in the 1840s and 1850s "felt that they were engaged in an honorable legitimate business, one which approximated near to philanthropy." He reported his personal experience:

> I can hardly avoid saying here that there has been no act of my life [now 71] performed with greater comfort . . . than when in the providence of God, I was the humble instrument in providing for an otherwise destitute family in the hour of their sad bereavement.[21]

A committed missionary was less harsh a replacement of the friendly neighbor or the concerned relative of yesteryear than a greedy salesman. Moreover, a missionary-convert type of interaction added greater credibility to the agent than a customer-seller relationship. Personal influence of the agent grew by minimizing personal interests. Commercial change agents suffer the "albatross of low credibility";[22] clients often suspect them of strictly mercenary concerns. Persuasive credibility is therefore more readily accorded to noncommercial change agents who have less to gain. Insurance writers upheld that "no field of philanthropy or enterprise offers a more useful calling," † declaring it unjust to attribute "interested motives" to a life agent, "as it is to attribute such motives to the teachings

* During the 1905 Armstrong investigation of New York State life insurance companies, Charles Evans Hughes, chief counsel of the committee, interrogated Richard A. McCurdy, president of the Mutual Life Insurance Co. on high agency expenses. McCurdy responded that life insurance was "a great beneficent missionary institution, to extend the benefits of life insurance as far as possible within the limits of safety." In what became probably the most publicized single statement of the hearings, Hughes retorted: "Treating it as a missionary enterprise, Mr. McCurdy, the question goes back to the salaries of missionaries"; cited by R. Carlyle Buley, *The American Life Convention*, p. 216.

† "Life Insurance as a Profession," *United States Insurance Gazette* (June 1868), 27:66. Life insurance histories characteristically romanticize the altruism of early salesmen. Stone

of a clergyman, the advice of the physician or the opinion of the lawyer who are all . . . paid for their services."[23] Knapp praised the natural congruence between a life agent's self-interest and that of the community:

> No agent of a correct Company ever persuades a person into the measure of insuring his life without conferring a public benefit upon society. He cannot perform the selfish act to obtain his commissions without doing a public good.[24]

An early instruction manual advised agents:

> Above all, be sure to remember that you will never be able to make any great progress until you are thoroughly imbued with the conviction that it is a great moral as well as a social reformation that you are engaged in carrying onward and that the principal reward you have to look forward to, is the pleasure and delight of accomplishing these grand and good designs, more than all the pecuniary recompense that you can ever receive for your labour.[25]

Later booklets similarly recommended agents to act "with the determination of the Apostle," reminding them that life insurance was "above an occupation of pure commercial nature," monetary rewards remaining secondary to the "higher motive of doing a service to society." One 1870 manual warned that "no agent will be successful who makes his agency a mere matter of business and overlooks the moral and philanthropic aspects of it."[26]

Even when life insurance became big business, the trade literature supported a noncommercial, altruistic role definition of its salesmen. A good agent was still expected to labor for the satisfaction that "the work he has achieved has been second to none other in its beneficial effect upon the afflicted and the distressed."[27] One manual explained: "Now there is a moral element in the business which we do not find anywhere else. The "drummer" or commercial traveler, who sells dry-goods, hardware or machinery, knows that he is conferring no such lasting benefit on the public as the life agent."[28] The life insurance agent "mitigates suffering and want . . . : he pleads the cause of every widow and orphan . . . in the prosecution of his work he confers ten times as much benefit as he receives."[29] Soliciting was a "missionary labor," and agents were praised as "persuaders of men and the missionaries of a noble propaganda."[30] The techniques of these "apostles of thrift and altruism"[31] were comparable to the priests, both demanding similar inspiration and faith:

---

writes: "Even life insurance peddlers were motivated by the good they saw resulting from their sales. . . . Men who sold even small contracts . . . knew that their work meant the difference between hope and despair." Mildred F. Stone, *A Calling and Its College*, p. 1.

> No man can understand life insurance and believe in it and who does not feel its driving power. The genuine life insurance man is a descendant of those men who have through all history accomplished something acting under the force of an impulse which is as much moral as mental.[32]

Industrial agents ranked above mere salesmen as well. They preached the "gospel of thrift" to their clients, becoming a "true friend."[33] The sacredness of all agency work was bolstered by vilifying "dishonorable" and "designing" solicitors concerned only with their commissions:

> They . . . do not care one brass button for your interests or for the risks that your wife and children may run through their evil machinations. These men are acutely alive to their own interest—the interest of dollars and cents. . . .[34]

But while life insurance proclaimed an ideology of altruism it institutionalized an openly commercial marketing structure. The rhetoric applauded the agent's missionary zeal. But the industry rewarded exclusively his talents as shrewd businessman. The earliest marketing goal of life managers was volume of production. Other issues, such as quality of risks solicited, concern with clients' needs, the persistency of policies or economy of agency management remained "lesser objectives."[35] Accordingly, the successful agent was the one who sold the most policies. The prevalent commission system of agency compensation reinforced the concern with mere quantity, making the agent's income directly dependent "upon the number of persons whom he can induce to insure their lives."* The expectation of larger commissions encouraged agents "to build up a large volume of new business irrespective of its quality."[36]

Critics warned unsuccessfully against a system that "does all it can to make rogues." Life insurance, "originally designed for one of the most laudable of objects," was becoming a highly commercialized "business of competition."[37] *Hunt's Merchants' Magazine* cautioned that agents dependent on commissions "have a direct pecuniary interest in obtaining clients and issuing policies, regardless of the soundness of the lives insured."[38] The advice was ignored. The overriding concern of life insur-

* "The Condition of Life Insurance Among Us," *Nation* (January 26, 1871), 12:54. The commission system had been severely criticized by English insurance experts, as allowing fraud and imposition. Babbage, a prominent authority, decried commissions as "bribes" to "mercenary agents." Solicitors were enticed to recommend the company rewarding them with highest commissions rather than the one offering clients the best policies. Charles Babbage, *A Comparative View of the Various Institutions for The Assurance of Lives*, pp. 133, 137.

ance officials was expanding sales. Increasingly large commissions were offered on first year premiums, with lesser ones on renewals, encouraging quantity of sales over persistency of placed business. Enough incoming business was expected to offset the high rate of lapses, keeping sufficient volume of net business in force.*

After the 1870s, mercenary inducements to agents intensified in quantity and form. Henry B. Hyde of Equitable led the way, offering his agents "extra-commissions," bonuses, and prizes to stimulate production.† He goaded salesmen:

> Make use of all your friends and associates. Get lists from your doctor of insurable people, and, if necessary make it an inducement to him to smooth the way. Make your clergyman help you insure his flock, join literary societies and clubs—in order that you may insure the members.[39]

Hyde's innovations, later adopted by the other companies, exploited every competitive device to spur agents. One of his earliest salesmen recalled:

> Mr. Hyde had many devices for stimulating agents. One was to pitch one man against another. Once he sent for me and said: "Miller, I can find a man who can do more business in thirty days than you can. . . ." Mr. Hyde went on to say that he thought McCorkle (who was one of the famous canvassers of the day) could beat me. At last he got me so stirred up that when he offered to bet me one hundred dollars that McCorkle could do more business than I could in a month, I took the bet.[40]

Hyde improvised contests between agents, rewarding them with cash or prizes. Another agent reminisced:

> Away back in the sixties, he [Hyde] met me at the door and slapping me on the shoulder, said: "Now here is a chance for you to win a prize—a silver pitcher and salver. . . ." The magnetism of the man made me feel that the

*Without cash surrender value, lapsed policies were a major source of profit to the companies. In 1873, more than 50 percent of the policies issued by Mutual lapsed and the company appropriated a million dollars. Wright and Wright, *Elizur Wright*, pp. 254, 255. Even after the nonforfeiture law of 1880, tontines (the most popular type of policy) had minimal cash-in value. In 1893, policies that lapsed for nonpayment of premiums due in the second year were worth $700 million. William T. Standen, *The Ideal Protection*, p. 154.

†Commission scales varied, favoring deferred dividend policies more profitable to the company. In 1893, Mutual Life offered 80 percent first-year commission and renewals on whole life policies where dividends remained in the company for at least twenty years. The same policy paid 35 percent first year and no renewals if dividends were distributed annually. The system was effective. Tontine policies constituted about three-quarters of the business under such compensation plans. Stalson, *Marketing Life Insurance*, pp. 528–29; Bain, *The Process of Professionalization*, p. 51.

prize was mine already; but I replied: "Mr. Hyde, I don't want a pitcher . . . !" Quick as a lightning he said: "We'll make the prizes two first class watches."[41]

Agents were also coached by mail. Hyde's circulars stressed invariably the importance of expanding sales:

> It is astonishing how much more a man can do if he has in his mind a definite object that he is striving to accomplish. . . . In other words, if an agent makes up his mind to write $100,000 of new assurance in a month he is certainly likely to write a larger amount than if he starts out with no definite aim, or if he is striving to write but one half that amount.[42]

No wonder that by 1886, Equitable became the largest life insurance company in the world.

Agents were caught in the ambivalence of the life insurance enterprise. On the one hand, they were verbally encouraged to serve as devoted missionaries of a beneficent institution; while on the other, the system rewarded the rapid, unconcerned salesman and penalized excessive client-orientation which distracted from the commercial goals of a profit-making business.

THE STIGMATIZED SALESMAN

> By life insurers . . .
> I'm intercepted, pestered, vexed
> Almost beyond endurance;
> And though their schemes appear unsound,
> Their advocates are seldom found
> Deficient in assurance.[43]

The life insurance agent in the United States fared no better with public opinion than his seventeenth century English predecessors. Life insurance could not have sold without them. Yet, agents have been characteristically regarded as a sort of "necessary evil, and even by many as an unnecessary evil."[44] Stalson notes: "He is traditionally an unwelcome person. The public has long since conceived an obstinate dislike for him; he is heir to a long-standing and strangely persistent disfavor."[45] Far from being a sacred mission,* life insurance soliciting in the nineteenth century

* The life agent has higher status among the lower-class than with his middle-class customers. Miller Lee Taylor, "The Life Insurance Man," p. 325. According to Weare, among

was disparaged as nothing more than an undignified "scramble for premiums."[46] Agents were unwelcome "intruders" and "disagreeable inflictions," in the category of lightning rod sellers or horse dealers.[47] The *Fireside Companion* conveyed in jest popular opinion on the "sleek-looking agent, with the smooth, oily voice":

> Did you ever happen to meet a "Life Insurance Agent?" If you haven't I should like to be allowed to ask where you've kept yourself, and whether there's room for one more, for turn which way you will, some spruce looking man stands before you with a policy to fill out for the benefit of your dear friends and relatives, whenever you may be so fortunate as to "shuffle off this mortal coil. . . ." They come smiling at a man, to tell how finely his family will be situated, if he only gets insured in his company, and then mercifully dies and leaves his widow to remark to the children, "How much better we get along now than when your poor, dear father was alive!"[48]

Cartoonists exploited this image of agents (see figures 7.1 to 7.3). At the first convention of the National Association of Life Underwriters, the main speaker recalled grievances endured by the members:

> Some of the gentlemen I see before me are old enough to remember a time when it was made a serious objection to canvassers for Life Insurance policies . . . that the whole business of Life Insurance was a gambling game. . . . I can remember very well, and it is not so long ago . . . when Life Insurance solicitors were turned out of houses and offices in the city of New York on conscientious grounds. . . .[49]

Already in 1852, Currie's *Insurance Agent's Assistant* warned readers about the "difficulties and obstacles" of that "peculiarly trying and disheartening occupation": "Your advances are met with coldness and reserve, your entreaties with scorn, your anxiety with indifference."[50] Insurance journals regularly published articles on "The Difficulties and Prejudices to be Overcome" by agents and the need to "dignify the profession of the solicitor."[51]

Agents resented the stigma of their occupation. Their plight was compared to the painful trials of "a Christian missionary in a heathen land. . . . He preached his gospel, worked it; and sometimes the scoffing forgotten, it was said he saved."[52] The agents' defensiveness inadvertently revealed their predicament more fully. The solicitation of policies was justified as "one of the first elements of a good Agent," never "a

---

blacks the industrial agent became a "minor folk figure," particularly welcome in remote rural areas. He was a symbol of black success. Walter B. Weare, *Black Business in the New South*, pp. 130, 184.

Figure 7.1

"You see, sir, you see, the incomparable benefits that I have triumphantly demonstrated, as accruing from . . ."

"Oh yes, I see, I yield, I cave, I climb down, I am yours, take me. Insure me, spare me, oh my! oh my!"

From *Fireside Companion*. Reprinted in *The Insurance Monitor* (May 1870).

Figure 7.2

"In the midst of life we are in death"

Figure 7.3

"You may drop off any minute and leave your family unprovided for."

From the *New York Journal*. Reprinted in Alexander, *How to Sell Assurance*.

beggarly business . . . ungenteel or undignified."[53] One angry salesman wrote to the *Insurance Monitor:*

> Mr. Editor: I have something to say, and I intend to say it plainly and to the point. If no other Life Insurance Solicitor raises his voice or hands in protest against the sneers and slanders heaped upon our profession, then upon me, Sir, shall devolve the duty of defending my class. . . . "Who is that?" says a merchant to his friend, "Oh he is a life insurance man." It is impossible to convey an idea of the sneering tone of the remark. Every Solicitor has felt it. . . .[54]

An 1867 *Manual of Life Assurance* reaffirmed the "value and moral grandeur" of an agent, lamenting the many "who seem to feel that they were doing a mean sort of work, and needed to beg pardon of all creation for being about such work. . . ."[55] Indeed, the work of an agent guaranteed "a character almost unequaled and unattainable in any other position or pursuit."[56] Equitable reminded its salesmen: "Though [the agent] may at first be coldly received by the thoughtless he still has the consciousness that, by his calling, he is conferring incalculable benefit."[57] An agent, vouched Phelps, "can hold up his head, look any man in the eye and, if necessary, like William Penn, may wear his hat in the presence of the king."[58]

Despite protestations and denials, selling life insurance remained an undesirable occupation. It attracted mostly older men who drifted from previous unsuccessful jobs. The agency soon became a sort of "asylum, a last refuge on the road to the poor house, a sanctuary for the lame, the halt, the blind, and the refuse of every calling."[59] One insurance spokesman later recalled: "There was a time when the life insurance agent's name was anathema, when men after making failures in other lines started out to solicit for ours."[60] Unaccomplished lawyers, teachers, and preachers turned to soliciting as a last resort. The difficulties of recruitment were particularly damaging to an industry whose very subsistence depended on extensive representation by agents. Life insurance companies tried every method of attracting salesmen: from circulars, letters, and advertising to personal interviews and traveling organizers. However, low public esteem acted as a powerful deterrent to the recruitment of good candidates. Officials were forced to settle for mediocre ones. Selection standards were practically nonexistent and even the most poorly qualified applicants were seldom refused an agency.* Hendrick reported in 1903:

* Apparently, one of the three largest companies at the turn of the century had planned to make every barber in Greater New York a solicitor. On the negative effects of shortage of

They employ men and women, educated and ignorant, high and low born, broken down clergymen superannuated college professors, briefless lawyers, bankrupt businessmen, cast-off politicians, actors, reporters, artists. . . . Evidently the managers argue that every man has a few friends; and is useful at least until he has exhausted them. "Anyone who has two hands and a hip pocket for a rate book can become an agent," so say life insurance men.[61]

Higher pay did not raise the agents' status nor make the occupation more appealing. The rate of turnover among life insurance agents was notoriously high. One observer was puzzled: "If the business is not comparatively difficult and commissions are high, why do not more take hold of it or those stick to it already in?"[62] In the 1840s, the agent received a 5 or 10 percent commission on first-year premiums and 5 percent on renewal premiums. In the next two decades it increased to 15 or 20 percent commission on first-year premiums. Many received higher first-year commissions, often as much as 50 percent. The increased competitive struggle between life insurance companies in the 1870s made manpower shortage still more acute. It was not uncommon for agents to receive as much as 80 percent commission on first-year premiums as well as renewal premiums and a variety of bonuses and prizes.[63] Hendrick ironically noted that the main rivalry was waged, "not over the solicitation of new business, but the solicitation of new agents."[64] In the 1900s the three leading life insurance companies promised their agents 100 percent commission on first-year premiums, plus renewals and a salary or bonus. Despite such financial inducements, the problem of attracting suitable men remained unsolved. The *Insurance Monitor* reported: "It is found impossible to get the requisite talents at any price, and companies are constantly advertising without success for successful agents."[65] Trade journals significantly carried more advertisements to lure prospective agents than to attract new customers. Another dramatic expression of manpower shortage was the widespread "agent stealing" after the 1870s. Life insurance companies ruthlessly bought off their rivals' best salesmen.

---

applicants on entry standards in other occupations, see Dan C. Lortie, "The Balance of Control and Autonomy in Elementary School Teaching," in Amitai Etzioni, ed., *The Semi-Professions and Their Organization* (New York: Free Press, 1969), p. 21.

THE "DIRTY WORKER"

Hughes distinguishes three forms of "dirty work": first, physically disgusting work; second, work that is a "symbol of degradation, something that wounds one's dignity," and finally, work that goes against "the more heroic of our moral conceptions."[66] The concept of "dirty work" helps us understand the occupational stigma of selling insurance. The relative prestige of an occupation is determined largely by its functional significance to the general society.* The two major dimensions of functional significance that order stratificational ranking of occupations are the degree of generalized and systematic knowledge and the amount of responsibility required by the occupational role. The low prestige of life insurance salesmen can be thereby inferred from the minimum degree of both knowledge and responsibility attached to the occupation. The life agent in the nineteenth century received no formal training.[67] He was expected to learn by doing. As late as 1891, Willey noted: "With no preliminary training or study . . . with no fixed ideas of insurance as a business, they stuff their pockets with pamphlets and commence soliciting."[68] "A preparation of the heart and a particular blending of all the faculties"[69] were considered more important for an effective solicitor than any specific knowledge. Above all, the agent required personal appeal:

> He must be diplomatic in his correspondence, conversation and intercourse with others; he must exercise an unusually high degree of skill in avoiding enmities; and by his affability, geniality and unquestioned honor, must always be in the position of deserving the friendship of those whose friendship can be of the greatest assistance to him.[70]

The only available sources of printed information for agents were the various articles in trade journals and company sales booklets. Insurance principles were only briefly discussed. Most of the space was reserved for the description and rates of the various policies, and responses to prevalent objections against insuring. Agents' manuals published in the 1850s and 1860s were hardly more instructive, dealing primarily with the histor-

* Barber defines functional significance as "the relative consequentiality of any occupational role for various other roles or for the various individual and shared goals and values that people in society have." Bernard Barber, "Inequality and Occupational Prestige," p. 78. Scarcity of available personnel does not necessarily determine occupational prestige. As in the case of the life insurance agent, it may increase the amount of material rewards for an occupational role without raising its prestige.

ical background and moral contributions of life insurance.[71] Beginning agents were occasionally advised by more experienced general agents. Yet even this was rare, since most agents worked alone in their communities.

As lower-echelon salesmen, subject to the decisions of general agents and home office management officials, the degree of responsibility of life insurance agents was minimal. Unlike fire and marine insurance solicitors authorized to countersign and deliver insurance policies legally binding on the insurer, life agents had no power to make a binding contract or settle claims.*

The low functional significance of selling life insurance, measured by the lack of required generalized and systematic knowledge and the low level of responsibility, explains its low occupational prestige. It does not fully account for the occupational stigma of the life insurance agent. Popular bias has been attributed by proinsurance ideologists to "the crusading methods required to break down prejudice and lack of understanding to get people to do the very obvious thing of insuring their lives."[72] Agents are "a man's own conscience."[73] Bain points out:

> He must continually . . . persuade another person to defer gratifications in order to assume future benefits. The feeling of guilt entertained by many men who do believe they should protect their family with life insurance but who are not quite able to bring themselves to the point of doing so often leads to hostility directed towards the person who intensifies this inner conflict—the agent.[74]

Traditionally, the aversion to life insurance agents has been explained by their closeness to death. They were a visible reminder of the "gloomy and disagreeable prospective" of death.[75] Riley interprets client reluctance as an expression of "the built-in cultural reluctance to consider the subject of death."[76] However, physicians and clergymen with similar intimate occupational involvement with death are universally held in high public esteem. The occupational stigma of selling insurance cannot therefore be explained away by an unqualified statement of its relation to death in general. It is the specific nature of that involvement which built its ill-repute. To life insurance salesmen, as to undertakers, death is a moneymaking business. As "businessmen" of death they are differen-

* Agents were not permitted to waive forfeitures, grant credit or modify the contract. Fouse, "The Organization and Management of the Agency System," p. 65. Their responsibilities were limited to soliciting applications, delivering policies, and accepting the first premium. E. Paul Huttinger, *The Law of Salesmanship* (New York: D. Appleton, 1927), p. 2; Edwin W. Patterson, *Cases and Materials on The Law of Insurance*, p. 626.

tiated from the "professionals" of death, physicians and clergymen, whose connection to death is made legitimate by their service orientation. Parsons and Merton distinguish between individual motivational patterns and the institutional structures of business and the professions.[77] Regardless of the individual motivations of the practitioners—their greed or beneficence—professions institutionalize altruism while business institutionalizes self-interest. To save and to heal is holier than to sell. The powerful normative stigma of the utilitarian association of money to death discussed in chapter 4 results in a negative evaluation of those occupationally involved in making money out of a death.[78] In sum, marketing life insurance is "dirty work." The "unwarrantable traffic in flesh and blood"[79] disgraced agents: "[Many] think that there is something sacred in human life which should not be made the subject of a policy of insurance. It is regarded as almost as bad as man-stealing or dissecting a human corpse."[80] The commercialization of death mocked the uniqueness and sanctity of each human life. The sense of personal tragedy was trampled by the objectivity and detachment of the business deal. In his analysis of occupations, Hughes notes the resentment of receivers of emergency services against the workers or practitioners who deal routinely with their crisis.[81] One humorous but revealing article complained against the agents' trivialization of death:

> There's a sort of melancholy satisfaction in thinking of one's self mourned and wept over, after death. But the life insurance agent takes even this grain of satisfaction away. He speaks of your being dead in very cheerful, lively tone of voice, setting forth in glowing colors the free and easy circumstances of your family after you are put away from its joys. . . . If the agent would only transact that part of the business in a voice of condolence and sympathy, it would make it a little easier to bear, but they won't.[82]

Funeral undertakers are similarly stigmatized. Warner describes their low status in Yankee City:

> Despite the fact that the undertaker performs a necessary, useful service . . . that he is usually well paid and is very often successful as an entrepreneur, there is considerable evidence that neither he nor his customers are content with his present status in the occupational hierarchy.

As with life insurers, undertakers attempt to legitimate their business by adopting a "sacred" role:

> There is an increasing tendency on the part of the undertaker to borrow the ritual and sacred symbols of the minister and other professionals to provide an

outward cover for what he is and does. His place of business is not a factory or an office but a "chapel" or a "home."*

Within the life insurance industry it was primarily the selling agent who bore the stigma, while higher echelon executive officers and managers achieved positions of high status and power. In fact, agents were no less denigrated by their superiors, who spoke of them as an "unpleasant but costly necessity," than by customers.†

The institutional ambivalence of the life insurance enterprise, divided between commerce and altruism, became partially resolved by relegating

*Lloyd W. Warner, *The Living and The Dead: A Study of the Symbolic Life of Americans*, p. 317. On the low social prestige of undertakers see Talcott Parsons and Victor Lidz, "Death in American Society," p. 158; Leroy Bowman, *The American Funeral*, p. 71; Robert L. Fulton, "The Clergyman and the Funeral Director: A Study in Role Conflict"; and John C. McKinney, ed., *Aging and Social Policy* (New York: Appleton-Century-Crofts, 1966). Beyond their commercial involvement with death, undertakers have the added stigma of their close physical contact with the dead. The aversion to the dead body is transferred to the persons in charge of it. Undertakers are often excluded from membership in clubs or social circles. Clergymen associate with undertakers in professional or associational contexts, but rarely for private social occasions. Funeral establishments are similarly segregated. Zoning laws bar them from public view. Even without regulations, undertaking parlors in residential areas are vigorously resisted and often closed down as "nuisances" and "offense" to neighbors. The occupational stigma of undertaking has made it difficult to recruit personnel, despite adequate financial rewards. At the 1974 meeting of the Jewish Funeral Directors of America a speaker referred to the longstanding difficulty in attracting young people to work in funeral parlors despite starting salaries of $15,000. *The Jewish Post*, Friday, December 6, 1974. Morgue attendants in hospitals are similarly stigmatized socially, although they earn higher salaries than other attendants or orderlies. David Sudnow, *Passing On* (Englewood Cliffs, N.J.: Prentice-Hall, 1967), pp. 53, 58. In the case of the physician, the "dirty work" of handling human bodies is integrated into his prestige-bearing role. Hughes explains:

"To bring back health (which is cleanliness) is the great miracle. Those who work the miracle are more than absolved from the potential uncleanliness of their tasks; but those who perform the lowly tasks without being recognized as among the miracle-workers fare badly in the prestige rating." Everett Cherrington Hughes, *Men and Their Work*, pp. 72–73.

†"Life Insurance Soliciting," *American Exchange and Review* (July 1878), 32:173, cited in Owen J. Stalson, *Marketing Life Insurance*, p. 536. Within the marketing branch of the company, home-office management officials and general agents had higher prestige than salesmen. Although involved in selling, general agents had management duties. They were responsible for the appointment of subagents and empowered to bind the company by statements made after the policy was delivered, or in transactions related to renewal premiums or waiving forfeiture. Huttinger, *The Law of Salesmanship*, p. 97. The National Association of Life Underwriters (1890) organized by general agents did not admit subagents until 1915.

the "dirty work" of commerce to the agent. While company officers were occupied with managing and investing, the agent alone handled the actual business transaction with the public, discussing and pricing the value of each client's life. Standen admitted: "It is a well recognized fact that the soliciting agent bears the heat and burden of the day."* The industry pursued its image of noble disinterestedness by deflecting the ignoble tasks on its salesmen, so that even when life insurance became fully adopted and its beneficence accepted by most, the agent remained stigmatized.

Like other "dirty workers," life agents were afforded considerable discretion.[83] As long as they sold, it did not matter greatly how they sold. New applications, "like a mantle of charity, covered a multitude of sins." One observer remarked:

> The agent is taught that his business is merely to get applications and forward the premium, no matter what statements have been made to procure them. . . . If the agent succeeds in bringing in a sufficient number of applications, he is honored with a front seat, if not he is of no importance.[84]

The successful agent was the successful salesman: "You will find agents who have been forgiven all the other offenses in the calendar, but nowhere will you find the agent who has been forgiven for not selling insurance."[85] Life insurance companies basically "washed their hands of the agent," preferring to maintain minimal contact with them.† Standen lamented: "Thousands of local and sub-agents are never taught to realize that in every detail of their work they should act as though they were held to a rigid personal accountability to the company they work for."[86] Lack of company supervision was compounded by the public's reluctance to plan their death. It was preferable to leave it all up to the specialist. The typical customer did not discriminate between life insurance companies or policies. Willey noted: "Most people, when called upon to

*Standen, *Ideal Protection*, p. 151. A similar differentiation of tasks occurs in the funeral. The minister controls the "clean and spiritual phases," while the undertaker handles the "unclean" and material aspects of death. Warner, *The Living and the Dead*, p. 317. There is indication that clergymen resent any attempt by undertakers to assume a "sacred" role. Robert Fulton, "The Clergyman and the Funeral Director," p. 319.

†Legally, the agent was not even an employee in his company. For most of the nineteenth century they were employed without written agreements. Only in recent times has the agent-principal arrangement become more of an employer-employee arrangement. Stalson, *Marketing Life Insurance*, pp. 161, 354; Solomon S. Huebner, *Life Insurance*, p. 417.

insure, know little or nothing of the kind of a policy they need. . . . They usually take such kind of a policy as the agent recommends to them."[87] The agent remained the final arbiter:

> That the results of an agency depend more upon the agent than even upon the nature and advantages of his Company, is clearly demonstrated by the numerous Companies whose claims upon the public are by no means powerful, while in the same town another office offering the greatest and most solid advantages effects scarcely a policy.*

Hyde of Equitable cynically advised his agents: "You will find, that nineteen men out of twenty will let you decide for them."[88]

Predictably, the overriding emphasis on the goal of expanding sales without similar concern with institutional means encouraged deviant selling practices.[89] After the 1870s, the growing competition between companies intensified the "sales-at-any-cost" philosophy of marketing without increasing supervision of agency methods by either companies or customers. Agents were clearly instructed: "Let the problem be to produce a given result in your agency. Consider all the present means of accomplishing it; go out of the old ruts . . . invent new ways."[90] Rebating and twisting became the way to sell. Rebating was price haggling. The agent deducted part of his commission in order to induce sales. Twisting was the replacement of a client's old policy by a new one and usually involved misrepresentation. The older policy in force for some time carried a lower premium rate than a new one issued to the customer at an older age.[91] The two techniques became so prevalent that the agent who did not rebate or twist did not sell.[92] Willey noted:

> The practice of giving a part or whole of the first commission to the insured in order to induce him to take a policy is what no honorable agent will allow . . . yet . . . if such practice is once commenced . . . in any town or city, other agents will have to make the same terms or lose some of their business.†

* "Suggestions on the Elements of Success of Life Assurance Agents," *United States Insurance Gazette* (August 1861), 12:206. To this day, there is little discrimination between life insurance companies. The agent remains the decisive factor in the sale. Evans, "Selling," p. 77. There is a similar lack of information regarding the funeral transaction. Robert Fulton, "The Sacred and the Secular: Attitude of the American Public toward Death, Funerals and Funeral Directors," in Robert Fulton, ed., *Death and Identity*, p. 94.

† N. Willey, *An Instruction Book for Life Insurance Agents* (New York: C. C. Hine, 1891), p. 65. In one noted case of twisting during the 1870s, an agent obtained a list of the insured from a rival company in the outskirts of New York that had some financial difficulties. He obtained copies of a New York paper with accounts of the recent problems and mailed

Thus, initially intense cultural bias against life insurance agents was reinforced by the vivid social reality of unethical salesmen. "Men of intelligence and respectability,"[93] chastised life insurance as "the meanest business a person could be engaged in who had the least claim to respectability." The agent became characterized as "that peculiar nondescript, whose home is everywhere, whose business is everywhere . . . who looks upon fraud and swindling "within the acts of incorporation" as domestic virtues . . . and who aids in all the deceptions practiced."[94] Some observers perceived the structural source of deviant selling practices: "Rebating becomes the logical consequence of an unrestrained and injudicious effort to secure the largest possible volume of new business which very erroneously is conceived to be the principal . . . element of successful field work." Standen insistingly warned against a "vicious and unreasonable" system which freed agents "from any feeling of personal responsibility such as would, and should restrain them from doing anything reprehensible."[95] However, the industry needed "hustling" agents to expand. Life insurance officers verbally condemned rebating and twisting but little was done to correct the system which created them.*

THE STRUGGLE FOR PRESTIGE

By the early years of the twentieth century, cultural aversion to life agents, compounded by the actual low quality of most salesmen and the delinquency of many, brought the prestige of soliciting to its lowest ebb.

---

them to each patron of the rival company. Within a few days, he took all their business away. The company complained to the agent's home office:

"Its complaint was received . . . and a promise was given to notify the special agent to desist; which notice was prepared and sent out, a copy no doubt being furnished to the other company; but that copy of course failed to contain a few words written after it was made. . . . 'Get all the business you can.' " Miles M. Dawson, *Things Agents Should Know*, p. 60.

* Proposals to reduce agents' first-year commissions and increase renewal commissions to discourage rebates and encourage persistency of sales were ignored. Bain, *The Process of Professionalization*, p. 91. Buley notes: "Considering that everyone opposed it . . . rebating, like sin showed remarkable powers of survival." Buley, *The American Life Convention*, p. 148.

The distasteful commercialism of life agents had been heightened by the redefinition of life insurance from protection to investment. The agents' instructions were "to eliminate sentiment and offer the assurance as you would offer a block of railroad bonds."[96] At one time the immorality of the product tainted its sellers. The situation reversed. The immorality of the salesmen now threatened the success of life insurance. Agents were accused of being "one of the greatest present curses of the business." Disreputable solicitors had a monopoly of the business:[97] "Gentlemen who have any self-respect will not consent to associate or be classed with the grade of men in whose company they now occasionally find themselves."[98]

The Armstrong investigation of 1905 completed the erosion of the agents' reputation by revealing the full extent of their occupational malpractices. After that climactic event there were attempts both from within the industry and from without to redeem the agents' status by restructuring the format and goals of life insurance marketing. In the first place, the 1905 legislative hearings resulted in remedial legislation that dampened the industry's unrestrained pursuit of size and volume. Limitations were imposed on the amount of new business a company was authorized to write yearly. All prizes, bonuses, and extra commissions for agents were ruled out. Uniform commission schedules were enforced, limited to 50 percent on first-year premiums and 7.5 percent on each successive renewal premium for nine years.[99] While the law set constraints on the operational framework of agents, the industry undertook a redefinition of their institutionalized goals. To salvage their prestige, the commercialism of nineteenth-century agents was replaced by a professional role-orientation. Life insurance salesmen became involved in the sociologically predictable behavior of all professionalizing occupations.[100] A professional organization, the National Association of Life Insurance Underwriters had been organized in 1890. Agents chose the more dignified title of life underwiter.* Their first code of ethics was passed in 1918, and a second in 1935. Formal training of life insurance agents was first introduced by Eq-

*Apparently in the 1890s the title salesman had become prevalent. Before that men "took out" insurance instead of buying it, and agents "took applications" instead of selling insurance. Dawson, *Things Agents Should Know*, p. 4. The terminological shift reflected the increasing commercialization of life insurance. In the 1870s there had been a series of short-lived organizational efforts by general agents. Their purpose was primarily to control the status-reducing competitive malpractices of agents.

uitable in 1902 in a series of three consecutive summer session classes at the home office.[101] In 1919 the first prominent school of life insurance salesmanship was founded at the Carnegie Institute of Technology in Pittsburgh. The trend toward emphasis on systematic knowledge increased in the 1920s,[102] leading to a "new salesmanship": "The knowledge necessary to carry on the profession of life underwriting comes as no natural gift. A knowledge of life insurance in general and what particular policies best fill specific needs comes only after long, patient and intensive study and practice."[103]

The American College of Life Underwriters was organized in 1927 to "recognize properly qualified life underwriters with a professional degree."[104] It instituted the designation of Chartered Life Underwriter for agents who met certain established requirements and passed a series of exams.* The development of more complex uses for life insurance justified the newfound claims to specialized knowledge. Huebner explained: "[Life insurance] deals intimately with credit and requires of the fieldman a knowledge of banking and commercial credit . . . [and] the organization and operation of partnerships and corporations."[105] Life insurance for business partnerships and for corporation indemnification began selling in 1909. After 1911, insurance purchases were coordinated with tax and inheritance laws to maximize the policyholder's potential estate.[106] The trend towards "informed marketing," as Stalson calls it, was accompanied by a redefinition of the customer-agent relation. Life insurance selling was "more than the mere effecting of a sale,"[107] and agents were more than mere salesmen. Beginners were advised to "forget about selling, to concentrate on becoming expert in the knowledge and skills which will make them good craftsmen in designing financial programs for clients."[108] A professional orientation was expected to capture "that general respect and confidence which life insurance should rightly have."[109] An earlier generation of life insurance agents defined themselves as priests and missionaries to legitimate their commercial involvement with death. Life insurance salesmen in the twentieth century claimed professional status based on knowledge and service to redeem their role. Soliciting was ranked alongside law, medicine, and teaching: "There are few callings, if any, which offer to the practitioner a greater opportunity for

*The CLU is a designation, not a degree. The college acts as an examining board in the field of life insurance. Bain, *Process of Professionalization*, p. 213. The first life insurance textbook was Dr. Huebner's *Life Insurance*, published in 1915. Huebner then became the editor of a series of eight books on life insurance published by D. Appleton.

service than life insurance. . . . Life insurance ranks in nobleness and possibility of service with the other time-honored professions."*

THE ENDURING STIGMA

Behind the rhetoric of professionalization and despite some actual improvements in training and recruitment of agents, the stigma of selling insurance remained. A 1914 questionnaire assessing the prestige of agents in Syracuse, New York turned out a large percentage of negative evaluations.† Another less formal inquiry among successful sales managers in various large concerns revealed widespread prejudice against selling life insurance.‡ Later occupational prestige studies confirmed the persistent low status of the insurance agent. A 1925 survey of 45 occupations by George S. Counts among college and high school students rated insurance agent 14, immediately below electrician and immediately above

*Solomon S. Huebner, *The Economics of Life Insurance*, p. 17. Recently, the agent has assumed a new role to increase his credibility with clients. From missionary and professional he has become "the good neighbor." The importance of primary-type relationships and personal influence to mediate the impersonal commercialism of the industry is clearly spelt out in contemporary advertisement:

"We wanted a big, financially sound insurance company . . . and a nearby agent who was known for taking good care of his policyholders. With Rod Mace, we have both. . . . He's right there in the neighborhood to give us personal service. . . . He really cares, and he's backed by State Farm. We have the best of both worlds." Advertisement for State Farm, in *Time*, June 14, 1976.

†The questionnaire was mailed to 230 persons; 50 each of physicians, lawyers, merchants and managers, and 30 bankers. Out of 62 responses, 28 were "negative." The questions were themselves revealing: "Have you any prejudice against the profession of Life Insurance salesmanship? If so, why?" Winslow Russell, "Report presented at the Twenty-Fifth Annual Convention of the NALU," *Proceedings* (New York: National Association of Life Underwriters, 1914), p. 152.

‡An ad was placed for salesmen with no mention of life insurance. A large number of initial respondents made no further inquiry after being informed of the nature of the position. A letter was sent out to them to investigate their rejection:

"We are seeking to locate the reasons which deter many a successful man from entering the ranks of the Life Insurance profession. . . . In order to learn something of the reason which induced you to drop the matter, you will render us a great service if you will complete the enclosed blank." Winslow Russell "Report," p. 152.

mail carrier.* In 1936 a comparison of occupational attitudes among three groups ranked insurance agents 21, 22, and 16 in a list of 30 occupations.[110] The status of insurance agent made only negligible advances in the 1940s. A 1947 rating found him up four ranks from Count's 1925 scale, still below machinist and directly above electrician.[111] In the more comprehensive survey of 90 occupations conducted by the National Opinion Research Center in 1947, insurance agent was placed in the upper percentile of the lower-half distribution, on a similar level with bookkeeper, tenant farmer, and wholesale traveling salesman.† As in the previous century, the agency remained a place for older men, with unsuccessful careers in other fields.‡ A 1917 manual observed: "It is quite unusual that a business of such ramifying importance in its economic and beneficent value to the public should be accorded to such prejudice and be so generally shunned as a vocation."[112] As late as 1963, only 10 per-

*A disadvantage of occupational ratings as indicators of social class are their broad categories, which often obscure differences between members of a same occupation. Bernard Barber, *Social Stratification*, p. 109. Insurance agent does not discriminate between type of agent. However, the term "insurance agent" is generally associated with life solicitors rather than fire or marine agents. See Bain, *The Process of Professionalization*, p. 235.

†National Opinion Research Center, "Jobs and Occupations: A Popular Evaluation," *Public Opinion News* (1947), 9:3–13; reprinted in Reinhard Bendix and Seymour Martin Lipset, eds., *Class, Status, and Power*, pp. 411–26. A 1937 article detected a less negative attitude toward life agents: "Doors are no longer slammed in his face—at least not often . . . the presentation of his card no longer evokes a rush of blood and a wild desire to escape." Victor H. Bernstein, "Doors Once Shut Open To Insurance Men," *New York Times Magazine*, May 16, 1937, 11. Other sources belie the article's optimism. Marriage manuals in the 1940s warned young couples against unscrupulous agents; see Judson T. Landis, *Building A Successful Marriage* (Englewood Cliffs, N.J.: Prentice-Hall, 1948), p. 361; Norman Himes, *Your Marriage* (New York: Farrar & Rinehart, 1940), p. 235.

‡All applicants were encouraged: "Don't think you will fail as a life insurance solicitor simply because you have never been a large success at anything else. . . . Prove up! Surprise your friends." Charles W. Pickell, *Plain Reasons*, p. 103.

One popular fable warned against indiscriminate recruitment: "*The Coon Dog.* Colonel Culpepper's friends . . . asked him to take them on a coon hunt. . . . He went to the village and bought a mongrel pup from a horse dealer who assured him that this pup was a good coon dog. . . . The next day the Colonel hunted up the horse dealer and asked him why he had lied to him. "I didn't," replied the dealer, "I knew he was good for nothin' else, and so I knowed he must be a good coon dawg." *Application.* The man who has failed in other callings and goes into the life insurance business under the impression that he will find it a soft snap, will be disappointed." William Alexander, *Insurance Fables for Life Underwriters*.

cent of a group of one hundred and twenty-five successful life insurance salesmen hoped their sons would follow in their footsteps.*

Despite self-ratings by life insurance underwriters that reveal a professional self-image, the occupation never became widely defined as a profession.[113] Its code of ethics served to enhance the self-esteem of salesmen, but did not serve as an operational guide to their behavior. The conception of service was openly utilitarian: "and always remember—Service. If we will always think of the other fellow before we think of the dollar, we will always have the dollar."[114] The selection and training of agents continued loose and ineffective. Sales ability was still the only real job requirement.† The twentieth-century life insurance underwriter remained a low-status stigmatized salesman. Renaming an occupational role without changing its functional significance will not increase its prestige.[115] For all his honorable title and noble professional ideology, the underwriter was involved in the same "dirty work" of the nineteenth-century life agent. The success of the industry still depended on aggressive salesmen, not educated financial advisors.‡ Volume of sales were rewarded above quality of service.

High first-year commissions and lesser renewal commissions en-

*Evans, "Selling," p. 78. A 1952 *Fortune* survey found college students "detest the idea of selling life insurance." "Help Wanted: Sales," *Fortune* (May 1952), 45:102. College placement bureaus in the 1940s reported graduates' dislike of the "unattractive social status" of the job. Stalson, *Marketing Life Insurance*, p. 620. Black life insurance companies were an exception. The lack of respectable occupations for black college graduates made selling insurance an attractive opportunity. Weare, *Black Business*, p. 115.

†Attempts to dismiss all part-time agents and improve recruitment standards failed. The CLU did not become a license to practice and most licensing regulations remained token. Bain, *The Process of Professionalization*, p. 313.

‡Only an elite minority of life agents do advanced estate planning for a restricted upper-class clientele. The average life insurance sale, for middle- to low-income customers requires little training or specialized knowledge, Taylor, *The Life Insurance Man*, pp. 327, 403. Taylor and Pellegrin suggest that professionalization is dysfunctional to life insurance by reducing agents' sales vitality; see M. Lee Taylor and Roland J. Pellegrin, "Professionalization: Its Functions and Dysfunctions for the Life Insurance Occupation," *Social Forces* (December 1959), 38:110–14. In another study, three-fourths of a group of 125 successful salesmen indicated no interest in the CLU degree, nor did they believe it would in any way help their selling. Evans, "Selling," p. 78.

In the 1920s, the NALU organized the Million Dollar Round Table, an honorary club of agents who sold a million or more dollars of insurance every year. High persistence of policies and low lapse rate were not a requirement for membership. Bain, *The Process of Professionalization*, p. 234.

couraged agents to secure new business, making it financially unwise to spend much time attending customers' individual needs. The "highway to success" remained commercial: "We know that there is a definite, constant cash value to every call and every interview, and that the more folks we see the more money we will make." The mark of fame of one particularly noted solicitor were his 38,753 "calls" over eighteen years, for which he received over $300,000 in first-year commissions alone.* The overtly mercenary involvement with their customers' death was only clumsily and inadequately disguised by the agents' professional rhetoric. The public bought life insurance, but despised the men who sold it.†

Stock companies in the early nineteenth century treated life insurance as regular merchandise. Their newspaper advertisements and company booklets were informative but powerless. Life insurance had raised the management of death to a new level of rationality and technical efficiency. But it could not sell without the personal influence of the agent. Agents walked into the homes and offices of prospective customers; explaining, insisting, and finally persuading. Although the expense of the agency system was criticized, every attempt to eliminate it failed. The agent was indispensable. His role, however, was ambiguous. Death could not be pushed and promoted as a common ware. The industry needed aggressive salesmen, yet it was sacrilegious to reduce the welfare of widows and orphans to a routine sales job. The dilemma of marketing life was evident in the ambivalent role definition of agents. Official rhetoric urged them to remain above materialistic concerns, performing their task with the spiritual devotion of a missionary. The rewards went to the successful salesmen who solicited the most policies.

Despite the agent's professed zeal, he was stigmatized as a "salesman" of death, making a profitable living off people's worst tragedy. He was convincing but condemnable. To the life insurance industry, the salesman was their indispensable and despisable "dirty worker." After the 1870s,

* Milton L. Woodward, *The Highway to Success*, pp. 15–16. The commission system remains unchanged despite the public's preference for salaried agents. In a 1973 survey by the Institute of Life Insurance, three out of four respondents questioned the agent's motive. Close to six in ten felt the agent should be paid a salary rather than receive a commission. *The Map Report*, pp. 54–55.

† The negative image of life insurance salesmen still permeates our popular culture. The closing lines of a 1975 movie, *Love and Death*, affirm that spending an evening with a life insurance agent is a fate worse than death itself. "Mortality merchants" remained stigmatized. G. Scott Reynolds, *The Mortality Merchants* (New York: David McKay, 1968), pp. 172–73.

increased competition between life insurance companies intensified the need for extensive representation. Unsupervised by his superiors or his customers, the agent became a hustler using a panoply of illegitimate techniques to sell the most policies. Public exposure by the Armstrong investigation of 1905 triggered deliberate efforts to erase the stigma of soliciting by upgrading the salesman into a professional. Illegitimate practices were abolished, codes of ethics were published, professional associations organized and agents better trained. Yet the stigma endured. Life agents retained low status because they remained "dirty workers," occupationally constrained to treat death as a business.

Conclusions

> So ends this chronicle of varied monetary provisions resting on the personal life duration and the death contingency. . . . It is a record of illusions vanished, of progress retarded, of aims defeated, but of security achieved. . . . The planting of the seed may be in or with much derision, but the reaping is in honor.[1]

The first life insurance organizations in the United States were formed in the latter years of the eighteenth century to assuage the economic distress of the widows and orphans of low-paid Presbyterian and Episcopalian ministers. The idea soon appealed to the secular community and by the early decades of the nineteenth century several companies had optimistically undertaken the business of insuring life. Legislatures were encouraging; special charters for the organization of the new companies were rapidly and eagerly granted by many states. Life insurance seemed the perfect solution for the increasing economic destitution of widows and orphans. The public, however, did not respond. Surprised and dismayed by their failure, many pioneering companies withdrew altogether or else turned to other business to compensate for their losses in life insurance. The contrasting success of savings banks and trust companies, as well as the prosperity of fire and marine insurance companies, attests to the fact that there was sufficient disposable income among the population at the beginning of the nineteenth century. In addition, the early companies offered a solid economic organization; no life insurance company failed before the 1850s. Epidemics and high mortality rates did not affect their stability; actuarial knowledge was sufficient to calculate adequate premium rates. Americans were offered sound policies which they needed and they could well afford. They did not, however, want them.

After the 1840s there was a drastic reversal of trends and life insurance began its fantastic history of financial success. Its sudden prosperity has puzzled insurance historians as much as the initial failure of the industry. The new companies were offering the same product; neither rates nor conditions of life insurance policies were significantly improved. The only major change was the adoption of aggressive marketing techniques. Stalson has argued persuasively that the "rags-to-riches" transformation of life insurance in mid-century can be unequivocally attributed to the employment of thousands of active, high-pressure salesmen. He never explains, however, why agents were so necessary when other types of insurance, such as marine or fire, sold with little effort. The struggles and the victories of life insurance have remained enigmatic and misunderstood because its historians systematically overlooked the nonmonetary factors involved in its acceptance and adoption.

In the first place, the development of the insurance industry reflected the struggle between fundamentalist and modernist religious outlooks that worked itself out in the nineteenth century. Contrasting theological perspectives divided the clergy into opposing groups; there were those who denounced life insurance to their congregations as a secular and sacrilegious device that competed against God in caring for the welfare of widows and orphans. Others, more attuned to the entrepreneurial spirit, supported the industry in words and in deeds. Convinced of the theological propriety of taking a more active participatory role in handling human affairs, many clergymen not only insured their own lives but became leading spokesmen for the growing industry, lauding it from their pulpits and writing congratulatory pamphlets and journal articles about life insurance.

The cultural incompatibility of life insurance with literalist and fundamentalist beliefs hindered its development during the first part of the century. In opposition, the emerging liberal theology tended to make the enterprise legitimate. Religious liberals supported insurance programs for practical considerations as well. Congregations which had been unwilling to raise the meager salaries of their underpaid pastors and ministers were more easily persuaded to pay the relatively small premiums of a policy on the life of the clergymen.

The history of life insurance helps us understand the problem of establishing monetary equivalents for relations or processes which are defined as being beyond material concerns, a problem of long-standing interest in sociological thought. With life insurance, money and man, the sacred and the profane, were thrown together; the value of man became measurable by money. The purely quantitative conception of human beings was acceptable in primitive society where only the gods belonged to the sacred sphere while men remained part of the profane world. For Durkheim and Simmel, one of the most significant alterations in the moral values of modern society has been the sacralizing of man, his emergence as the "holy of holies."[2] The growth of individualism resulted in a new respect for the infinite worth of human personality, displacing the earlier utilitarianism with an absolute valuation of human beings. In an increasingly industrialized market economy dominated by the "cash nexus," human life and human feelings were culturally segregated into their separate incommensurable realm. Life insurance threatened the sanctity of life by pricing it. Insurance was uncomfortably reminiscent of the primitive institution of the wergild, or "blood-money," when the murder of a man was restituted with the payment of money. Thus, the financial evaluation of a man's life introduced by the industry was initially rejected by many as a profanation which transformed the sacred event of death into a vulgar commodity. By the latter part of the nineteenth century, the economic definition of the value of death finally became more acceptable, legitimating the life insurance enterprise. However, the monetary evaluation of death did not de-sacralize it; far from "profaning" life and death, money became sacralized by its association with them. Life insurance took on symbolic values quite distinct from its utilitarian function, emerging as a new form of ritual with which to face death and a processing of the dead by those kin left behind.

Another cultural factor explored is the impact of changing ideologies of risk and speculation. We have shown how certain practices considered to be deviant speculative ventures by a traditional economic morality were redeemed and transformed into legitimate, even noble investments by a different entrepreneurial ethos. Much of the opposition to life insurance resulted from the apparently speculative nature of the enterprise; the insured were seen as "betting" with their lives against the company. The instant wealth reaped by a widow who cashed her policy seemed suspiciously similar to the proceeds of a winning lottery ticket. Traditionalists upheld savings banks as a more honorable economic institution than life insurance because money was accumulated gradually and soberly. After the 1870s, as the notion of economic risk and rational speculation grew progressively more acceptable, the slower methods of achieving wealth lost some of their luster and life insurance gained prominence and moral respectability. The changing attitude toward insurance after 1870 corresponds, more or less precisely, with the "takeoff" period in American industry following the American Civil War. Traditional attitudes generally crumble after a major conflict, and the same was true following the War between the States. In the last third of the nineteenth century, "A new society—an industrial society—was being created, and its creation involved the uprooting and transplanting of millions of people, the raising of new groups to power and the decline of the once-powerful, the learning of new routines and habits and disciplines, the sloughing off of old ideas."[3]

The adoption of life insurance was influenced by cultural factors such as religious beliefs, values, and ideologies. Its pattern of diffusion demonstrates the limitations of an exclusively economic analysis of social behavior. Life insurance historians characteristically concentrate on economic determinants of the industry's development, overlooking as a consequence certain fundamental elements of that history external to the economic sphere. Barber has criticized the "absolutization" of the market as an analytical tool for social analysis in most social science disciplines.[4] Our study emphasizes the inadequacy and theoretical naivetè of single-factor theories; we have stressed the importance of developing less simplistic multidimensional explanatory models. There is no claim made that the vicissitudes of the life insurance business can be attributed to those cultural factors alone, or that economic and technological variables are irrelevant analytical tools. There is little doubt that the higher degree of economic development and the increased urbanization of mid-century America were necessary to the development of life insurance. They were not, however, sufficient for its adoption.

Our study of life insurance also takes into account selected socio-structural variables such as the strain in shifting a social practice from an altruistic type of exchange to a market exchange. The economic protection of widows and orphans was not easily reduced to pure economic exchange. Life insurance offers a prototype of what Robert K. Merton has called structured ambivalence at the institutional level, in which the simultaneous goals of business and altruism created a continuing tension between their contradictory demands and expectations. As in status-and-role ambivalence, contradictory demands result in oscillation of behavior. Periodic attempts by the life insurance enterprise to emphasize either its commercial or its altruistic goals were traced. Life agents were caught in the ambivalence of the life insurance enterprise; their careers marked by conflicting role expectations and definitions. Agents were torn between a self-image of beneficent missionaries assuaging the trials of death and helping out distressed widows and orphans, and a public image of greedy salesmen cashing in on people's misery and exploiting the bereaved. The agent was stigmatized because, despite his protestations to the contrary, he remained a "businessman" of death, making a living out of others' tragedies. Attempts to professionalize agents by improving and extending their training and organizing professional associations were frustrated by the ultimate reality that the industry did not need discreet professionals. The success of life insurance depended on aggressive salesmen to do the "dirty work" of persuading reluctant customers to do business with their death.

The emergence of life insurance companies also provides a useful indicator of functional changes in the family. The care of widows and orphans, previously the responsibility of the community, became defined as the obligation of the nuclear family with the assistance of paid professionals. A similar process occurred with the physical care of the dead at the beginning of the nineteenth century, when the family turned to professional undertakers for all burial arrangements.

America was, and remains, a land of economic magic. In the case of life insurance the trick was to sell futures—pessimistic futures. The task of selling a commodity to a materialist civilization was relatively simple. The task of converting human life and death into commodities, however, was highly complex. The universe of believers and theologians became involved with another universe of hard-headed businessmen. Out of this interaction emerged a compromise credo which was a far cry from vulgar marketplace linkages and at the same time a giant step beyond simplified heavenly rewards. Theology yielded to the capitalist ethos—but not without compelling the latter to disguise its materialist mission in spiritual garb.

Notes

Acknowledgments

1. Kurt H. Wolff, ed., *The Sociology of Georg Simmel* (New York: Free Press, 1950), pp. 392–93.

Introduction

1. Lester W. Zartman, "History of Life Insurance in the United States," p. 86.
2. J. Owen Stalson, *Marketing Life Insurance*, p. 666.
3. There are a few exceptions. See, for example, John W. Riley, Jr., "Basic Social Research and the Institution of Life Insurance," pp. 6–9. That entire issue of the magazine was devoted to social research and life insurance. Two doctoral dissertations have been written on the life insurance agent: M. Lee Taylor, "The Insurance Man: A Sociological Analysis of the Occupation"; Robert Ketcham Bain, "The Process of Professionalization: Life Insurance Selling."
4. Richard M. Titmuss, *The Gift Relationship*, p. 198. According to a recent report, the nation appears to be shifting toward amost total reliance on volunteer, nonpaid donors. *New York Times*, June 19, 1977.
5. Karl Marx, *The Economic and Philosophic Manuscripts of 1844* (New York: International, 1964), p. 151. See also *The Communist Manifesto*. Above all, money for Marx destroys individuality by enabling its possessor to achieve objects and qualities which bear no connection to individual talents or capacities.
6. Peter M. Blau, *Exchange and Power in Social Life* (New York: Wiley, 1967), p. 63.

1. Historical and Economic Background

1. *United States Insurance Gazette* (May 1861), 13:7.
2. United States Life Insurance and Trust Co. of Philadelphia, 1850 booklet.
3. New York Life Insurance Co. *Almanac*, 1869.
4. "Life insurance as it was—and as it is," *Insurance Monitor* (October 1871), 19:848.

5. Reported in the *Insurance Monitor* (April 1853), 1:1.

6. E. W. Stoughton, "Life Insurance," p. 222.

7. Mutual Life Insurance Co. of New York, between February 1843 and August 1844, reported in *Hunt's Merchants' Magazine* (October 1844), 11:340.

8. Lord vs. Dall, *12 Mass. Reports 115.*

9. Walter S. Nichols, *Insurance Blue Book, 1876–77.*

10. Even historians who are aware of these issues do not investigate them systematically. See Lester Zartman, "History of Life Insurance in the United States," p. 86; Owen J. Stalson, *Marketing Life Insurance,* p. 666; R. Carlyle Buley, *The Equitable Life Assurance Society of the United States,* p. 30; Shepard B. Clough, *A Century of American Life Insurance,* p. 13; James H. Cassedy, *Demography in Early America,* p. 44. Henrietta M. Larson laments the mostly "superficial and uncritical" characteristics of most insurance histories. Henrietta M. Larson, *Guide to Business History,* p. 194.

11. See Alexander Mackie, *Facile Princeps,* p. 64; Zartman, "History of Life Insurance," p. 80.

12. Margaret G. Myers, *A Financial History of the United States.* The conflict between the definition of life insurance as business or charitable enterprise persists throughout its history. I will deal with it in chapter 6.

13. Nichols, *Insurance Blue Book,* p. 9.

14. From *Fundamental By-Laws and Tables of Rates for the Corporation for the Relief of the Widows and Children of Clergymen in the Communion of the Protestant Episcopal Church,* with Preface by Horace Binney, p. 13. On the lack of response of Episcopalian ministers to life insurance, see also John William Wallace, *Historical Sketch of The Corporation for the Relief of the Widows and Orphans of Clergymen in the Communion of the Protestant Episcopal Church,* pp. 13–15.

15. Nichols, *Insurance Blue Book,* pp. 10–11.

16. Thomas H. Montgomery, *A History of the Insurance Company of North America,* p. 72.

17. Mackie, *Facile Princeps,* p. 126.

18. Nichols, *Insurance Blue Book,* pp. 37–38.

19. Gerald T. White, *A History of the Massachusetts Hospital Life Insurance Company,* p. 27.

20. From a letter written by one of the first directors of the Union Insurance Co., October 8, 1873, quoted in J. H. Van Amringe, *A Plain Exposition of the Theory and Practice of Life Assurance,* p. 55.

21. Quoted in F. F. Stevens, *Reminiscences of the Past Half Century,* p. 30.

22. *Hunt's Merchants' Magazine* (February 1843), 8:109; *Edinburgh Review,* 1827, quoted in Nichols, *Insurance Blue Book,* p. 17.

23. From the minutes of the Board of The Pennsylvania Co., 1814, quoted in Stalson, *Marketing Life Insurance,* p. 51.

24. *Legislative Documents of the Senate and Assembly of New York, 53d session, 1830,* vol. 2, no. 84, p. 3.

25. Zartman, "History of Life Insurance," p. 86.

26. "Life Insurance Profession and Life Insurance Literature—Their Rise and Progress," *United States Insurance Gazette* (May 1861), 13:8.

27. *United States Insurance Gazette* (May 1855), 1:iv.

2. The Persistent Puzzle

1. Nineteenth-century insurance historians were more sensitive to the importance of cultural resistance and popular prejudice; see "Life Insurance Profession and Life Insurance Literature—Their Rise and Progress," *United States Insurance Gazette* (May 1861), vol. 8; J. H. Van Amringe, *A Plain Exposition of the Theory and Practice of Life Assurance;* and Walter S. Nichols, *Insurance Blue Book, 1876–77.* Alfred Mannes is one contemporary writer who recognizes among the prerequisites for the development of life insurance "certain subjective limits arising from the ethical outlook of the individual and of his social group." Alfred Mannes, "Principles and History of Insurance," p. 97. In his book *Ethics, Morality, and Insurance,* John D. Long, a professor of insurance, discusses the ethical foundations of life insurance. Unfortunately, his data are largely impressionistic. The role of religious prejudice in retarding the growth of the industry is acknowledged by some historians but not systematically analyzed. See J. Owen Stalson, *Marketing Life Insurance;* Charles Knight, *History of Life Insurance to 1870;* Nichols, *Insurance Blue Book;* G. A. MacLean, *Insurance Up Through the Ages.* Joseph MacLean, *Life Insurance,* p. 511, suggests that "this foolish prejudice was responsible in large measure for the slow growth of the business."

2. T.R. Jencks, "Life Insurance in the United States," pp. 109–31 and 227–41. See also R. Carlyle Buley, *The Equitable Life Assurance Society of the United States,* pp. 34–35; Shepard B. Clough, *A Century of American Life Insurance,* pp. 4 and 41; Douglass C. North and Lance E. Davis, *Institutional Change and American Economic Growth,* p. 169; and Alfred Mannes, "Outlines of a General Economic History of Insurance," p. 40.

3. W. W. Rostow, *The Stages of Economic Growth,* p. 40.

4. See Douglass C. North, *Growth and Welfare in the American Past,* p. 75; S. Bruchey, *The Roots of American Growth,* p. 85; and Paul David, "The Growth of Real Product in the United States Before 1840: New Evidence, Controlled Conjectures."

5. Gerald T. White, *A History of the Massachusetts Hospital Life Insurance Company,* p. 17.

6. *Ibid.,* p. 28. See also W. H. Kniffin, *The Savings Bank and Its Practical Work,* p. 16; Nichols, *Insurance Blue Book,* p. 16; Lance E. Davis and Peter L. Payne, "From Benevolence to Business: The Story of Two Savings Banks," p. 387; and *Statistical Abstract of the United States, 1938* (U.S. Dept. of Commerce, Bureau of the Census), p. 257.

7. Quoted in James G. Smith, *The Development of Trust Companies in the United States,* p. 235.

8. Douglass C. North, "Capital Accumulation in Life Insurance Between the Civil War and the Investigation of 1905," p. 239. See also Buley, *Equitable Life Assurance Society,* p. 30; Clough, *A Century of American Life Insurance,* pp. 6–9; and Morton Keller, *The Life Insurance Enterprise, 1885–1910,* p. 9.

9. Dexter Reynolds, *A Treatise on the Law of Life Assurance,* p. 9.

10. E. W. Stoughton, "Life Insurance," p. 231.

11. "Life Insurance for Farm Families" (U.S. Dept. of Agriculture: Agricultural Research Service, 1959), p. 2. See also Clough, *A Century of American Life Insurance,* pp. 6–9.

12. W. S. Rossiter, *A Century of Population Growth,* p. 15.

13. North and Davis, *Institutional Change and Economic Growth*, p. 169. Mortality tables are used to calculate adequate premiums. They summarize the mortality experience of a single generation or cohort with a set of constant age-specific death rates.

14. Frederick H. Ecker, *The Great Provider*, p. 31; and Irving Pfeffer and David R. Klock, *Perspectives on Insurance*, p. 33.

15. C. F. Trenerry, *The Origin and Early History of Insurance*, p. 157. Actuarial science consists in applying the laws of probability to insurance. Probability theory was first developed in 1665 by Blaise Pascal.

16. MacLean, G. A., *Insurance Up Through the Ages*, p. 35.

17. Maris A. Vinovskis, "The 1789 Life Table of Edward Wigglesworth," pp. 570–583.

18. Miles M. Dawson, "The Development of Insurance Mathematics," p. 115.

19. See J. A. Fowler, *History of Insurance in Philadelphia for Two Centuries*, p. 647; Buley, *The Equitable Life Assurance Society*, p. 33; Lester Zartman, "History of Life Insurance in the United States," p. 80; and Terence O'Donnell, *History of Life Insurance in Its Formative Years*, p. 439.

20. Yasukichi Yasuba, *Birth Rates of the White Population in the United States, 1800–1860*, pp. 82–96. Vinovskis found relatively constant rates of mortality up to 1860, Maris Vinovskis, "Mortality Rates and Trends in Massachusetts before 1860," pp. 184–213.

21. *Ibid.*, p. 204.

22. Rossiter, *A Century of Population Growth*, p. 93; U.S. Bureau of the Census, *Historical Statistics of the United States: Colonial Times to 1957* (Washington, D.C., 1960), p. 24.

23. *House Journal Penna.* (1811–12), p. 157; quoted in Smith, *The Development of Trust Companies*, p. 235.

24. Report of the committee on banks and insurance companies in reference to the business of life insurance. *Documents of the Assembly of the State of New York*, 75th session, 1852.

25. Spencer L. Kimball, *Insurance and Public Policy*, p. 8.

26. Oscar Handlin and Mary F. Handlin, *Commonwealth—A Study of the Role of Government in the American Economy: Massachusetts 1774–1861*, p. 139.

27. *House Journal Penna.* (1811–12); quoted in Smith, *The Development of Trust Companies*, p. 235.

28. Stalson, *Marketing Life Insurance*, p. 74. This book has been rightfully called "the most valuable work in the history of life insurance." Henrietta M. Larson, *Guide to Business History*, p. 464.

29. See Stalson, *Marketing Life Insurance*, pp. 66, 81, 201, 662; Gerald T. White, *A History of the Massachusetts Hospital Life Insurance Company*, pp. 32, 83. By 1878, the Pennsylvania Co., the Massachusetts Co., New York Life, and Girard Life had all left the life insurance business.

30. Mannes, "Principles and History of Insurance," p. 97.

31. Quoted in Mildred F. Stone, *Since 1845: A History of the Mutual Benefit Life Insurance Company*, p. 19.

32. *Hunt's Merchants' Magazine* (October 1844), pp. 342–43.

33. Stalson, *Marketing Life Insurance*, p. 105.

34. Quoted in Harrison S. Morris, *A Sketch of the Pennsylvania Company for Insurances On Lives and Granting Annuities*, p. 96.

35. Quoted in Stalson, *Marketing Life Insurance*, p. 152.

36. *Insurance Monitor* (March 1853), 1:1.

37. *Prospectus of The Union Insurance Company, Incorporated by The Legislature of the State of New York, for Making Insurance on Lives, and Granting Annuities* (New York, 1818), p. 1.

38. *Hunt's Merchants' Magazine* (October 1844), 11:342.

39. See White, *Massachusetts Hospital Life Insurance Company*, p. 31; Stalson, *Marketing Life Insurance*, p. 220; and *United States Life Insurance Co.* in Philadelphia, 1850 booklet.

40. Fowler, *History of Insurance in Philadelphia*, p. 655; Marquis James, *The Metropolitan Life*, p. 16; Stalson, *Marketing Life Insurance*, p. 327. Of the effect of the panic of 1857 on life insurance companies, Knight points out: "While other institutions and mercantile establishments whose credit had up to that time been unimpaired were failing daily, the life insurance companies stood prominently as the only source of financial protection to many who had lost all in other enterprises." Knight, *History of Life Insurance*, p. 117.

41. Stalson, *Marketing Life Insurance*, p. 55. The impressionistic basis for these assumptions leads to polar interpretations of the same variable. Zartman claims that the "almost universal ignorance" of its principles benefited life insurance, by allowing certain shady tactics crucial to its success to remain undiscovered. Zartman, *History of Life Insurance*, p. 86.

42. Alexander C. Campbell, *Insurance and Crime*, p. 187.

43. James Gollin, *Pay Now, Die Later*, p. 3.

44. *Consumer's Union Report on Life Insurance*, p. ix.

45. J. Brainbridge, *Biography of an Idea: The Story of Mutual Fire and Casualty Insurance*, p. 17.

46. A. C. Dollarhide, *Facts and Fallacies of Life Insurance*, p. 5.

47. Burton Hendricks, "The Story of Life Insurance," p. 68.

48. *New York Daily Tribune* (June 6, 1874), p. 6.

49. Brainbridge, *Biography of an Idea*, p. 17.

50. *Ibid.*

51. *The Map Report*, p. 44.

52. *New York Times*, Feb. 23, 1974.

53. Jeffrey O'Connell, "Living with Life Insurance," p. 34.

54. Stone, *Mutual Benefit Life Insurance Company*, p. 15.

55. Everett M. Rogers with F. Floyd Shoemaker, *Communication of Innovations*, p. 108.

56. Jencks, "Insurance in the United States," p. 119.

57. Stalson, *Marketing Life Insurance*, pp. 321–22.

3. A Comparative Perspective

1. T. R. Jencks, "Life Insurance in the United States," p. 124.

2. Portalis, from *Recueil Complet des Travaux Préparatoires du Code Civil XIV*, quoted

by I. Tournan, "L'Assurance sur la Vie en France au XIX Siècle," p. 24. *Note:* Translations from the French, except when otherwise indicated, are my own.

3. Rogers and Shoemaker suggest cross-cultural testing as one way of determining the importance of different variables in explaining the success or failure of diffusion of an innovation. Everett M. Rogers with Floyd Shoemaker, *Communication of Innovations*, p. 52. On comparative analysis, see Ivan Vallier, ed., *Comparative Methods in Sociology*.

4. Jencks, "Life Insurance in the United States," p. 110. On the development of fire and marine insurance, see also Stuart Bruchey, *The Roots of American Economic Growth*, p. 145; Terence O'Donnell, *History of Life Insurance in Its Formative Years*, p. 439; R. Carlyle Buley, *The Equitable Life Assurance Society of the United States*, p. 20; Joseph S. Davis, *Essays in the Earlier History of American Corporations*, p. 245; Solomon Huebner, "History of Marine Insurance," p. 18.

5. P. Henry Woodward, *Insurance in Connecticut*, p. 11.

6. Davis, *Essays in the Earlier History of American Corporations*, pp. 234, 245.

7. Walter S. Nichols, *Insurance Blue Book, 1876–77*, pp. 7, 13–14.

8. *Ibid.*, p. 12.

9. Marquis James, *Biography of a Business*, p. 43; Davis, *Essays in the Earlier History of American Corporations*, pp. 234–236.

10. Nichols, *Insurance Blue Book*, p. 8. See also James G. Smith, *The Development of Trust Companies in the United States*, p. 235.

11. *The American Life Assurance Magazine and Journal of Actuaries* (July 1859–April 1860), 1:12.

12. *Ibid.*, pp. 11–12.

13. Woodward, *Insurance in Connecticut*, p. 14.

14. Hawthorne, *The Hartford of Hartford*, p. 75. Likewise, a major London fire in 1666 led to the formation of the first English fire insurance company. James, *Biography of a Business*, p. 140.

15. See S. Huebner, *Marine Insurance*, p. 32; James L. Athearn, *General Insurance Agency Management*, p. 30; and William D. Winter, *Marine Insurance*, p. 342.

16. Miller Lee Taylor, "The Life Insurance Man: A Sociological Analysis of the Occupation," p. 284.

17. Legislative Documents of the Senate and Assembly of New York 53d Sess., 1830, vol. 2, no. 84, pp. 3–7, quoted in Smith, *The Development of Trust Companies in the United States*, p. 254.

18. E. W. Stoughton, "Life Insurance," p. 227.

19. William T. Standen, *The Ideal Protection*, p. 84.

20. "Which is the Greater Duty," *Insurance Journal* (October 1882), 10:276.

21. Rev. S. A. Hodgman, *Father's Life Boat*, p. 8.

22. Standen, *The Ideal Protection*, p. 84. The emphasis on self-denial was only temporary; by the end of the nineteenth century self-interest was upgraded by life insurance publications as the leading motivation to purchase life policies. This ambivalence between altruism and self-interest will be analyzed in chapter 6.

23. Editorial, *New York Journal of Commerce*, December 30, 1863.

24. Nichols, *Insurance Blue Book*, p. 20.

25. Woodward, *Insurance in Connecticut*, p. 13. Also in F. C. Oviatt, "History of Fire Insurance in the United States," p. 77; Richard M. Bissell, "Fire Insurance: Its Place in the Financial World," p. 28.

26. Nichols, *Insurance Blue Book*, p. 21. See also Bissell, "Fire Insurance," p. 29.

27. "Which is the Greater Duty," *Insurance Journal*, (October 1882), 10:2; "The *New York Times* on Insurance," *Insurance Monitor* (April 1853), 1:1.

28. Bissell, "Fire Insurance," pp. 29, 34–35.

29. Huebner, "History of Marine Insurance," pp. 18–21.

30. Freeman Hunt, *Worth and Wealth*, pp. 38, 346, 386.

31. Editorial, *New York Times*, February 23, 1853, p. 4.

32. Jencks, "Insurance in the United States," p. 112.

33. Jules Lefort, *Traité du Contrat d'Assurance sur La Vie*, pp. 38–39.

34. Some companies operate without legal recognition, but their contracts may be cancelled at any time, forcing them to return all premiums. M. A. Wahab, "Insurance Development in Iraq and the U.A.R.," p. 6. See also *Insurance Markets of the World*, p. 497.

35. Marco Besso, "Progress of Life Assurance Throughout the World, from 1859 to 1883," p. 427; *Insurance Markets*, pp. 36–37, 83, 98, 120–21, 152, 158.

36. Henry S. Washburne, *Something About the Business of Life Assurance in Germany*, p. 7; Lefort, *Traité du Contrat d'Assurance*, pp. 79, 84.

37. P. G. M. Dickson, *The Sun Insurance Office*, p. 167.

38. Suketaro Hirose, *Development and Present Conditions of Life Insurance in Japan* (Osaka: Nippon Life Assurance Society, 1935), p. 1.

39. G. Jacquemyns, *Lagrand Dumoneau*, p. 49; *Insurance Markets*, pp. 36–37, 64–65, 120–21, 142–43, 152.

40. John Long, *Ethics, Morality and Insurance*, p. 15.

41. See, for instance, Jencks, "Life Insurance in the United States," p. 111; "Life Insurance," *Banker's Magazine* (February 1852), 6:662.

42. Edmond Reboul, *Du Droit des Enfants Bénéficiares d'Une Assurance sur La Vie Contractée par Leur Père*, p. 21.

43. "Life Insurance in France," *Banker's Magazine* (September 1861), 16:215.

44. Barry Supple, *The Royal Exchange Assurance*, p. 112.

45. Jencks, "Life Insurance in the United States," p. 112.

46. "Life Assurance in France," *Insurance Monitor* (August 1861), 9:179.

47. See P. J. Richard, *Histoire des Institutions d'Assurance en France*, p. 49; and Lefort, *Traité du Contrat d'Assurance*, p. 72.

48. *Proceedings of the Second Annual Meeting of the Nautilus Mutual Life Insurance Company*, p. 14.

49. Quoted in Lefort, *Traité du Contrat d'Assurance*, pp. 39, 46.

50. Quoted in Supple, *Royal Exchange Assurance*, p. 117.

51. Cornelius Walford, "Early History of Life Insurance in Great Britain," in Lester W. Zartman, and William H. Price, eds., *Life Insurance* (New Haven: Yale University Press, 1914), p. 67. Membership was to be limited to 2,000.

52. Supple, *Royal Exchange Assurance*, pp. 100, 110. Two important life insurance companies were organized in 1721, the Royal Exchange and the London Assurance. Although most of their profit came from fire and marine insurance they developed a moderate life business.

53. Owen J. Stalson, *Marketing Life Insurance*, p. 41.

54. Supple, *The Royal Exchange Assurance*, pp. 10, 110–11.

55. Besso, "Progress of Life Assurance," p. 431.

56. "Principles of Life Insurance," *Banker's Magazine* (April 1859), 13:810.

57. Dickson, *Sun Insurance Office*, p. 101.

58. Supple, *Royal Exchange Assurance*, p. 56.

59. From *Spéctateur Politique et Litteraire* (November 1818), quoted in J. B. Juvigny, *Coup d'Oeil sur les Assurances sur La Vie des Hommes*, p. 81.

60. "Life Insurance in France," *Banker's Magazine* (September 1861), 16:214.

61. Buley, *The Equitable Life Assurance Society*, p. 283.

62. Lefort, *Traité du Contrat d'Assurance*, pp. 47–49.

63. Quoted in Touman, *L'Assurance sur la Vie*, p. 49.

64. Lefort, *Traité du Contrat d'Assurance*, p. 54.

65. Henry S. Washburne, *Something About the Business of Life Assurance in France*, p. 34; Buley, *The Equitable Life Assurance Society*, p. 28; Alfred Mannes, "Outlines of a General Economic History of Insurance," p. 43.

66. Jencks, "Life Insurance in the United States," p. 110. The French government made life insurance illegal in 1793.

67. F. Chevert, *L'Assurance sur la Vie*, booklet 187?, p. 62. On French fire insurance see "Fire Insurance in France," *United States Insurance Gazette* (October 1856), 3:326; Richard, *Institutions d'Assurance en France*, p. 48.

68. Alois de Meuron, "Du Contrat d'Assurance sur la Vie," p. 13. See also Lefort, *Traité du Contrat d'Assurance*, p. 61; René Goupil, *De La Consideration de la Mort des Personnes dans les Actes Juridiques*, p. 2.

69. "Life Insurance in France," *Banker's Magazine*, p. 214.

70. Juvigny, *Assurance sur la Vie des Hommes*, pp. 2, 94.

71. Jencks, "Life Insurance in the United States," p. 112.

72. Buley, *The Equitable Life Assurance Society*, p. 96; Lefort, *Traité du Contrat d'Assurance*, p. 54; Touman, *L'Assurance sur la Vie*, p. 63.

73. Goupil, *La Consideration de la Mort*, p. 125; Miles W. Dawson, "The Development of Insurance Mathematics," in Lester W. Zartman, ed., *Personal Insurance*, p. 106.

74. "Life Insurance in France," *Banker's Magazine* (November 1857), 12:379.

75. Michel Pascan, "*Les Pactes sur Succession Future*," p. 103.

76. *Ibid.*, pp. 105–6.

77. Goupil, *La Consideration de la Mort*, pp. 131, 195; Lefort, *Traité du Contrat d'Assurance*, p. 76; Pierce Pelerin, *The French Law of Wills, Probates Administration and Death Duties*, pp. 8–9.

78. Quoted in Lefort, *Traité du Contrat d'Assurance*, pp. 38, 41.

79. Quoted in *ibid.*, p. 47.

80. Quoted in Richard, *Institutions d'Assurance en France*, p. 37.

81. Quoted in Touman, *L'Assurance sur la Vie*, p. 24.

82. Quoted in Jencks, "Life Insurance in the United States," p. 112.

83. See Lefort, *Traité du Contrat d'Assurance en France*, p. 65.

84. Goupil, *La Consideration de la Mort*, p. 35.

85. Lefort, *Traité du Contrat d'Assurance*, p. 6.

4. The Impact of Values and Ideologies on the Adoption of Social Innovations

1. *Insurance Monitor* (August, 1863), 11:183.

2. Douglass C. North and Lance E. Davis, *Institutional Change and American Economic Growth*, p. 39. See also Everett M. Rogers with F. Floyd Shoemaker, *Communication of Innovations*, p. 144.

3. Bernard Barber, "Function, Variability, and Change in Ideological Systems," p. 259.

4. James Coleman refers to the conjectural quality of most discussions on the emergence of social innovations. "Social Inventions," p. 172. There are exceptions. One study of the acceptance of old age and survivor's insurance concluded that social innovations are particularly influenced by affective rather than cognitive factors. Ward Bauder, "Iowa Farm Operators' and Farm Landlords' Knowledge of, Participation in and Acceptance of the Old Age and Survivors' Insurance Program." In *The Struggle for Social Security*, Roy Lubove illustrates the impact of ideological opposition on the efforts to introduce social insurance. Social security was not attacked on economic grounds, but as a challenge to the ideologies of voluntarism and individualism. Benjamin Nelson, in *The Idea of Usury*, shows another case of an innovation opposed on moral grounds.

5. Surprisingly, while funeral expenditures and wills have been used as indicators of attitudes toward death, life insurance material has remained mostly unexplored. On funeral expenditures, see Vanderlyn R. Pine and Derek L. Phillips, "The Cost of Dying," pp. 130–39; and William M. Kephart, "Status After Death," pp. 635–43. On wills, see Thomas L. Schaffer, *Death, Property, and Lawyers* and Michel Vovelle, *Piété Baroque et Déchristianisation en Provence au XVIII Siècle*.

6. From the *Rules and Constitutions* of various eighteenth-century voluntary associations (on microfilm at the Columbia University Library): Society of the Sons of St. George, 1772, 1774, 1778 (English); Friendly Brothers of St. Patrick, 1775 (Irish); Baltimore Benevolent Society, 1796 (Catholic); Scots Society, New York City, 1744; Fellowship Society of Charleston, South Carolina, 1769; Society for the Relief of Poor, Aged and Infirm Masters of Ships, their Widows and Children, 1800; and Moravian Brotherly Association for the Support of Widows, 1771. An entrance fee and monthly or yearly dues paid by the members provided the basic funds with which to offer benefits. An average entrance fee was 30 shillings in 1780 and the average annual dues were also about the same. Other monies were obtained from various fines for misbehavior, absence from meetings, or not attending a fellow member's funeral. The average benefits paid by these societies were limited to 10 pounds per person or family. Although often self-defined as charities, these mutual aid societies were not limited to the indigent.

7. Gerald T. White, *A History of the Massachusetts Hospital Life Insurance Company*, p. 3.

8. Leroy Bowman, *The American Funeral*, p. 113; Robert Habenstein and William M. Lamers, *The History of American Funeral Directing*, pp. 220, 235.

9. Lawrence M. Friedman, "Patterns of Testation in the 19th Century," p. 39.

10. James T. Phelps, *Life Insurance Sayings*, pp. 12—13.

11. Rev. Henry Ward Beecher, *Truth in a Nutshell*.

12. Emile Durkheim, *The Elementary Forms of the Religious Life*, p. 55.

13. Georg Simmel, *Philosophie des Geldes*, pp. 387–437. Little attention has been given by sociologists to this book; its first translation appeared only in 1978. See Georg Simmel, *The Philosophy of Money*, Tom Bottomore and David Frisby, trans. (London: Routledge and Kegan Paul, 1978). See also S. P. Altmann, "Simmel's Philosophy of Money," pp. 46–48; Donald Levine, ed., *Georg Simmel on Individuality and Social Forms*, (Chicago: University of Chicago Press, 1971); P. A. Lawrence, *Georg Simmel: Sociologist and European* (New York: Harper & Row, 1976); and Peter Etzkorn, *Georg Simmel: Conflict in Modern Culture and Other Essays* (New York: Teacher's College Press, 1968). The wergild still survives in some countries; see Jacques El-Hakim, *Le dommage de source delictuelle en droit musulman*, p. 110.

14. Quoted in Altmann, "Simmel's Philosophy of Money," p. 58. Parsons and Lidz also attach the conception of the sanctity of life to the stress on individualism; see Talcott Parsons and Victor Lidz, "Death in American Society," p. 163.

15. *Ibid.*, p. 133.

16. Michel Pascan, "Les Pactes sur Succesion Future," p. 2.

17. René Goupil, *De La Consideration de la Mort des Personnes Dans Les Actes Juridiques*, pp. 139, 183. See also Vovelle, *Piété Baroque et Déchristianisation*.

18. Oscar T. Schultz, *The Law of the Dead Human Body*, p. 5.

19. Richard M. Titmuss, *The Gift Relationship*, p. 198. The offensiveness of prostitution is also related by Simmel to its reduction of human values to dollars and cents. Altmann, "Simmel's Philosophy of Money," p. 59.

20. "Tax Consequences of Transfers of Bodily Parts," pp. 862–63.

21. Talcott Parsons, Renée C. Fox, and Victor M. Lidz, "The Gift of Life and Its Reciprocation." p. 46. Renée Fox refers to the magico-religious aspects of heart transplants in particular; see "A Sociological Perspective on Organ Transplantation and Hemodialysis," p. 422.

22. "Transfers of Bodily Parts," pp. 843–45, 863. The Uniform Anatomical Gift Act is the legal vehicle through which post-mortem gifts of parts of the body or of the body itself are made to different institutions. It was drafted by the Commission on Uniform State Laws in 1968 and as of June 1971 was adopted by forty-eight states and the District of Columbia.

23. George Albree, *The Evils of Life Insurance*, p. 18. Mennonites, vehemently opposed to life insurance cited similar reasons: "It is equivalent to merchandising in human life; it is putting a monetary price on human life which is considered unscriptural since man is the "temple of the Holy Ghost." "Life Insurance," *Mennonite Encyclopedia*, 3:343.

24. Beecher, *Truth in a Nutshell*.

25. Walter S. Nichols, *Insurance Blue Book, 1876–77*, p. 37.

26. William T. Standen, *The Ideal Protection*, pp. 44–45. See also Moses Knapp, *Lectures on the Science of Life Insurance*, p. 207.

27. Norman O. Brown, *Life Against Death*, pp. 239–48.

28. Durkheim, *The Elementary Forms of the Religious Life*, p. 466.

29. Kephart, "Status After Death," p. 636.

30. Bowman, *The American Funeral*, p. 47. Legally, the cost of funerals takes priority even over the claims of creditors. New York Public Health Law 4200, in William Mark McKinney, *Consolidated Laws of New York Annotated*, Book 44, p. 401. See also Allison Dunham, "The Method, Process and Frequency of Wealth Transmission at Death," p. 273.

31. George Russell and Kenneth Black, *Human Behavior and Life Insurance*, p. 203.

32. *Practical Points for Practical Persons*, p. 57.

33. Funeral expenses became so great that the General Court of Massachusetts passed laws in 1721, 1724, and 1842 prohibiting "Extraordinary Expenses at Funerals." Habenstein and Lamers, *History of American Funeral Directing*, pp. 203–4. On this subject see also *Hunt's Merchants' Magazine* (1855), 32:519. On criticism of modern funeral undertakers, see Jessica Mitford, *The American Way of Death*; Ruth Mulvay Harmer, *The High Cost of Dying*.

34. Frederick L. Hoffman, *History of The Prudential Insurance Company of America*, p. 4. John F. Dryden, president of Prudential Life Insurance Co. in 1909, also saw that "deep at the root of the problem of life insurance for the poor lies their abhorrence of a pauper burial." John F. Dryden, *Addresses and Papers on Life Insurance and Other Subjects*, p. 75. See also Charles R. Henderson, *Industrial Insurance in the United States*, p. 150; John F. Dryden, "Burial or Industrial Insurance," p. 394.

35. Marilyn G. Simmons, "Funeral Practices and Public Awareness," pp. 10, 19; Habenstein and Lamers, *Funeral Customs the World Over*, p. 449.

36. James Gollin, *Pay Now, Die Later*, p. 210.

37. Parsons and Lidz, "Death in American Society," p. 156.

38. Pine and Phillips, "The Cost of Dying," p. 138. Ariès similarly suggested that the money earned by funeral undertakers "would not be tolerated if they did not meet a profound need." Phillipe Ariès, *Western Attitudes Toward Death*, p. 100.

39. William Graham Sumner, *Folkways*, p. 26.

40. Bronislaw Malinowski, *Magic, Science, and Religion*, p. 31.

41. Charles W. Wahl, "The Fear of Death," p. 17.

42. Habenstein and Lamers, in *Funeral Customs the World Over*, offer countless examples of the use of magic at the time of death, pp. 85, 165, 465, 482 and many others. See also "Death and its Superstitions," *Eclectic Magazine* (January 1881), 96:396–400; Leo W. Simmons, *The Role of the Aged in Primitive Society*, pp. 221–22; Robert Blauner, "Death and Social Structure," p. 382.

43. Friedman, "*Patterns of Testation*," p. 37.

44. Theo P. Otjen and Arthur J. Pabst, "Updating Life Insurance Settlement Options (A Comparison with Wills)," *Journal of Insurance* (December 1960), 27:75–76. See also Dunham, "Wealth Transmission," p. 279.

45. New York Life Insurance Company newsletter, May 1869, p. 3.

46. "A Thought for Life Insurance," *Insurance Monitor* (May 1854), 1:43.

47. Knapp, *Science of Life Insurance*, p. 207.

48. "The Usual Objections To Life Insurance Answered," *United States Insurance Gazette* (November 1859), 10:19.

49. "Thirty Short Answers to Thirty Common Objections to Life Insurance."

50. T. R. Jencks, "Life Insurance in the United States," p. 111.

51. *Duty and Prejudice—an Interesting and Truthful Narrative*, p. 1.

52. Ibid.

53. Judah T. Pompilly, *Watchman! What of The Night? Or Rejected Blessings. For Wives and Mothers*, p. 5.

54. New York Life Insurance Company newsletter, May 1869, p. 3.

55. *A Query for Women*, p. 18.

56. *Duty and Prejudice*, p. 1.

57. *Our Mutual Friend* (New York: Equitable Life Assurance Co., June 1867), p. 3.

58. Pompilly, *Watchman! What of The Night?* p. 8.

59. Rev. Henry Clay Fish, *Word to Wives*, p. 5.

60. "Woman's Agency," *Insurance Monitor* (September 1855), 3:69.

61. Standen, *Ideal Protection*, pp. 44–45.

62. Phelps, *Life Insurance Sayings*, p. 87.

63. *A Query for Women*, p. 18.

64. Standen, *Ideal Protection*, pp. 44–45.

65. Phelps, *Life Insurance Sayings*, p. 27.

66. Rogers and Shoemaker, *Communication of Innovations*, p. 188.

67. Charles E. Rosenberg, *The Cholera Years*. Previously many diseases were seen as "inevitable and unavoidable and try to escape them would be to defy Providence"; see R. Carlyle Buley, "Pioneer Health and Medical Practices in the Old Northwest Prior to 1840," p. 501. Insanity was likewise considered the result of God's will; see David J. Rothman, *The Discovery of the Asylum* (Boston: Little, Brown, 1971), p. 109.

68. Parsons and Lidz, "Death in American Society," p. 139.

69. "A Thought for Life Insurance," p. 38.

70. Albree, *The Evils of Life Insurance*, p. 11.

71. *Nile's Weekly Register* (February 8, 1823), 1:354.

72. Gerald J. Gruman, "A History of Ideas about the Prolongation of Life," p. 86. See also James H. Cassedy, *Demography in Early America*, pp. 262–64; and T. H. Hollingsworth, *Historical Demography*, p. 219.

73. D. R. Jacques, "Mutual Life Insurance," p. 164.

74. "Why Should I Insure My Life?" *American Life Assurance Magazine*, (January 1860), 1:185.

75. Phelps, *Life Insurance Sayings*, pp. 33, 83.

76. Irving Fisher, "Economic Aspects of Lengthening Human Life," p. 20. In 1914, the insurance industry organized the Life Extension Institute for the conservation of life; it offered policyholders of all companies a centralized center for periodic health examinations as well as an educational program of personal hygiene. By 1919, they had examined over 600,000 insurance policyholders. See Irving Fisher, "The Life Extension Institute," and *Prolonging Life As A Function of Life Insurance* (New York: Life Extension Institute, 1919); and Edward A. Woods, *The Sociology of Life Insurance*. Some life insurance companies were sponsoring longevity studies as early as 1869, such as T. S. Lambert's *Biometry: The Measure of the Span of Life*.

77. Glenn Vernon, *The Sociology of Death*, p. 13. See also Geoffrey Gorer, *Death, Grief, and Mourning in Contemporary Britain*, pp. 110–16.

78. William A. Faunce and Robert L. Fulton, "The Sociology of Death: A Neglected Area of Research," p. 207; Pine and Phillips, "The Cost of Dying," p. 138; Blauner, "Death and Social Structure," p. 286.

79. Parsons and Lidz, "Death in American Society," p. 156.

80. Gollin, *Pay Now, Die Later*, p. 205.

81. Pine and Phillips, "The Cost of Dying," p. 138; Bowman, *American Funeral*, p. 118. Ariès sees the contemporary American funeral rites as a compromise between de-ritualization and traditional forms of mourning. Phillipe Ariès, "The Reversal of Death: Changes in

Attitudes Toward Death in Western Societies," in David E. Stannard, ed., *Death in America*, pp. 154–55. Group therapy and family reunions have also been suggested as secular rituals; see Raul R. Patterson, "Children and Ritual of the Mortuary," p. 86.

82. Alexander Welsh, "The Religion of Life Insurance," p. 1576.

83. David N. Holwig, *The Science of Life Insurance*, p. 22.

84. Morris Franklin, speech delivered at the First Annual Session of the Convention of Life Assurance Underwriters, May 26, 1859, in *American Life Assurance Magazine* (January 1860), 1:34.

85. *In Life Prepare for Death*, p. 24.

86. *American Life Assurance Magazine* (January 1860), 1:180.

87. Lewis O. Saum, "Death in the Popular Mind of Pre-Civil War America," in David E. Stannard, ed., *Death in America*, pp. 44–46.

88. "Life Insurance as a Duty," *Insurance Journal* (October 1882), 10:313.

89. Life Insurance (booklet published by the Manhattan Life Insurance Co., 1852), p. 19.

90. Knapp, *Science of Life Insurance*, p. 226.

91. "Life Insurance-Present Time and its Requirements," *United States Insurance Gazette* (June 1868), 27:6.

92. New York Life Insurance Co., *Almanac*, 1869, p. 6.

93. *Insurance Journal* (May 1882), 10:105.

94. Standen, *Ideal Protection*, pp. 40, 194.

95. Beecher, *Truth in a Nutshell*.

96. From a sermon delivered by T. DeWitt Talmage, editor of the *Christian Herald* and *Signs of Our Times*; quoted in Roger Hull, "Immortality Through Premiums," *Christian Century* (February 19, 1964), 81:240.

97. "The Ethics Of Life Insurance," *Catholic World* (March 1897), 64:820.

98. A fifth mode of immortality, which they call experiential, is achieved through specific transcendental experiences in life. Robert J. Lifton and Eric Olson, *Living and Dying*, pp. 79–82. For an interesting commentary on autobiography as a form of social immortality, see Irving Louis Horowitz, "Autobiography as the Presentation of Self for Social Immortality," *New Literary History* (1977–78), 9:173–79.

99. Carl Becker, *The Heavenly City of Eighteenth-Century Philosophes*, particularly his last chapter, "The Uses of Posterity."

100. Vovelle, *Piété Baroque et Déchristianisation*, pp. 57–59, 63–65, 111, 113, 119, 274.

101. Quoted in "Attitudes Towards Death Grow More Realistic," *New York Times* (July 21, 1974), p. 34. See also Herman Feifel, "Death," p. 17.

102. E. W. Stoughton, "Life Insurance," p. 223. On the importance of leaving an estate in the nineteenth century, see Henry Steele Commager, *The American Mind*, p. 50. For Puritan conceptions of death and dying, see Stannard, "Death and Dying in Puritan New England," pp. 1305–30.

103. Textbook definitions reinforce the symbolism by describing life insurance as perpetuating "the earning capacity of the life for the benefit of those dependent on it." S. Huebner and Kenneth Black, Jr., *Life Insurance*, p. 20.

104. Booklet published by the United States Life Insurance, Annuity and Trust Company of Philadelphia (New York, 1850).

105. Standen, *Ideal Protection*, p. 46.

106. New York Life Insurance Company *Almanac*, 1869, p. 6.

107. *Our Mutual Friend* (June 1867), p. 1.

108. Goody, *Death, Property, and the Ancestors*, pp. 375–78.

109. "A Ghostly Argument," *Insurance Monitor* (November 1894), 42:447.

110. C. Stephen H. Tyng, "Life Insurance Does Assure," p. 4.

111. Joe B. Long, *The Adventures of a Life Insurance Salesman*, pp. 78–79.

112. Schaffer, *Death, Property, and Lawyers*, p. 82.

113. Blauner, "Death and Social Structure," p. 387.

114. *Insurance Monitor* (February 1863), 11:34.

115. See Kurt W. Back and Hans W. Baade, "The Social Meaning of Death and the Law," in Lewis M. Simes, *Public Policy and the Dead Hand*, p. 1; Dunham, "Wealth Transmission," p. 255. As early as the seventeenth century, many will bequests to children were made contingent on their maintaining certain modes of behavior, see John Demos, *A Little Commonwealth*, p. 103. Unlike common law, civil law provides for an undefeasible share—légitime—of the offspring in their parents' estate.

116. Goody, *Death, Property, and the Ancestors*, pp. 328, 394, 407, 414.

117. Quoted in the *Insurance Monitor* (August 1870), 18:4.

118. For other attempts to evaluate the economic value of human life, see Louis I. Dublin and Alfred J. Lotka, *The Money Value of Man*, pp. 6–21.

119. Knapp, *Science of Life Insurance*, p. 227.

120. "The Money or Commercial Value of a Man," *Hunt's Merchants' Magazine*, (July 1856), 35:34.

121. Holwig, *The Science of Life Assurance*, 1856, p. 4.

122. "The Philosophy of Life Insurance," *United States Insurance Gazette* (May 1868), 26:2.

123. Beecher, *Truth in a Nutshell*.

124. Dr. C. C. Pierce, "Human Life as a National Asset," p. 386.

125. S. Huebner, in *Proceedings of the 35th Annual Convention of the National Association of Underwriters* (Los Angeles, 1924), p. 18. The speech received wide notice in California newspapers, and was distributed in pamphlet form to life underwriters. The human life value concept "caught fire"; soon most agents were using the idea in selling. Mildred F. Stone, *The Teacher Who Changed An Industry: A Biography of Dr. Solomon S. Huebner* (Homewood, Ill.: R. D. Irwin, 1960), pp. 150–51.

126. S. Huebner, *The Economics of Life Insurance*, pp. 55, 195. Woods had estimated the money value of the American population in 1926 at $1,650,000,000,000. Woods, *The Sociology of Life Insurance*, p. 22.

127. Huebner, *The Economics of Life Insurance*, p. 22 (1959 ed.).

128. Huebner and Black, *Life Insurance*, p. 36.

129. Dublin and Lotka, *The Money Value*, pp. 70, 80, 82, 91.

130. *Ibid.*, p. 3. Even economists were reluctant to include life insurance in their general discussions of production, exchange, and consumption and treated it in a separate chapter. Huebner, *Proceedings of the 35th Annual Convention*, p. 21. See also S. Huebner, "Human Life Values," in *Life and Health Insurance Handbook*, Davis W. Gregg, ed. (Homewood, Ill.: R. Irwin, 1959), p. 8.

131. Huebner, *Proceedings of the 35th Annual Convention*, p. 21.

5. Life, Chance, and Destiny

1. Freeman Hunt, ed., *Worth and Wealth*, p. 345.

2. John Samuel Ezell, *Fortune's Merry Wheel: The Lottery in America*, pp. 205, 274. While Ezell explains the decline of lotteries mostly as the result of corruption in the system, Stuart Bruchey suggests that it was partially the consequence of the moral crusade against gambling in the 1830s as well as the rise of other investment possibilities such as stocks and bonds. Bruchey, *The Roots of American Economic Growth*, p. 145.

3. A. M. Sakolski, *The Great American Land Bubble*, pp. 232, 234, 250.

4. From the minutes of a shareholders' meeting of the Universal Tontine Association, November 3, 1972, quoted by J. A. Fowler in *History of Insurance in Philadelphia*, p. 43. See also Charles K. Knight, *History of Life Insurance to 1870*, p. 69. Tontines were devised in the mid-seventeenth century by Lorenzo Tonti who suggested them as a fund-raising scheme to solve the financial problems of the government of Louis XIV. A. Fingland Jack, *An Introduction to the History of Life Assurance*, p. 211. Tontines were introduced in the United States in the late eighteenth century mainly for the accumulation of funds for the construction of special buildings. They were mostly unsuccessful. Two prominent failures were the Boston Tontine, organized in 1791, and the Universal Tontine of Philadelphia, in 1792. Marquis James, *Biography of a Business*, pp. 12, 15.

5. On the success of European Tontines, see R. Carlyle Buley, *The Equitable Life Assurance Society of the United States*, p. 96; Terence O'Donnell, *History of Life Insurance in Its Formative Years*, p. 163; Jules Lefort, *Traité du Contrat d'Assurance sur La Vie*, p. 54.

6. *Life Insurance Illustrated and Objections Considered From A Business Standpoint*, booklet, 1870. For other lists see William Alexander, *What Life Insurance Is and What It Does*, p. 107; Owen J. Stalson, *Marketing Life Insurance*, p. 278.

7. Charles Norton, *Life Insurance*, p. 63. This was probably the first life insurance text published in the United States.

8. Elizur Wright, "Life Insurance For the Poor," *Journal of Social Science* (1876), no. 8, p. 148.

9. William T. Standen, *The Ideal Protection*, p. 224.

10. "An Examination and Defense of Life Insurance," *United States Insurance Gazette* (July 1857), 5:151. See also George W. Gordon, *Lecture before the Boston Young Men's Society*, p. 13.

11. "The Difference Between Life and Fire Insurance," *Insurance Monitor* (November 1895), 43:455.

12. George Albree, *The Evils of Life Insurance*, p. 2.

13. Johan Huizinga, *Homo Ludens*, p. 73.

14. Alexander Colin Campbell, *Insurance and Crime*, p. 195. See also A. Fingland Jack, *An Introduction to the History of Life Assurance*, p. 200, and Florence Edler de Roover, "Early Examples of Marine Insurance," p. 196.

15. "The Romance of Life Insurance," *Harper's New Monthly Magazine* (October 1859), 19:664–65. The article lists some of these companies: an insurance office for horses dying natural deaths, Assurance of Female Chastity, Insurance from housebreakers, Assurance from Lying, Plummer and Petty's Insurance from death by drinking, Geneva. A few

insured against the contingency of having children. Barry Supple, *The Royal Exchange Assurance*, p. 9.

16. *Public Advertiser* (December 6, 1771), quoted in Cornelius Walford, *Insurance Guide and Handbook*, pp. 27–28.

17. John Francis, *Annals, Anecdotes, and Legends*, p. 144.

18. Heineccius in *Pandectes*, 2, tit. 5, no. 258, quoted by Raymond Kahn, *L'Aléa Dans Les Contrats*, p. 93.

19. Samuel Williston, *A Treatise on the Law of Contracts*, p. 571.

20. Edward C. Devereux, Jr., "Gambling," p. 53.

21. I Couch on Insurance 79.

22. Paul Swadener, "Gambling and Insurance Distinguished," p. 463.

23. Gerald J. Nolan, "Fact or Fiction? The Relationship Between Insurance and Gambling," p. 27. For a thorough analysis of similarities between insurance and gambling, see Camilo Viterbo, *Ensayos de Derecho Comercial y Económico*, pp. 148–53, 283–87.

24. Charles O. Hardy, *Risk and Risk-Bearing*, p. 70.

25. St. 14 Geo. III, c. 48 (1774).

26. Warnock v. Davis, 104 U.S. 775 (1881).

27. Allan H. Willet, "The Economic Theory of Risk and Insurance," p. 116.

28. Wright, "Rights and Wrongs of Policy-Holders," from the *New York Daily Tribune Supplement*, March 15, 1873; reprinted in Elizur Wright, *Politics and Mysteries of Life Insurance*, p. 171.

29. *Hunt's Merchants' Magazine* (May 1849), 20:499.

30. William T. Standen, *The Ideal Protection*, p. 119. See also Moses L. Knapp, *Lectures on the Science of Life Insurance*, p. 207.

31. Albree, *The Evils of Life Insurance*, pp. 6, 10.

32. William Graham Sumner and Albert Keller, *The Science of Society*, p. 749.

33. John Angell James, *The Widow Directed to the Widow's God*, pp. 81, 83, 84. According to its introduction, this booklet was the first widow's guide published in the United States. See also A. C. Rose, *The Widow's Souvenir* (New York: Lane & Scott, 1852). On the surge of consolation literature between 1830 and 1880, see Ann Douglas, "Heaven Our Home: Consolation Literature in the Northern United States, 1830–1880," in David E. Stannard, ed., *Death in America*, pp. 49–68.

34. Albree, *The Evils of Life Insurance*, p. 11.

35. Nautilus Mutual Life Insurance Co., Second Annual Report, May 1847, p. 33.

36. "The Morality of Life Insurance," *Hunt's Merchants' Magazine* (January 1850), 22:117.

37. "Converting A Deacon," *Practical Points for Practical Persons*, p. 20. See also *United States Insurance Gazette* (July 1857), 5:152–53.

38. Myles A. Tracy, "Insurance and Theology," p. 86.

39. Jacob Viner, *The Role of Providence in the Social Order*, pp. 5–11, 32–42, 88, 99.

40. Albree, *The Evils of Life Insurance*, p. 19.

41. David J. Rothman, *The Discovery of the Asylum*, p. 156.

42. P. Henry Woodward, *A History of Insurance in Connecticut*, p. 62.

43. Albree, *The Evils of Life Insurance*, p. 19.

44. From a sermon by Elder Swan quoted in Woodward, *A History of Insurance in Connecticut*, p. 62.

45. Quoted by Terence O'Donnell, *History of Life Insurance*, p. 726.

46. Knapp, *Lectures on the Science of Life Insurance*, p. 207.

47. "Life Insurance," *Mennonite Encyclopedia*, 3:343.

48. *Insurance Monitor* (January 1899), 47:21. The official Lutheran Encyclopedia no longer condemns life insurance, declaring it is "part of the wisdom to prepare for the inevitable." "Insurance," *Encyclopedia of the Lutheran Church 1965*, 2:1152–53.

49. Rev. D. D. Lore, *Address to Christian Pastors and Churches on Life Assurance*, p. 4.

50. Rev. Henry Ward Beecher, *Truth in a Nutshell*.

51. *Practical Points for Practical Persons*, p. 10. Some companies employed ministers as an "auxiliary agency staff" to sell policies among their parishioners. O'Donnell, *History of Life Insurance*, pp. 684, 726. See also R. Carlyle Buley, *The Equitable Life Assurance Society*, 1:71. Life insurance writings supplemented the work of clergymen in convincing their customers of man's duty to provide for the economic contingencies of death:

"Men have lived long enough to know that a suitable provision for the future is not distrusting Providence but it is a wise forecast. . . . It is a mean, selfish, inconsiderate and procrastinating spirit . . . that induces a man to start on that long voyage from which there is no return and provide nothing for a wife and children." Burleigh, *The Sunny Side of Life Insurance*, p. 9.

52. James T. Phelps, *Life Insurance Sayings*, p. 78.

53. "Does a Man Shorten His Life by Insuring It?" *Hunt's Merchants' Magazine* (July 1856), 35:110.

54. Henry Mayhew, "An Inquiry into the Number of Suspicious Deaths Occurring in Connection with Life Insurance Offices," p. 73. Another popular prey for speculative insurers were their own wives. Many insurance offices refused to insure them, surgeons' wives in particular. *Insurance Monitor* (September 1856), 4:100.

55. *A Letter from Uncle John to his nephew Richard on Speculative Insurance*, p. 2.

56. Brockway v. Mutual Benefit Life Insurance Co. 9 Fed. Rep. 249, quoted in "Insurable Interest in Life," *Albany Law Journal* (November 1885), 32:386.

57. Brockway v. Mutual Benefit Life Insurance, *Albany Law Journal*, pp. 368, 385.

58. John F. Onion, "Insurable Interest in Life," p. 11.

59. Williston, *A Treatise on the Law of Contracts*, p. 649. Public policy against gambling is so strong that in most states wagering contracts condemned by the laws of the state will not be enforced by its courts, even when the contract was valid where it was entered into.

60. St. 14 Geo. III, c. 48 (1774). See also Edwin W. Patterson, *Cases and Materials on the Law of Insurance*, p. 114. Frivolity has also been charged against wagering agreements by American courts in selected instances. In Love v. Harvey, 114 Mass. 80 (1873), plaintiff and defendant had placed a bet concerning the place of burial of one Dr. Cahill. The judge objected: "It is inconsistent alike with the policy of our laws . . . that judges and juries should be occupied in answering every frivolous question upon which idle or foolish persons may choose to lay a wager" (p. 82).

61. Williston, *A Treatise on the Law of Contracts*, p. 649.

62. Irvin G. Wyllie, *The Self-Made Man in America*, p. 77. On the influence of the Protestant ethic on economic life, see Max Weber, *The Protestant Ethic and the Spirit of Capitalism*. See also Edmund S. Morgan, *The Puritan Family*, p. 71.

63. Ezell, *Fortune's Merry Wheel: The Lottery in America*, pp. 16, 53, 272.

64. Richard Weiss, *The American Myth of Success*, p. 37. See also Wyllie, *The Self-Made Man*, p. 79.

65. *Hunt's Merchants' Magazine* (November 1839), 5:447.

66. Hunt, *Worth and Wealth*, pp. 72, 104–5. Freeman Hunt was one of the leading pre-Civil war spokesmen of self-help. In 1839, he founded *Hunt's Merchants' Magazine*. The magazine conveyed his views, advising readers that although a bird in the hand was not always worth two in the bush: "Inasmuch . . . as the proverb also means to exhort us not to give up a good certainty for a tempting uncertainty, we do most fully coincide in its prudence and sound sense. . . ." *Hunt's Merchants' Magazine*, (May 1852), 26:50.

67. Editorial, *New York Times*, February 23, 1853, p. 4.

68. Hunt, *Worth and Wealth*, p. 345.

69. Editorial, *New York Times*, February 23, 1853, p. 4.

70. Standen, *The Ideal Protection*, p. 228.

71. Hunt, *Worth and Wealth*, pp. 38, 196.

72. Editorial, *New York Times*, February 23, 1853, p. 4.

73. Hunt, *Worth and Wealth*, p. 352.

74. A. B. Johnson, "The Relative Merits of Life Insurance and Savings Banks," p. 673.

75. A. B. Johnson, *A Guide to the Right Understanding of Our American Union* (New York: Derby & Jackson, 1857).

76. "Life Insurance Investment," *Banker's Magazine*, (May 1856), 16:273.

77. "The *New York Times* on Insurance," *Insurance Monitor* (April 1853), 1:1.

78. George Cardwell, *A Month in a Country Parish*, p. 43.

79. Hunt, *Worth and Wealth*, p. 346.

80. Gilbert Currie, *A Popular Essay on Life Assurance*, p. 159.

81. Donald McConnell, *Economic Virtues in the United States*, p. 59.

82. Standen, *The Ideal Protection*, pp. 69–70. Late nineteenth-century fraternal societies likewise upheld the greater morality of cooperativism over the individualism of savings banks: "Thrift alone is not enough. . . . There is a kind of thrift such as New England thrift which is a mean egoism. . . . The savings bank is a purely individualistic society and . . . is outside the truly social development of modern life." *Lend a Hand* (1892), 8:292, quoted by Hace Sorel Tishler, *Self-Reliance and Social Security*, p. 24.

83. Henry Crosby Emery, *Speculation on the Stock and Produce Exchanges of the United States*, p. 8. Emery also distinguishes between gambling and legitimate speculation that serves economic needs of the society. His book is considered one of the major works on speculation of that period.

84. "Cause for the Popularity of Life Assurance," *Prospectus for 1885*, Equitable Life Assurance Society, p. 5.

85. Burton Hendrick, "The Story of Life Insurance," p. 411. This feature made tontines attractive to wives who had objected to benefit from their husband's death. From a circular letter, Equitable's *Scrapbook*, 1885, quoted in Owen J. Stalson, *Marketing Life Insurance*, p. 506.

86. Hendrick, "Story of Life Insurance," p. 411. Initially, tontine policies had no surrender or cash value. In 1871, Equitable introduced the "Tontine Savings Fund Policy" which provided for a small cash surrender value and thereby increased sales significantly.

6. Marketing Life: Moral Persuasion and Business Enterprise

1. Statement by the French Revolutionary government in 1789, cited by P. J. Richard, *Histoire des Institutions d'Assurance en France*, p. 37.

2. Richard M. Titmuss, *The Gift Relationship*, p. 23. For an analysis of the types and functions of the different forms of economic and social exchange, see Bernard Barber, "The Absolutization of the Market." On the shift from "status" to "contract," see Henry Sumner Maine, *Ancient Law* (New York: Dutton, 1961).

3. George Albree, *The Evils of Life Insurance* (Pittsburgh: Bakewell and Mathers, 1870), p. 28.

4. "Life Insurance," *Mennonite Encyclopedia*, 3:344.

5. Frederick L. Hoffman, *History of the Prudential Insurance Co. of America*, p. 7. The first fraternal insurance society was the Ancient Order of United Workmen, organized in 1868 in Meadville, Pennsylvania. Fraternal societies functioned as religious, social, and charitable entities, offering, beyond insurance, "the attractions of lodge and club house, of ritual and organization, of familiar faces and customs." Morton Keller, *The Life Insurance Enterprise*, p. 10. They also served as halfway houses for the adaptation of immigrants to an alien land. On social functions of fraternal societies, see also Richard De Raismes Kip, *Fraternal Life Insurance in America*, pp. 4, 148; Charles O. Hardy, *Risk and Risk-Bearing*, p. 286; and Charles R. Henderson, *Industrial Insurance in the United States*, pp. 63–64.

6. Hoffman, *History of the Prudential*, p. 34. Recognizing the attraction of fraternalism, the Prudential started business as The Prudential Friendly Society. Only in 1877, two years later, did it shed all pretense of fraternalism; it was renamed The Prudential Insurance Company of America.

7. *Insurance Monitor* (May 1854), 2:38.

8. Moses L. Knapp, *Lectures on the Science of Life Insurance*, p. 18.

9. "Life Insurance—Present Time and Its Requirements," *United States Insurance Gazette* (June 1868), 27:81. Likewise, fire insurance substituted the more informal and less adequate assistance of neighbors.

10. "The Power of Association Illustrated by the System of Life Insurance," *United States Insurance Gazette* (November 1870), 32:4.

11. "Life Insurance," *United States Insurance Gazette* (June 1868), 27:82.

12. "The Relation Between Life Assurance and Natural Law," *United States Insurance Gazette* (November 1873), 38:33.

13. Rev. Dr. Cook, "Life Insurance," *Banker's Magazine* (October 1849), 4:375.

14. *Importance of Life Assurance*, 1861 booklet published by Equitable.

15. Elias Heiner, "An Examination and Defense of Life Insurance," p. 146. See also *The Advantage of Life Insurance* (New York: Mutual Life Insurance Co. of New York, 1855), and "The Moral Duty of Life Assurance," *Insurance Monitor* (August 1863), 11:183.

16. *Importance of Life Assurance* and "Life Insurance as a Duty," *Insurance Journal* (October 1882), 10:313. One writer noted that "when a brother . . . comes to the help of brother's destitute widow or of an own sister . . . the very commendation he receives for his generosity is proof of the absence of this virtue." "Power of Association," p. 2.

17. Knapp, *Science of Life Insurance*, p. 29.

18. "The Moral Duty."

19. "The Philosophy of Life Insurance," *United States Insurance Gazette* (May 1868), 26:3.

20. "Why Should I Insure My Life?" *American Life Assurance Magazine* (January 1860), 1:176.

21. Heiner, "Defense of Life Insurance," p. 143.

22. Knapp, *Science of Life Insurance*, p. 204.

23. Hon. Morris Franklin, President of the New York Life Insurance Company, cited by *United States Insurance Gazette* (May 1859), 9:138.

24. Knapp, *Lectures on the Science of Life Insurance*, p. 28.

25. *Ibid.*, p. 25.

26. *Mutual Life Insurance Company*.

27. Heiner, "An Examination and Defense of Life Insurance," pp. 82–83, 152.

28. "Life Insurance—Its Importance and Necessity," *United States Insurance Gazette* (June 1855), 1:117.

29. "The Moral Duty."

30. Heiner, "An Examination and Defense of Life Insurance," p. 143.

31. Knapp, *Lectures on the Science of Life Insurance*, p. 60.

32. "Why Should I Insure My Life?" p. 179.

33. Knapp, *Lectures on the Science of Life Insurance*, p. 227.

34. Cook, "Life Insurance," p. 377.

35. Knapp, *Lectures on the Science of Life Insurance*, p. 209.

36. "Why Should I Insure My Life?" p. 179.

37. *Importance of Life Assurance*.

38. *Fifteen Good Reasons for Insuring My Life*.

39. Knapp, *Lectures on the Science of Life Insurance*, p. 27.

40. George Cardwell, *A Month in a Country Parish*, p. 17.

41. *United States Insurance Gazette* (May 1868), 27:2.

42. *Insurance Monitor* (August 1863), 11:183. Similarly industrial insurance in later years claimed as one of its social contributions the substantial savings to taxpayer and community resulting from the reduction of pauper burials. Hoffman, *History of the Prudential*, p. 307.

43. Knapp, *Lectures on the Science of Life Insurance*, p. 27.

44. "Why Should I Insure My Life?" p. 177. See also *Fifteen Good Reasons for Insuring My Life*, 1860 booklet, on the social duty to prevent dependents from "becoming a tax on the charity of others."

45. "Life Assurance," *Hunt's Merchants' Magazine* (August 1870), 68:120.

46. Darwin P. Kingsley, "Life Insurance—Its Service and Its Leadership," *Independent* (1900), 52:2827; cited by Morton Keller in *The Life Insurance Enterprise*, p. 29.

47. S. E. Mulford, *A Reply to Colonel Greene*.

48. "Life Assurance," *Hunt's Merchants' Magazine*.

49. *Insurance Journal* (October 1880), 8:409.

50. William T. Standen, *The Ideal Protection*, p. 80.

51. There was a growing conviction among the public that policy terms and conditions were unfair, and that company managers were "too arbitrary, too extravagant or too ruthlessly selfish." Owen J. Stalson, *Marketing Life Insurance*, p. 406.

52. Dr. T. M. Coan, "Does Life Insurance Insure?" p. 279.

53. J. A. Fowler, *History of Insurance in Philadelphia*, p. 659.

54. From the first prospectus issued by the Mutual Benefit Life Insurance Company in 1845, cited by Mildred F. Stone, *Since 1845*, p. 9; see also *Fifteen Good Reasons to Insure My Life*.

55. *Journal of Insurance* (October 1858), 39:498.

56. "A Thought for Life Insurance," *Insurance Monitor* (May 1854), 2:43.

57. *Insurance Monitor* (May 1854), 2:37. See also Stalson, *Marketing Life Insurance*, p. 275.

58. Stephen H. Tyng, *Life Insurance Does Assure*, pp. 14–15.

59. The deferred dividend policy of tontines required policyholders to forgo dividends for extended periods in return for the prospect of benefiting at the term's end from the company's greater investment flexibility as from other policyholders' lapses and policy surrenders. Stalson, *Marketing Life Insurance*, p. 487; Keller, *Life Insurance Enterprise*, p. 56.

60. *A Fortune for Everybody—How It Pays or the Best Investment for Business Men*, pp. 15, 19.

61. E. A. Rollins, *The Business Worth of Life Insurance; A Fortune for Everybody—How It Pays or the Best Investment for Business Men*.

62. Rev. H. C. Fish, *The American Manual of Life Assurance*, p. 9. See also Burleigh, *Life Insurance Illustrated and Objections Considered from a Business Standpoint*, p. 20.

63. "Hints to Life Insurance Agents," from a New York Life Insurance Company newsletter, April, 1868, p. 4.

64. S. S. Huebner, *The Economics of Life Insurance*, p. 120.

65. William Alexander, *How To Sell Life Assurance*, p. 195.

66. *How To Sell Life Assurance* (instruction booklet), p. 18.

67. "Auger Holes and Gimlets," *Insurance Monitor* (January 1899), 47:35.

68. Burton Hendrick, *The Story of Life Insurance*, p. 36.

69. Solomon S. Huebner and Kenneth Black, Jr., *Life Insurance*, p. 21. The new literature encouraged the redefinition of the family as a business that should be protected against "needless bankruptcy." *Ibid.*, p. 27.

70. C. Wright Mills, "Situated Actions and Vocabularies of Motive," *American Sociological Review* (December 1940), 5:904–13.

71. *A Brief History* (New York: Mutual Life Insurance Co., 1857), p. 1.

72. Fowler, *History of Insurance in Philadelphia*, p. 659.

73. Heiner, "Defense of Life Insurance," p. 146.

74. Knapp, *Lectures on the Science of Life Insurance*, p. 224.

75. See Mutual Benefit Life Insurance Company booklet, 1858, cited by Stone in *Since 1845*, p. 51; see also Knapp, *Lectures on the Science of Life Insurance*, p. 225; and "Mrs. Buffon's Nerves," *New York Life Insurance Co. Newsletter* (March 1868).

76. *Insurance Journal* (October 1882), 10:277. To similar criticisms of savings banks as selfish, life insurance opponents responded that selflessness was inadequate motivation: "A man who labors to purchase an insurance on his life for the future benefit of his widow and orphans, cannot command the energy he would feel were he laboring for his own present affluence." A. B. Johnson, "The Relative Merits of Life Insurance and Savings Banks," p. 672.

77. Cook, "Life Insurance," p. 378.

78. Editorial, *New York Evangelist*, September 21, 1876.

79. Standen, *The Ideal Protection*, p. 25.

80. Elizur Wright, "The Regulation of Life Insurance," p. 541. Jencks similarly noted how the "little premiums" paid were well worth "the comfortable feeling that death itself could not beggar our trusting friend or our dependent relatives." T. R. Jencks, "Life Insurance in the United States," p. 124.

81. Brainbridge explains how "aside from his policy, put away in a drawer or file, the purchaser of insurance has no concrete evidence of what he has bought." J. Brainbridge, *Biography of an Idea*, p. 18. On the intangibility of life insurance, see Mark Greene, *Risk and Insurance*, p. 168; Kimball, *Insurance*, p. 4. Early life insurance companies actively sought the endorsement of prominent community leaders as another way to reassure customers of the legitimacy of their enterprise. Stalson, *Marketing Life Insurance*, pp. 70, 145; Gerald T. White, *A History of the Massachusetts Hospital Life Insurance Company*, p. 5.

82. *Remarks of the Late Dr. Norman MacLeod on Life Assurance.*

83. Everett Rogers with F. Floyd Shoemaker, *Communication of Innovations*, pp. 22–23, 155.

84. On the role of public exposure of deviance as a mechanism for the enforcement of social norms, see Paul F. Lazarsfeld and Robert K. Merton, "Mass Communication, Popular Taste and Organized Social Action," in David Rosenberg and D. M. White, eds., *Mass Culture*, pp. 102–4.

85. "Power of Association," p. 4.

86. *Insurance Journal* (October 1882), 10:314.

87. *Practical Points for Practical Persons*, p. 60.

88. Standen, *The Ideal Protection*, p. 238. Earlier epithets were reversed, turning the uninsured into a "desperate gambler." *Insurance Monitor* (November 1895), 43:456.

89. "The Moral Duty," p. 183.

90. "The Power of Association," p. 4. Some even suggested life insurance as an obligatory requirement for marriage. "The Duty of the Hour," *Insurance Journal* (September 1880), 8:369.

91. "The Moral Duty," p. 183.

92. Standen, *The Ideal Protection*, p. 94.

93. Elias Heiner, "An Examination and Defense of Life Insurance," p. 143.

94. "Why Should I Insure My Life?" p. 177. See also *U.S. Insurance Gazette* (June 1868), 27:81; Letter to the editor, *Equitable Record* (August 1, 1888). Rev. T. DeWitt Talmage, D.D., in a sermon delivered in 1894 said that a man who died uninsured was a defalcator and a swindler: "He did not die, he absconded." Cited by R. Carlyle Buley, *The Equitable Life Assurance Society of the United States*, p. 395.

95. Cash surrender values were predictably opposed by those who upheld life insurance as a purely unselfish act meant to have no benefits for the policyholder. Ironically, some spokesmen of life insurance as a business also attacked cash-in policies, as "unheard of favors and gratuities" more appropriate to charitable organizations. Hoffman, *History of the Prudential*, p. 41, and Hendrick, *Story of Life Insurance*, p. 547.

96. Hoffman, p. 36.

97. Huebner, *The Economics of Life Insurance*, p. 145.

98. *Ibid.*, p. 144.

99. Knapp, *Lectures on the Science of Life Insurance*, p. 205.

100. Darwin P. Kingsley, *Militant Life Insurance*, p. 16.

101. F. Robertson Jones, ed., *History and Proceedings of the World's Insurance Congress*, p. 3.

102. Standen, *The Ideal Protection*, p. 76. Standen attributed widespread criticism of the high salaries of company officers to that resistance against treating rationally "the company that carries the risk of your death," pointing to the easier acceptance of profits in other businesses:

"When you have bought your bread and boots in the cheapest market; when you have paid good money and received genuine articles in return . . . you don't care a snap of your finger whether your baker is putting in a new storefront or whether your bootmaker is indulging in the luxury of a new sign." *Ibid.*, p. 77.

103. Fowler, *History of Insurance*, p. 822.

104. "The Ethics of Life Insurance," *Catholic World* (March 1897), 64:817, 821.

105. Kingsley, *Militant Life Insurance*, p. 13.

106. Tyng, *Life Insurance Does Assure*, p. 25. See Keller, *The Life Insurance Enterprise*, p. 39. On the symbolism of physical places, see Bernard Barber, "Place, Symbol, and Utilitarian Function in War Memorials," pp. 328–44.

107. Geo. Rowland, ed., *Advice to the Holders of Life Insurance Policies, by a Practical Observer*, p. 7.

108. "A Popular Error Corrected," *United States Insurance Gazette* (May 1870), 31:18.

109. "Solid Facts," *Insurance Times* (May and June 1868), 1:202.

110. "Popular Error Corrected," p. 18.

111. Coan, "Does Life Insurance Insure?" p. 279.

112. Hardy, *Risk and Risk-Bearing*, p. 285; Kip, *Fraternal Life Insurance*, p. 99.

113. Henderson, *Industrial Insurance*, p. 119.

114. Robert K. Merton and Elinor Barber, "Sociological Ambivalence," in Edward A. Tyrakian, ed., *Sociological Theory, Values, and Socio-Cultural Change* (New York: Free Press, 1963), p. 96.

115. Charles L. Sanford, "The Intellectual Origins and New-Worldliness of American Industry," pp. 1–16. On this subject, see also Richard Hofstadter, *Anti-Intellectualism in American Life* (New York: Vintage Books, 1963), p. 251. The accumulation of great fortunes was justified by the ultimate social and philanthropic purposes to which the money was put. See Sigmund Diamond, *The Reputation of the American Businessman*, pp. 13–15.

7. The Life Insurance Agent

1. Burton Hendrick, *The Story of Life Insurance*, p. 65.

2. "Advice to Life Insurance Agents," *United States Insurance Gazette* (February 1859), 8:189. As one example of the efficacy of agents, of the $296,908,000 of insurance issued between 1843 and 1868 by the Mutual Life Insurance Co. of New York, only $17,402,000

came to the office unsolicited. Shepard B. Clough, *A Century of American Life Insurance*, pp. 89–90.

3. New York Life Insurance Co. newsletter (June 1871).

4. "Suggestions on the Elements of Success of Life Insurance Agents," *United States Insurance Gazette* (August 1861), 13:202.

5. N. Willey, *An Instruction Book for Life Insurance Agents* (New York: C. C. Hine, 1891), p. 66.

6. *Ibid.*, p. 64.

7. "Life Assurance," *Hunt's Merchants' Magazine* (August 1870), 63:123.

8. William T. Standen, *The Ideal Protection*, p. 232.

9. John F. Dryden, *Addresses and Papers on Life Insurance*, p. 106. Industrial insurance companies adapted the agency system to their lower-class clientele. Premiums were collected weekly (or monthly) in person by the agent at the home of the insured.

10. Burton Hendrick, *The Story of Life Insurance*, p. 65.

11. "Life Assurance," *Hunt's Merchants' Magazine*, p. 122.

12. Dr. T. M. Coan, "Does Life Insurance Insure?" p. 277.

13. "Commissions to Agents," *Insurance Monitor* (September 1870), 18:719.

14. Louis D. Brandeis, *Business—A Profession*, p. 149.

15. Darwin P. Kingsley, *Militant Life Insurance*, p. 73.

16. "Commissions to Agents," *Insurance Monitor* (November 1870), 18:881.

17. Miles M. Dawson, *Things Agents Should Know*, p. 20.

18. Everett Rogers with F. Floyd Shoemaker, *Communication of Innovations*, p. 255.

19. Elihu Katz and Paul F. Lazarsfeld, *Personal Influence*, p. 178.

20. James T. Phelps, *Life Insurance Sayings*, p. 17.

21. "Life Insurance as It Was—and As It Is: The Views of an Old Time Worker," *Insurance Monitor* (October 1871), 19:848.

22. Rogers and Shoemaker, *Communication of Innovations*, p. 246.

23. *Our Mutual Friend* (April 1867), p. 7.

24. Moses L. Knapp, *Lectures on the Science of Life Insurance*, p. 230.

25. Gilbert E. Currie, *The Insurance Agent's Assistant*, p. 174.

26. *How To Sell Life Assurance*, pp. 18, 42.

27. Standen, *Ideal Protection*, p. 180.

28. Willey, *An Instruction Book*, p. 40.

29. Standen, *The Ideal Protection*, p. 232.

30. Solomon S. Huebner, "How the Life-Insurance Salesman Should View His Profession." An address delivered before the Annual Meeting of the Baltimore Life Underwriters Association on February 20, 1915, reprinted in Solomon S. Huebner, *Life Insurance: A Textbook*, p. 436.

31. Hugh D. Hart, *Life Insurance as a Life Work*, p. 202.

32. Kingsley, *Militant Life Insurance*, p. 79. The methods of "the divine and the solicitor" are compared by William Alexander, *How To Sell Assurance*, p. 180.

33. Frederick L. Hoffman, *History of the Prudential Insurance Company of America*, p. 148.

34. Standen, *The Ideal Protection*, pp. 201, 204.

35. Owen J. Stalson, *Marketing Life Insurance*, p. 526.

36. Standen, *The Ideal Protection*, p. 151.

37. "A Dishonesty in High Walk," *Banker's Magazine* (July 1848), 3:46, 47.

38. "Life Assurance," *Hunt's Merchants' Magazine*, p. 123.

39. Henry B. Hyde, "Hints to Agents," cited by Burton Hendrick, *The Story of Life Insurance*, p. 244.

40. "Reminiscences of the Oldest Agents," *Henry Baldwin Hyde: A Biographical Sketch*, p. 195.

41. *Ibid.*, p. 197.

42. *Ibid.*, pp. 228–29.

43. An allegedly seventeenth-century English sonnet, quoted in "The Romance of Life-Insurance," *Harper's New Monthly Magazine* (October 1859), 19:664.

44. Warren Horner, *Training for a Life Insurance Agent*, p. 16.

45. Stalson, *Marketing Life Insurance*, p. 26.

46. *Insurance Monitor* (January 1899), 45:35.

47. See J. A. Fowler, *History of Insurance in Philadelphia*, p. 660; New York Life Insurance Company newsletter (December 1870); *Proceedings of the Fifth Annual Convention of the National Association of Life Insurance Underwriters*, June 20–21, 1894 (Boston, Mass.: Standard Publishing Co., 1894), p. 38.

48. Reprinted in *The Insurance Monitor* (May 1870), 18:405.

49. Charlton Lewis, *Proceedings of the First Annual Convention of the NALU, 1890* (Boston, Mass.: Standard Publishing Co., 1890), p. 39. The sign "No peddlers, solicitors, or insurance agents allowed," was found as late as 1900 in lobbies of office buildings. Mildred F. Stone, *A Calling and Its College*, p. 1.

50. Currie, *Insurance Agent's Assistant*, p. 173. Although published originally in England, it was widely read in the United States. Stalson, *Marketing Life Insurance*, p. 251. It was used by Equitable's agents in the 1860s. R. Carlyle Buley, *The Equitable Life Assurance Society of the United States*, p. 72.

51. "Life Insurance Solicitations—The Difficulties And Prejudices to Be Overcome," *Insurance Times* (August 1868), 355; see also "Difficulties of a Life Insurance Agency," *Insurance Monitor* (February 1863): 11–12:39; "Life Insurance as a Profession," *United States Insurance Gazette* (June 1868), 27:64.

52. Fowler, *History of Insurance*, p. 660.

53. The American Mutual Life Insurance and Trust Co., New Haven, Conn. (1860), sales booklet, p. 23, cited by Stalson, *Marketing Life Insurance*, p. 367.

54. *Insurance Monitor* (October 1868), 16:653, cited by Stalson, *Marketing Life Insurance*, p. 512.

55. Henry C. Fish, *Agent's Manual of Life Assurance* (New York, 1867), p. 57, cited by Stalson, *Marketing Life Insurance*, p. 371.

56. "Life Insurance as a Profession," p. 66.

57. *Our Mutual Friend* (April 1867), p. 7.

58. Phelps, *Life Insurance Sayings*, p. 20.

59. From a speech by Richard A. McCurdy quoted by *Weekly Statement*, issued by the Mutual Life Ins. Co. of New York, p. 18, cited by Stalson, *Marketing Life Insurance*, p. 510. Originally, agents had been upper- and middle-class professionals or businessmen who devoted a few hours a year to underwriting policies. When life insurance became a full-time occupation, they were replaced by individuals of low socioeconomic status.

60. Wilson Williams, "The Great Opportunity for Trained Men," *Proceedings of The Fourth Annual Meeting of the Association of Life Insurance Presidents*, p. 96. Another speaker at that meeting also referred to the time when life insurance "was evidence of total

depravity," and agents "were . . . men who had failed in everything else." Sylvester C. Dunham, "The Systematic Training of Agents," *ibid.*, p. 88.

61. Burton Hendrick, *The Story of Life Insurance*, p. 65.

62. "Commissions to Agents," p. 881.

63. Robert Ketcham Bain, *The Process of Professionalization: Life Insurance Selling*, pp. 41, 51; Stalson, *Marketing Life Insurance*, pp. 254–57, 374, 529.

64. Hendrick, *The Story of Life Insurance*, p. 66.

65. "Commissions to Agents," p. 881.

66. Everett Cherrington Hughes, *Men and Their Work*, pp. 49–52.

67. The amount of formal education and training required for an occupational role is considered a valid measure of the degree of generalized and systematic knowledge required for its performance. Bernard Barber, "Inequality and Occupational Prestige," p. 79. See also Bernard Barber, *Social Stratification*, p. 24.

68. Willey, *An Instruction Book*, p. 51.

69. "Life Insurance as a Profession," p. 65.

70. Standen, *The Ideal Protection*, p. 179.

71. Henry C. Fish's *Agent's Manual of Life Assurance*, published in 1867, included more practical information. However, personal qualities remained the author's parameters of a good agent.

72. Horner, *Training for a Life Insurance Agent*, p. 16.

73. New York Life Insurance Co. newsletter (December 1870).

74. Bain, *The Process of Professionalization*, p. 46.

75. "Difficulties of A Life Insurance Agency," *Insurance Monitor* (February 1863), 11–12:39.

76. John W. Riley, "Basic Social Research and the Institution of Life Insurance," *American Behavioral Scientist* (May 1963), 6:8.

77. Talcott Parsons, "The Professions and Social Structure," and Robert K. Merton, "The Uses of Institutionalized Altruism," pp. 110–11.

78. On the symbolic indignity of certain occupational roles, see Barber, *Social Stratification*, p. 143. Goffman defines stigma as an "undesired differentness." It ranges from physical forms of stigma to national, race, religious, and tribal stigma. Erving Goffman, *Stigma*, pp. 4–5. Life insurance agents and undertakers are cases of occupational stigma.

79. Charles W. Pickell, *Plain Reasons*, p. 31.

80. Willey, *An Instruction Book for Life Insurance Agents*, p. 95.

81. Hughes, *Men and Their Work*, pp. 54–55.

82. *The Fireside Companion*, reprinted in *Insurance Monitor* (May 1870), 18:405.

83. On the discretion of "dirty workers," see Everett C. Hughes, "Good People and Dirty Work," pp. 30–32.

84. Willey, *An Instruction Book*, pp. 9, 46.

85. Dawson, *Things Agents Should Know*, p. 4.

86. Standen, *The Ideal Protection*, p. 149.

87. Willey, *An Instruction Book*, p. 61.

88. Hendrick, *The Story of Life Insurance*, p. 244.

89. On the malintegration of the cultural goals and institutionalized means of a social structure as a source of deviant behavior, see "Social Structure and Anomie," in Robert K. Merton, *Social Theory and Social Structure* (New York: Free Press, 1968), pp. 185–214.

90. From a circular sent by Henry B. Hyde of Equitable to his agents, February 1, 1871, in *Henry Baldwin Hyde*, p. 213.

91. Bain, *The Process of Professionalization*, pp. 51, 54.

92. Standen, *The Ideal Protection*, p. 152. Agents also commonly resorted to derogatory pamphlets and articles published by their companies attacking competitors with no restraints. R. Carlyle Buley, *The American Life Convention*, p. 147.

93. "Life Insurance as It Was," p. 848.

94. *Tuckett's Monthly Insurance Journal* (February 15, 1855), p. 12, cited in Stalson, *Marketing Life Insurance*, p. 268.

95. Standen, *Ideal Protection*, pp. 151, 157, 174.

96. Alexander, *How to Sell Assurance*, p. 179.

97. Willey, *Instruction Book*, p. 44.

98. "The Character of Life Solicitors," *Insurance Monitor* (October 1870), 18:804.

99. Bain, *The Process of Professionalization*, pp. 115, 121. The legislation was passed first in New York and then in other states. Stalson, *Marketing Life Insurance*, p. 552.

100. On the recurrent patterns of emerging or aspiring professions, see Bernard Barber, "Some Problems in the Sociology of the Professions," 676–768; William Goode, "The Theoretical Limits of Professionalization," *Explorations in Social Theory* (New York: Oxford University Press, 1973). For detailed analysis of the professionalization attempts of life insurance agents, see Bain, *The Process of Professionalization*, and Miller Lee Taylor, *The Life Insurance Man*. Our interest in the professionalization of life agents is limited to its functions as a mechanism for status enhancement. Stalson suggests that professionalization was deliberately undertaken to salvage the prestige of agents after the Armstrong investigations. Stalson, *Marketing Life Insurance*, p. 579.

101. According to Stalson, the first university course in insurance was given at Harvard University in 1897. *Ibid*., p. 578.

102. There were correspondence or self-study courses, home-office schools, traveling home-office instructors who lectured for agencies, adult education night classes in colleges and YMCA's as well as "sales congresses" sponsored by the companies or the local underwriters' associations. Bain, *The Process of Professionalization*, pp. 161, 199.

103. Edward A. Woods, *Life Underwriting as a Career*, p. 59.

104. From its bylaws, cited in Stone, *A Calling and Its College*, p. 69.

105. Solomon S. Huebner, *The Economics of Life Insurance*, p. 19. Huebner became the most prominent teacher of life insurance in the country.

106. After 1914, life insurance was also used to make charitable bequests.

107. Huebner, *Life Insurance*, p. 431. See also William Alexander, *How to Sell Insurance*, p. 5.

108. Quoted by Stalson, *Marketing Life Insurance*, p. 635.

109. Huebner, *Life Insurance*, p. 427.

110. Kenneth Evans, Vernon Hughes, and Logan Wilson, "A Comparison of Occupational Attitudes," *Sociology and Social Research* (November/December 1936), 21:147. They were, respectively, college students from East Texas State Teachers College, CCC workers in several camps, and employed men and women from five northeast Texas towns.

111. M. E. Deeg and D. G. Patterson, "Changes in Social Status of Occupations," *Occupations* (1947), 25:205–18, reprinted in Barber, *Social Stratification*, p. 101.

112. Horner, *Training for a Life Insurance Agent*, p. 15.

113. On agents' professional self-image; see Taylor, *The Life Insurance Man*, p. 287; Evans, "Selling as a Dyadic Relationship," p. 78. Two extensive studies conclude that life insurance is not a profession: Bain, *The Process of Professionalization*, p. 379; Taylor, *The Life Insurance Man*, pp. 401–2. Undertakers also saw professionalization as a means of status enhancement. However, public opinion rates them far below any group of professional workers (*NORC survey*). Funeral directing, like insurance remains a business. Leroy Bowman, *The American Funeral*, pp. 81–83. On the social and cultural constraints against the professionalization of business in general, see Bernard Barber, "Is American Business Becoming Professionalized?"

114. Milton L. Woodward, *The Highway to Success* (Cincinnati: Diamond Life Bulletins, 1934), p. 18. Prestige building was approached with similar pragmatism as "shrewd self-promotion." Lorraine Sinton, *Practical Prestige Building* (Indianapolis: R & R Publications, 1937), p. 5.

115. Barber, "The Limits of Equality," p. 38.

Conclusions

1. J. A. Fowler, *History of Insurance in Philadelphia*, p. 822.
2. Ernest Wallwork, *Durkheim: Morality and Milieu*, p. 145. See Georg Simmel, *Philosophie des Geldes*, pp. 387–437.
3. Sigmund Diamond, ed., *The Nation Transformed*, p. 6.
4. Bernard Barber, "The Absolutization of the Market," p. 16.

Selected Bibliography

Primary Sources

Newspapers, Journals, and Magazines

American Life Assurance Magazine and Journal of Actuaries I. July 1859; April 1860.

Banker's Magazine, July 1848; February 1852; December 1854; May 1856; April 1859; September 1861.

Catholic World, March 1897.

Harper's New Monthly Magazine, October 1859; January–April 1881.

Hunt's Merchants' Magazine, October, November 1839; February 1843; October 1844; April 1846; May 1849; May 1852; April, October 1855; July 1856; February 1857; January 1858; February, April, October 1860; January 1861; May 1862; September 1865; August 1870.

Insurance Journal, October 1880; October 1882.

Insurance Monitor, April, June 1853; May 1854; September 1855; August 1861; February, July–August 1863; May–November 1870; March, October 1871; February 1873; November 1894; August, November 1895; January 1899.

Insurance Times, May–June, August 1868.

Journal of Commerce, December 30, 1863.

Journal of Insurance, October 1858.

Nation, January 1871.

New York Evangelist, September 1876.

New York Times, February 21, 23, 1853; July 21, 1974; August 11, 1976.

Nile's Weekly Register, February 1823.

Our Mutual Friend, June–September 1867.

Proceedings of the First, Fifth, Twenty-Fifth and Thirty-Fifth Annual Conventions of the National Association of Life Underwriters. Boston, Mass., 1890, 1894, 1914, 1924.

United States Insurance Gazette, May, June 1855; October 1856; January, July 1857; February, May, November 1859; May, August 1861; May, June 1868; May, November 1870; November 1873.

Articles

Coan, Dr. T. M. "Does Life Insurance Insure?" *Harper's Monthly Magazine* (January 1881), 62:273–77.

Cook, Rev. Dr. "Life Insurance." *Banker's Magazine* (October 1849), 4:370–82.

Corliss, Guy C. H. "Insurable Interest in Life." *Albany Law Journal* (November 1885), 32:385–88.

Fisher, Irving. "The Life Extension Institute," *Proceedings from the Insurance Institute of Hartford*. Hartford, Conn.: 1914.

Heiner, Elias. "An Examination and Defense of Life Insurance." *United States Insurance Gazette* (August 1863), 11:138–46.

Hendricks, Burton. "The Story of Life Insurance." *McClures*, May to November 1906.

Homans, Sheppard. "The Banking Element in Life Insurance." *Banker's Magazine* (July 1875), 30:49–52.

Jacques, D. R. "Mutual Life Insurance." *Hunt's Merchants' Magazine* (February 1847), 16:152–65.

Jencks, T. R. "Life Insurance in the United States." *Hunt's Merchants' Magazine* (February 1843), 8:109–30.

Johnson, A. B. "The Relative Merits of Life Insurance and Savings Banks." *Hunt's Merchants' Magazine* (December 1851), 25:670–77.

Lottin, J. "La Statistique Morale et le Determinisme." *Journal de la Société de Statistique de Paris* (October 1905), 10:21–34.

Mayhew, Henry. "An Inquiry into the Number of Suspicious Deaths Occurring in Connection with Life Insurance Offices." *Insurance Monitor* (July 1856), 4:73, 99–100.

Onion, John F. "Insurable Interest in Life." *Proceedings of the Legal Section of the American Life Convention*, Chicago, 1918.

Quételet, Adolphe Jacques. "Sur la Statistique Morale." *Nouveaux Mémoires de L'Académie Royale de Bruxelles* (Brussels: M. Hayez, 1848), 21:1–111.

Riley, George D. "Aiding Humanity to Meet Disaster." *United States Daily*, December 15, 1932.

Russell, Winslow. "Report." *Proceedings of the Twenty-Fifth Annual Convention of Life Underwriters*. New York, 1914.

Stoughton, E. W. "Life Insurance." *Hunt's Merchants' Magazine* (March 1840), 2:222–33.

Tyng, Stephen H. "Life Insurance Does Assure." *Harper's Monthly Magazine* (April 1881), 62:754–63.

Williams, Wilson. "The Great Opportunity for Trained Men." *Proceedings of the Fourth Annual Meeting of the Association of Life Insurance Presidents*. Chicago, 1910.

Wright, Elizur. "The Regulation of Life Insurance." *Hunt's Merchants' Magazine* (November 1852), 27:541–45.

Yartman, John V. "Principles of Assurance." *Insurance Monitor* (October 1854), 2:77.

Books and Life Insurance Pamphlets

A Fortune for Everybody—How It Pays or the Best Investment for Business Men. New York: J. H. and C. M. Goodsell, 1871.

Albree, George. *The Evils of Life Insurance*. Pittsburgh: Bakewell and Mathers, 1870.

A Letter from Uncle John to His Nephew Richard on Speculative Insurance. A pamphlet published in 1880 and found in the New York Public Library.

Alexander, William. *How To Sell Life Assurance.* New York: Winthrop Press, 1902.

—— *What Life Insurance Is and What It Does.* New York: Spectator, 1917.

—— *Insurance Fables for Life Underwriters.* New York: Spectator, 1924.

A Query for Women. New York: Equitable Life Insurance Co., 1882.

Babbage, Charles. *A Comparative View of the Various Institutions for the Assurance of Lives.* London: J. Manman, 1826.

Beecher, Rev. Henry Ward. *Truth in a Nutshell.* New York: Equitable Life Insurance Co., 1869.

Burleigh. *Life Insurance Illustrated and Objections Considered From a Business Standpoint.* New York, 1870.

—— *The Sunny Side of Life Insurance.* New York: S. W. Green, 1873.

Cardwell, George. *A Month in a Country Parish.* New York: Dana, 1856.

Currie, Gilbert E. *The Insurance Agent's Assistant.* London: H. G. Collins, 1852.

—— *A Popular Essay on Life Assurance.* London: H. G. Collins, 1852.

Dawson, Miles M. *Things Agents Should Know.* New York: Insurance Press, 1898.

de Meuron, Alois. "Du Contrat d'Assurance sur la Vie." Ph.D. diss., Faculté de Droit de l'Académie de Lausanne, 1877.

Documents of the Assembly of the State of New York 75th session, 1852, vol. 5, no. 111, April 7, 1852.

Dollarhide, A. C. *Facts and Fallacies of Life Insurance.* Ohio: American Actuarial Bureau, 1926.

Dryden, John F. *Addresses and Papers on Life Insurance and Other Subjects.* Newark: Prudential Press, 1909.

Duty and Prejudice-an Interesting and Truthful Narrative. New York: J. H. and C. M. Goodsell, 1870.

Emery, Henry Crosby. *Speculation on the Stock and Produce Exchanges of the United States.* New York: Columbia University Press, 1896.

Fifteen Good Reasons for Insuring My Life. New York: Equitable Life Insurance Co., 1860.

Fish, Rev. H. C. *The American Manual of Life Assurance.* New York: Equitable Life Assurance Society of the United States, 1885.

—— *Word to Wives.* New York: Equitable Life Insurance Co., 1872.

Fisher, Irving. *Prolonging Life as a Function of Life Insurance.* New York: Life Extension Institute, 1919.

Fundamental By-Laws and Tables of Rates for the Corporation for the Relief of the Widows and Children of Clergymen in the Communion of the Protestant Episcopal Church, with preface by Hon. Horace Binney. Philadelphia: Sherman, 1851.

Gabelli, Aristide. *Gli Scettici della Statistica.* Rome: Libreria A. Manzoni, 1878.

Gordon, George W. *Lecture before the Boston's Young Men's Society.* Boston: Temperance Press, 1833.

Goupil, René. *De la Consideration de La Mort des Personnes dans les Actes Juridiques.* Ph.D. diss., Université de Caen, Faculté de Droit, 1905.
Graham, William. *The Romance of Life Insurance.* Chicago: The World To-day, 1909.
Hart, Hugh D. *Life Insurance as a Life Work.* New York: F. S. Crofts, 1928.
Henry Baldwin Hyde: A Biographical Sketch. New York: De Vinne Press, 1901.
Hodgman, Rev. S. A. *Father's Life Boat.* Saint Louis: Western Insurance Review Printing House, 1871.
Holwig, David N. *The Science of Life Assurance.* Boston, Mass.: Provident Life and Trust Co., 1886.
Horner, Warren. *Training for a Life Insurance Agent.* Philadelphia: J. B. Lippincott, 1917.
How To Sell Life Assurance. New York: Equitable Life Insurance Co. instruction booklet, 1870.
Huebner, Solomon S. *Life Insurance, A Textbook.* New York: D. Appleton, 1921.
Hunt, Freeman. *Worth and Wealth: A Collection of Maxims, Morals, and Miscellanies for Merchants and Men of Business.* New York: Stringer and Townsend, 1856.
Importance of Life Assurance. New York: Equitable Life Insurance Co., 1861.
In Life Prepare for Death. New York: Manhattan Life Insurance Co., 1852.
James, John Angell. *The Widow Directed To The Widow's God.* New York: D. Appleton, 1844.
Juvigny, J. B. *Coup d'Oeil sur les Assurances sur la Vie des Hommes.* Paris: Librairie de Commerce, 1825.
Kingsley, Darwin P. *Militant Life Insurance.* New York Life Insurance Co., 1911.
Knapp, Moses L. *Lectures on the Science of Life Insurance.* Philadelphia: E. J. Jones, 1851.
Lambert, T. S. *Biometry: The Measure of the Span of Life.* New York: American Popular Life Insurance, Co., 1869.
Lefort, Jules. *Traité du Contrat d'Assurance sur la Vie.* Paris: Ancienne Librairie Thorin et Fils, 1893.
Long, Joe B. *The Adventures of a Life Insurance Salesman.* Barre, Mass.: State Mutual Life Assurance Co. of America, 1966.
Lore, Rev. D. D. *Address to Christian Pastors and Churches on Life Insurance.* Home Life Insurance Co., 1861.
Mulford, S. E. *A Reply to Colonel Greene.* Philadelphia, 1885.
Mutual Life Insurance Company: A Brief History. New York: published by the company, 1857.
New York Life Insurance Company newsletters. March 1868; April 1868; May 1869; December 1870; June 1871.
Norton, Charles B. *Life Insurance: Its Nature, Origin, and Progress.* New York: Irving Bookstore, 1852.
Pascan, Michel. "Les Pactes sur Succession Future." Ph.D. diss. Faculté de Droit, Université de Paris, 1907.
Phelps, James T. *Life Insurance Sayings.* Cambridge, Mass.: Riverside Press, 1895.

Pickell, Charles W., *Plain Reasons*. New York: Spectator, 1912.
Pompilly, Judah T. *Watchman! What of the Night? or Rejected Blessings: For Wives and Mothers*. New York: English & Rumsey, 1869.
Practical Points for Practical Persons. New York: Matthew Griffin, 1882.
Reboul, Edmond. *Du Droit des Enfants Bénéficiaires d'Une Assurance sur la Vie Contractée par Leur Père*. Paris: Librairie Nouvelle de Droit, 1909.
Remarks of the late Dr. Norman MacLeod on Life Assurance. New York: July 15, 1872.
Reynolds, Dexter. *A Treatise on the Law of Life Assurance*. New York: Banks, Gould, 1853.
Rollins, E. A. *The Business Worth of Life Insurance*. New York: J. H. and C. M. Goodsell, 1872.
Rowland, Geo., ed. *Advice to the Holders of Life Insurance Policies, by a Practical Observer*. New York: Office of *Insurance Monitor*, 1871.
Sayle, Philip. *Practical Aids for Life Assurance Agents*. London: Simpkin, Marshall, 1879.
Sinton, Lorraine. *Practical Prestige Building*. Indianapolis, Ind.: R & R Publications, 1937.
Standen, William T. *The Ideal Protection*. New York: U.S. Life Insurance Co., 1897.
Stevens, B. F. *Reminiscences of the Past Half Century*. Boston: New England Mutual Life Insurance Co., 1897.
Thirty Short Answers to Thirty Common Objections to Life Insurance. New York: Manhattan Life Insurance Co., 1860.
Touman, I. *L'Assurance sur la Vie en France au XIX Siècle*. Ph.D. diss., L'Université de Paris, 1906.
Tuckett, Harvey. *Practical Remarks on the Present State of Life Insurance*. New York, 1850.
Tyng, Stephen H. *Life Insurance Does Assure*. New York: Coby, 1881.
United States Life Insurance and Trust Company of Philadelphia, 1850 booklet.
Van Amringe, J. H. *A Plain Exposition of the Theory and Practice of Life Assurance*. New York: Charles A. Kittle, 1874.
Wallace, John William. *Historical Sketch of the Corporation for the Relief of the Widows and Orphans of Clergymen In the Communion of the Protestant Episcopal Church*. Philadelphia: Collin Printing House, 1870; reprinted with additions in 1889.
Willey, N. *An Instruction Book for Life Insurance Agents*. New York: C. C. Hine, 1891.
Woods, Edward A. *Life Underwriting as a Career*. New York: Harper, 1923.
Woodward, Milton L. *The Highway to Success*. Cincinnati, Ohio: The Diamond Life Bulletins, 1934.
Wright, Elizur. *Politics and Mysteries of Life Insurance*. New York: Lee, Shepard, and Dillingham, 1873.

Legal Sources—Cases

37	California Reports	670
9	Federal Reporter	249
136	Florida Reports	188
114	Mass.	80
12	Mass. Reports	115
23	N.Y. Reports	523
94	U.S. Reports	460
104	U.S. Reports	188

Secondary Sources

Articles

Altmann, S. P. "Simmel's Philosophy of Money." *American Journal of Sociology* (July 1903), 9:46–68.

Barber, Bernard. "Inequality and Occupational Prestige: Theory, Research and Social Policy." *Sociological Inquiry*, 48(2):75–88.

—— "Some Problems in the Sociology of the Professions." *Daedalus* (Fall 1963), 92:669–88.

Bauder, Ward. "Iowa Farm Operators' and Farm Landlords' Knowledge of, Participation in, and Acceptance of the Old Age and Survivors' Insurance Program." *Agricultural and Home Economics Experiment Station*, Iowa State University, Research Bulletin 479, Ames, Iowa, June 1960.

Becker, Howard. "On Simmel's Philosophy of Money." In Kurt H. Wolff, ed., *Georg Simmel*. Columbus: Ohio State University, 1959.

Berekson, Leonard L. "Birth Order, Anxiety, Affiliation and the Purchase of Life Insurance." *Journal of Risk and Insurance* (March 1972), 39:93–108.

Besso, Marco. "Progress of Life Assurance Throughout the World, from 1859 to 1883." *Journal of the Institute Of Actuaries* (October 1887), 26:426–35.

Blauner, Robert. "Death and Social Structure." *Psychiatry* (November 1966), 29:378–94.

Bloch, Herbert A. "The Sociology of Gambling." *American Journal of Sociology* (November 1951), 57:215–21.

Buley, R. Carlyle. "Pioneer Health and Medical Practices in the Old Northwest Prior to 1840." *Journal of American History* (1933–34), 20:497–520.

Chinard, Gilbert. "Eighteenth-Century Theories on America as a Human Habitat." *American Philosophical Society Proceedings* (1947), 91:27–57.

Coleman, James. "Social Inventions." *Social Forces* (December 1970), 39:164–72.

Curti, Merle. "The Changing Concept of 'Human Nature' in the Literature of American Advertising." *Business History Review* (Winter 1967), 41:335–57.

David, Paul A. "The Growth of Real Product in the United States Before 1840: New Evidence, Controlled Conjectures." *Journal of Economic History* (June 1967), 27:151–95.

Davis, Lance E. and Peter L. Payne. "From Benevolence to Business: The Story of Two Savings Banks." *Business History Review* (Winter 1958), 30:386–91.

de Roover, Florence Edler. "Early Examples of Marine Insurance." *Journal of Economic History* (May 1945), 5:172–97.

Devereux, Jr., Edward C. "Gambling." *International Encyclopedia of Social Science*. 2d ed., vol. 6.

Dunham, Allison. "The Method, Process, and Frequency of Wealth Transmission at Death." *University of Chicago Law Review* (Winter 1963), 30:241–85.

Evans, F. B. "Selling as a Dyadic Relationship." *The American Behavioral Scientist* (May 1963), 6:76–79.

Faunce, William A. and Robert L. Fulton. "The Sociology of Death: A Neglected Area of Research." *Social Forces* (October 1957), 36:205–9.

Fox, Renèe C. "A Sociological Perspective on Organ Transplantation and Hemodialysis." *New Dimensions in Legal and Ethical Concepts For Human Research*, Annals, New York Academy of Sciences (January 2, 1970), 169:406–28.

Friedmann, Lawrence M. "The Dynastic Trust." *Yale Law Journal* (March 1964), 73:547–81.

—— "Patterns of Testation in the 19th Century: A Study of Essex County (New Jersey) Wills." *American Journal of Legal History* (1964), pp. 34–53.

Fulton, Robert L. "The Clergyman and the Funeral Director: A Study in Role Conflict." *Social Forces* (May 1961), 39:317–23.

Gruman, Gerald J. "A History of Ideas about the Prolongation of Life." *Transactions of the American Philosophical Society* (1966), 56:5–91.

Hellner, Ian. "The Scope of Insurance Regulation." *American Journal of Comparative Law* (1963), 12:494–543.

Hollenberg, Richard H. "Is a Uniform Statute on Insurable Interest Desirable?" *Proceedings of the Section on Insurance Law of the American Bar Association*. Cincinnati, December 1945.

Hull, Robert. "Immortality Through Premiums?" *The Christian Century* (February 19, 1964), 31:239–40.

Kephart, William M. "Status After Death." *American Sociological Review* (October 1950), 15:635–43.

"Life Insurance." *Mennonite Encyclopedia*. Scottsdale, Pa.: Mennonite Publishing House, 1957.

Manes, Alfred. "Outlines of a general economic history of insurance." *Journal of Business of the University of Chicago* (January 1942), 15:30–47.

—— "Principles and History of Insurance." *International Encyclopedia of The Social Sciences*, vol. 8. New York: MacMillan, 1932.

Merton, Robert K. "The Unanticipated Consequences of Purposive Social Action." *American Sociological Review* (1936), 1:894–904.

Merton, Robert K. "The Uses of Institutionalized Altruism." *Seminar Reports*, pp. 105–13. New York: Columbia University, 1975.

Mills, C. Wright. "Situated Actions and Vocabularies of Motive." *American Sociological Review* (December 1940), 5:904–13.

Moore, Wilbert E. "Time-The Ultimate Scarcity." *American Behavioral Scientist* (May 1963), 6:58–60.

Nolan, Gerald J. "Fact or Fiction? The Relationship Between Insurance and Gambling." *Insurance Advocate* (April 24, 1965), 76:26–29.

O'Connell, Jeffrey. "Living with Life Insurance." *New York Times Magazine* (May 19, 1974), pp. 34–102.

Parsons, Talcott. "Death in American Society-A Brief Working Paper." *American Behavioral Scientist* (May 1963), 6:61–65.

Patterson, Edwin W. "Hedging and Wagering on Produce Exchanges." *Yale Law Journal* (April 1931), 40:843–53.

Pine, Vanderlyn R. and Derek L. Phillips. "The Cost of Dying: A Sociological Analysis of Funeral Expenditures." *Social Problems* (Winter 1970), 17:131–39.

Ploscowe, Morris. "The Law of Gambling." *The Annals of the American Academy of Political and Social Science*, Philadelphia (May 1950), 269:1–19.

Riley, John W. "Basic Social Research and the Institution of Life Insurance." *American Behavioral Scientist* (May 1963), 6:6–9.

Sanford, Charles L. "The Intellectual Origins and New-Worldliness of American Industry." *Journal of Economic History* (1958), 18:1–15.

Simmons, Marylin G. "Funeral Practices and Public Awareness." *Human Ecology Forum* (Winter 1975), 5:9–13.

Smith, Robert S. "Life Insurance in 15th Century Barcelona." *Journal of Economic History* (May 1941), 1:57–59.

Stannard, David E. "Death and Dying in Puritan New England." *American Historical Review* (December 1973), 78:1305–30.

Swadener, Paul. "Gambling and Insurance Distinguished." *Journal of Risk and Insurance* (September 1964), 31:463–68.

"Tax Consequences of Transfers of Bodily Parts." *Columbia Law Review* (April 1973), 73:842–65.

Tracy, Myles A. "Insurance and Theology." *Journal of Risk and Insurance* (March 1966), 33:85–93.

Vinovskis, Maris A. "Mortality Rates and Trends in Massachusetts before 1860." *Journal of Economic History* (March 1972), 32:184–213.

—— "The 1789 Life Table of Edward Wigglesworth." *Journal of Economic History* (September 1971), 31:570–83.

Welsh, Alexander. "The Agent as Priest." *Christian Century* (December 18, 1963), 80:1574–76.

—— "The Religion of Life Insurance." *Christian Century* (December 11, 1963), 80:1541–43.

Books

Ariès, Phillipe. *Western Attitudes Towards Death*. Baltimore, Md.: Johns Hopkins University Press, 1974.

Athearn, James L. *General Insurance Agency Management*. Homewood, Ill.: Richard D. Irwin, 1965.

Aubert, Vilhem. "Chance in Social Affairs." *The Hidden Society*. Totowa, N.J.: Bedminster Press, 1965.

Back, Kurt W. and Hans W. Baade. "The Social Meaning of Death and the Law." In John C. Kinney, ed., *Aging and Social Policy*. New York: Appleton-Century-Crofts, 1966.

Bain, Robert Ketcham. "The Process of Professionalization: Life Insurance Selling." Ph.D. diss., University of Chicago, 1959.

Barber, Bernard. "The Absolutization of the Market: Some Notes on How We Got From There to Here." In G. Dworkin, G. Bermant, and P. Brown, eds. *Markets and Morals*. Washington, D.C.: Hemisphere, 1977.

—— "Function, Variability, and Change in Ideological Systems." In Bernard Barber and Alex Inkeles, eds. *Stability and Social Change*. Boston: Little, Brown, 1971.

—— "Is American Business Becoming Professionalized? Analysis of a Social Ideology." In E. A. Tiryakian, ed., *Sociocultural Theory, Values, and Sociocultural Change*. Glencoe, Ill.: Free Press, 1963.

—— "Place, Symbol, and Utilitarian Function in War Memorials." In Robert Gutman, ed., *People and Buildings*. New York: Basic Books, 1972.

—— *Social Stratification*. New York: Harcourt, Brace & World, 1957

Becker, Carl. *The Heavenly City of Eighteenth-Century Philosophes*. New Haven: Yale University Press, 1932.

Bendix, Reinhard and Seymour Martin Lipset, eds. *Class, Status, and Power: A Reader in Social Stratification*. Glencoe, Ill.: Free Press, 1953.

Bissell, Richard M. "Fire Insurance: Its Place in the Financial World." *Yale Insurance Lectures*. New Haven: Tuttle, Morehouse, and Taylor Press, 1903–4.

Bowman, Leroy. *The American Funeral*. Washington, D.C.: Public Affairs Press, 1959.

Brainbridge, J. *Biography of an Idea: The Story of Mutual Fire and Casualty Insurance*. New York: Doubleday, 1952.

Brandeis, Louis D. *Business—A Profession*. Boston: Small, Maynard, 1925.

Brown, Norman O. *Life Against Death*. Middletown, Conn.: Wesleyan University Press, 1959.

Bruchey, S. *The Roots of American Economic Growth, 1607–1861*. New York: Harper and Row, 1965.

Buley, Carlyle R. *The American Life Convention, 1906–1952*. New York: Appleton-Century-Crofts, 1953.

—— *The Equitable Life Assurance Society of the United States*. New York: Appleton-Century-Crofts, 1967.

Buttrick, George A. *The Interpreter's Bible*. New York: Cokesbury Press, 1953.

Cahn, William. *A Matter of Life and Death*. New York: Random House, 1970.

Campbell, Alexander Colin. *Insurance and Crime*. New York: Putnam, 1902.

Cassedy, James H. *Demography in Early America*. Cambridge: Harvard University Press, 1969.

Clough, Shepard B. *A Century of American Life Insurance: A History of The Mutual Life Insurance Company of New York*. New York: Columbia University Press, 1946.

Colton, John W. *The First Century*. Hartford: Connecticut Life Insurance Co., 1946.

Commager, Henry Steele. *The American Mind*. New Haven: Yale University Press, 1950.

Consumer's Union Report on Life Insurance. New York: Bantam Books, 1972.

Corcoran, Charles. *Search for a Sign*. New York: Equitable Life Assurance Society of the United States, 1961.

Couch Encyclopedia of Insurance Law. 2d ed., 1960.

Cowing, Cedric B. *Populists, Plungers, and Progressives*. Princeton: Princeton University Press, 1965.

Davis, Joseph S. *Essays in the Earlier History of American Corporations*. Cambridge: Harvard University Press, 1917.

Dawson, Miles M. "The Development of Insurance Mathematics." In Lester W. Zartman, ed., *Yale Readings in Life Insurance*. New Haven: Yale University Press, 1914.

Demos, John. *A Little Commonwealth*. New York: Oxford University Press, 1970.

Diamond, Sigmund. *The Nation Transformed: The Creation of an Industrial Society*. New York: George Braziller, 1963.

—— *The Reputation of the American Businessman*. Cambridge: Harvard University Press, 1955.

Dickson, P. G. M. *The Sun Insurance Office*. London: Oxford University Press, 1960.

Dodd, Edwin Merrick. *American Business Corporations until 1860*. Cambridge: Harvard University Press, 1954.

Donohue, Sister J. H. *The Irish Catholic Benevolent Union*. Washington, D.C.: Catholic University of America, 1953.

Dryden, John. "Burial or Industrial Insurance." In Lester W. Zartman and William H. Price, eds., *Life Insurance*. New Haven: Yale University Press, 1914.

Dublin, Louis I. and Alfred J. Lotka. *The Money Value of Man*. New York: Ronald Press, 1930.

Durkheim, Emile. *The Elementary Forms of the Religious Life*. New York: Free Press, 1965.

Ecker, Frederick H. *The Great Provider*. Hartford, Conn.: Industrial Publication Co., 1959.

El-Hakim, Jacques. *Le dommage de source delictuelle en droit musulman*. Paris: R. Pichon et Durand Auzias, 1971.

Ezell, John Samuel. *Fortune's Merry Wheel: The Lottery in America*. Cambridge: Harvard University Press, 1960.

Feifel, Herman. "Death." In Norman Farberow, ed., *Taboo Topics*. New York: A. Thernton Press, 1963.

Fisher, Irving. "Economic Aspects of Lengthening Human Life." In Lester W. Zartman and William H. Price, eds., *Life Insurance*. New Haven: Yale University Press, 1914.

Fouse, L. G. "The Organization and Management of the Agency System." In *Insurance*. Philadelphia: American Academy of Political and Social Science, 1905.

Fowler, J. A. *History of Insurance in Philadelphia for Two Centuries*. Philadelphia: Review Publishing and Printing Co., 1888.

Francis, John. *Annals, Anecdotes, and Legends*. London: Longman, Brown, Green, and Longmans, 1853.

Fulton, Robert, ed. *Death and Identity*. New York: Wiley, 1965.

Gamble, Philip. *Taxation of Insurance Companies*. Albany: J. B. Lyon, 1937.

Garcia-Amigo, M. *Condiciones Generales de los Contratos*. Madrid: Editorial Revista de Derecho Privado, 1969.

Goffman, Erving. *Stigma*. Englewood Cliffs, N.J.: Prentice-Hall, 1963.

Goldsmith, R. W. *A Study of Savings in the United States*. Princeton: Princeton University Press, 1955.

Gollin, Gillian Lindt. *Moravians in Two Worlds*. New York: Columbia University Press, 1967.

Gollin, James. *Pay Now, Die Later*. New York: Penguin Books, 1969.

Goody, Jack. *Death, Property, and the Ancestors*. Stanford, Calif.: Stanford University Press, 1962.

Gorer, Geoffrey. *Death, Grief, and Mourning in Contemporary Britain*. London: Cresset Press, 1965.

Greene, Marc. *Risk and Insurance*. Cincinnati, Ohio: Southwestern Publishing Co., 1962.

Habenstein, Robert and William M. Lamers. *The History of American Funeral Directing*. Milwaukee, Wisc.: Bulfin Printers, 1955.

Handlin, Oscar and Mary F. Handlin. *Commonwealth: A Study of the Role of Government in the American Economy: Massachusetts 1774–1861*. New York: New York University Press, 1947.

Hardy, Charles O. *Risk and Risk-Bearing*. Chicago: University of Chicago Press, 1923.

Harmer, Ruth Mulvey. *The High Cost of Dying*. New York: Crowell-Collier Press, 1963.

Hawthorne, Daniel. *The Hartford of Hartford*. New York: Random House, 1960.

Henderson, Charles R. *Industrial Insurance in the United States*. Chicago: University of Chicago Press, 1909.

Hendrick, Burton. *The Story of Life Insurance*. New York: McClures, Phillips, 1906.

Hirose, Suketaro. *Development and Present Conditions of Life Insurance in Japan*. Osaka: Nippon Life Assurance Society, 1935.

Hoffman, Frederick L. *History of the Prudential Insurance Company of America*. Newark: Prudential Press, 1900.

Hollingsworth, T. H. *Historical Demography*. New York: Cornell University Press, 1969.

Huebner, Solomon S. "History of Marine Insurance." In Lester W. Zartman, ed., *Property Insurance*. New Haven: Yale University Press, 1909.

—— "Human Life Values." In Davis W. Gregg, ed., *Life and Health Insurance Handbook*. Homewood, Ill.: Richard D. Irwin, 1959.

—— *Marine Insurance*. New York: D. Appleton, 1919.

—— *The Economics of Life Insurance*. New York: Appleton-Century-Crofts, 1927.

Huebner, Solomon S. and Kenneth Black Jr. *Life Insurance*. New York: Appleton-Century-Crofts, 1969.

Hughes, Everett Cherrington. "Good People and Dirty Work." In Howard S. Becker, ed., *The Other Side*. New York: Free Press, 1964.

—— *Men and Their Work*. Glencoe, Ill.: Free Press, 1958.

Huizinga, Johan. *Homo Ludens*. New York: Harper and Row, 1970.

Hunter, Rudolf. *A Short Survey of Swedish Insurance Activity*. Stockholm: Swedish Insurance Association, 1930.

Ibsen, H. *Four Great Plays*. New York: Bantam Books, 1971.

Insurance Markets of the World. Zurich: Swiss Reinsurance Co., 1964.

Jack, A. Fingland. *An Introduction to the History of Life Assurance*. London: P. S. King, 1912.

Jackson, Kenneth T. and Stanley K. Schultz, ed. *Cities in American History*. New York: Knopf, 1972.

Jacquemyns, G. *Lagrand Dumoneau*. Brussels: Centre d'Histoire Economique et Sociale de l'Université Libre de Bruxelles, 1960.

James, Marquis. *Biography of a Business*. New York: Bobbs-Merrill, 1942.

—— *The Metropolitan Life*. New York: Viking, 1947.

James, William. *Essays in Pragmatism*. New York: Hafner, 1948.

Johnson, Donald R. *Savings Bank Life Insurance*. Homewood, Ill.: Richard D. Irwin, 1963.

Jones, F. Robertson, ed. *History and Proceedings of the World's Insurance Congress*. San Francisco: National Insurance Council, 1917.

Kahn, Raymond. *L'Aléa Dans Les Contrats*. Paris: Librairie de la Societé du Reccueil Sirey, 1924.

Katz, Elihu and Paul F. Lazarsfeld. *Personal Influence*. New York: Free Press, 1955.

Keller, Morton. *The Life Insurance Enterprise*. Cambridge: Harvard University Press, 1963.

Kimball, Spencer L. *Insurance and Public Policy*. Madison: University of Wisconsin Press, 1960.

Kip, Richard de Raismes. *Fraternal Life Insurance in America*. Philadelphia: College Offset Press, 1953.

Kniffin, William H. Jr. *The Savings Bank and its Practical Work*. New York: Bankers, 1912.

Knight, Charles K. *History of Life Insurance to 1870*. Philadelphia: by the author, 1920.

Koren, John, editor. *The History of Statistics*. New York: Macmillan, 1918.

Larson, Henrietta M. *Guide to Business History*. Cambridge: Harvard University Press, 1948.

Lebrun, François. *Les Hommes et La Mort en Anjou Aux 17ᵉ et 18ᵉ Siècles*. La Haye: Mouton, 1971.

Life Insurance Consumers. Hartford: Life Insurance Agency Management Association, 1973.

Life Insurance Statistical Highlights. New York: Institute of Life Insurance, 1974.

Lifton, Robert J. and Eric Olson. *Living and Dying*. New York: Praeger, 1974.

Linton, M. Albert. "Life Annuities." In S. S. Huebner, ed., *Modern Insurance Problems*. Philadelphia: American Academy of Political and Social Science, 1917.

Long, John. *Ethics, Morality, and Insurance*. Bloomington: Indiana University, Bureau of Business Research, 1971.

Lubove, Roy. *The Struggle for Social Security*. Cambridge: Harvard University Press, 1968.

Mackie, Alexander. *Facile Princeps: The Story of the Beginning of Life Insurance in America*. Lancaster, Pa.: Lancaster Press, 1956.

MacLean, G. A. *Insurance Up Through the Ages*. Louisville, Ky.: Dunne Press, 1938.

McLean, Joseph. *Life Insurance*. New York: McGraw-Hill, 1945.

Malinowski, Bronislaw. *Magic, Science, and Religion*. New York: Doubleday, 1954.

May, Henry F. *Protestant Churches and Industrial America*. New York: Harper, 1949.

McConnell, Donald. *Economic Virtues in the United States*. New York: by the author, 1930.

McKinney, William Mark. *Consolidated Laws of New York Annotated*. Minneapolis, Minn.: West Publishing Co., 1971.

Meitzin, August. *History, Theory, and Techniques of Statistics*. Philadelphia: American Academy of Political and Social Science, 1891.

Mitford, Jessica. *The American Way of Death*. Greenwich, Conn.: Fawcett Crest Books, 1963.

Moir, Henry. "Mortality Tables." In Lester W. Zartman and W. H. Price, eds., *Life Insurance*. New Haven: Yale University Press, 1914.

Montgomery, Thomas H. *A History of the Insurance Company of North America*. Philadelphia: Review Publishing and Printing Company, 1885.

Morgan, Edmund S. *The Puritan Family*. New York: Harper and Row, 1966.

Morley, John. *Death, Heaven and the Victorians*. Pittsburgh: University of Pittsburgh Press, 1971.

Morris, Harrison S. *A Sketch of the Pennsylvania Company for Insurance On Lives and Granting Annuities*. Philadelphia: Lippincott, 1896.

Myers, Margaret G. *A Financial History of the United States*. New York: Columbia University Press, 1970.

Nelson, Benjamin. *The Idea of Usury*. Chicago: University of Chicago Press, 1969.

Nichols, Walter S. *Insurance Blue Book, 1876–77*. New York: C. C. Hine, 1877.

North, Douglass C. "Capital Accumulation in Life Insurance between the Civil War and the Investigation of 1905." In William Miller, ed., *Men in Business*. Cambridge: Harvard University Press, 1952.

North, Douglass, C. *The Economic Growth of the United States, 1790–1860.* New York: Norton, 1966.

—— *Growth and Welfare in the American Past.* Englewood Cliffs: Prentice Hall, 1966.

North, Douglass C. and Lance E. Davis. *Institutional Change and American Economic Growth.* Cambridge: Harvard University Press, 1971.

O'Donnell, Terence. *History of Life Insurance in its Formative Years.* Chicago: American Conservation Co., 1936.

Oviatt, F. W. "History of Fire Insurance in the United States." In Lester W. Zartman, ed., *Property Insurance.* New Haven: Yale University Press, 1909.

Parsons, Talcott. "The Professions and Social Structure." In Talcott Parsons, ed., *Essays in Sociological Theory.* New York: Free Press, 1949.

Parsons, Talcott, Reneé C. Fox, and Victor Lidz. "The Gift of Life and Its Reciprocation." In Arien Mack, ed., *Death In American Experience.* New York: Schocken Books, 1973.

Parsons, Talcott and Victor Lidz. "Death in American Society." In Edwin S. Schneidman, ed., *Essays in Self Destruction.* New York: Science House, 1967.

Passamaneck, Stephen M. *Insurance in Rabbinic Law.* Edinburgh: University of Edinburgh Press, 1974.

Patterson, Edwin W. *Cases and Materials on the Law of Insurance.* New York: Foundation Press, 1955.

Patterson, Raul R. "Children and Ritual of the Mortuary." In Otto S. Margolis, ed., *Grief and the Meaning of the Funeral.* New York: MAS Information Corporation, 1975.

Pelerin, Pierre. *The French Law of Wills, Probates, Administration and Death Duties.* London: Stevens, 1958.

Pfeffer, Irving and David R. Klock. *Perspectives on Insurance.* Englewood Cliffs, N.J.: Prentice-Hall, 1974.

Pierce, Dr. C. C. "Human Life as a National Asset." In F. Robertson Jones, ed., *History and Proceedings of the World's Insurance Congress,* San Francisco: National Insurance Council, 1915.

Presbrey, A. *The History and Development of Advertising.* New York: Greenwood Press, 1968.

Richard, P. J. *Histoire des Institutions d'Assurance en France.* Paris: L'Argus, 1956.

Rogers, Everett M. with F. Floyd Shoemaker. *Communication of Innovations.* New York: Free Press, 1971.

Rosenberg, Charles. *The Cholera Years.* Chicago: University of Chicago Press, 1962.

Rosenberg, David and D. M. White. *Mass Culture.* New York: Free Press, 1957.

Rossiter, W. S. *A Century of Population Growth.* U.S. Bureau of the Census. Washington D.C.: Government Printing Office, 1909.

Rostow, W. W. *The Stages of Economic Growth.* London: Cambridge University Press, 1971.

Rothman, David J. *The Discovery of the Asylum.* Boston: Little, Brown, 1971.

Russell, George and Kenneth Black. *Human Behavior and Life Insurance.* Princeton: Princeton University Press, 1963.

Sakolski, A. M. *The Great American Land Bubble.* New York: Harper and Row, 1932.

Schaffer, Thomas L. *Death, Property, and Lawyers.* New York: Dunellen, 1970.

Schultz, Oscar T. *The Law of the Dead Human Body.* Chicago: American Medical Association, 1930.

Simes, Lewis M. *Public Policy and the Dead Hand.* Ann Arbor: University of Michigan Law School, 1955.

Simmel, Georg. *Philosophie des Geldes.* Leipzig: Duncker and Humblot, 1900.

—— *The Philosophy of Money.* Tom Bottomore and David Frisby, trans. London: Routledge and Kegan Paul, 1978.

Simmons, Leo W. *The Role of the Aged in Primitive Society.* New Haven: Yale University Press, 1945.

Smith, James G. *The Development of Trust Companies in the United States.* New York: H. Holt, 1927.

Stalson, Owen J. *Marketing Life Insurance.* Bryn Mawr, Pa.: McCahan Foundation, 1969.

Stannard, David E. editor. *Death in America.* Philadelphia: University of Pennsylvania Press, 1975.

Stone, Mildred F. *A Calling and Its College.* Homewood, Ill.: Richard D. Irwin, 1963.

—— *Since 1845: A History of the Mutual Benefit Life Insurance Company.* New Brunswick, N.J.: Rutgers University Press, 1957.

Sumner, William Graham. *Folkways.* New York: New American Library, 1940.

Sumner, William Graham and Albert Keller. *The Science of Society.* New Haven: Yale University Press, 1927.

Supple, Barry. *The Royal Exchange Assurance.* London: Cambridge University Press, 1970.

Sussman, Marvin B., Judith N. Cates, and David T. Smith. *The Family and Inheritance.* New York: Russell Sage Foundation, 1970.

Taeuber, C. and Irene B. Taeuber. *The Changing Population of the United States.* New York: Wiley, 1958.

Taylor, Miller Lee. "The Life Insurance Man: A Sociological Analysis of the Occupation." Ph.D. diss., Louisiana State University and Agricultural and Mechanical College, 1958.

Teweley, Richard J., Charles U. Harlow, and Herbert L. Stone. *The Commodity Futures Game.* New York: McGraw Hill, 1974.

The Map Report. New York: Institute of Life Insurance, 1973.

The Nature of the Whole Life Contract. New York: Institute of Life Insurance, 1974.

Tishler, Hace Sorel. *Self-Reliance and Social Security 1870–1917.* New York: Kennikat Press, 1971.

Titmuss, Richard M. *The Gift Relationship.* New York: Random House, 1971.

Trenerry, C. F. *The Origin and Early History of Insurance.* London: P. S. King, 1926.

U.S. Bureau of the Census. *Historical Statistics of the United States: Colonial Times to 1957*. Washington, D.C.: Government Printing Office, 1960.

Vallier, Ivan. *Comparative Methods in Sociology*. Berkeley: University of California Press, 1971.

Vernon, Glenn M. *The Sociology of Death*. New York: Ronald Press, 1970.

Viner, Jacob. *The Role of Providence in the Social Order*. Philadelphia: American Philosophical Society, 1972.

Vinovskis, Maris A. "Angels' Heads and Weeping Willows: Death in Early America." In Michael Gordon, ed., *The American Family in Social-Historical Perspective*. New York: St. Martin's Press, 1978.

Viterbo, Camilo. *Ensayos de Derecho Comercial y Económico*. Buenos Aires, Argentina: Tea Tipográfica, 1948.

Vovelle, Michel. *Piété Baroque et Déchristianisation en Provence au XIII Siècle*. Paris: Plon, 1973.

Wahab, M. A. "Insurance Development in Iraq and the U.A.R." Master's thesis, New York, College of Insurance, May 1969.

Wahl, Charles W. "The Fear of Death." In Herman Feifel, ed., *The Meaning of Death*. New York: McGraw Hill, 1959.

Walford, Cornelius. *Insurance Guide and Handbook*. London: Charles & Edwin Layton, 1901.

Wallwork, Ernest. *Durkheim: Morality and Milieu*. Cambridge: Harvard University Press, 1972.

Ward, William M. *Down The Years*. Newark, N.J.: Mutual Benefit Life Insurance Co., 1932.

Warner, Lloyd W. *The Living and The Dead: A Study of the Symbolic Life of Americans*. New Haven: Yale University Press, 1959.

Washburne, Henry S. *Something About the Business of Life Assurance in France*. Boston: Franklin Press, 1879.

—— *Something About the Business of Life Assurance in Germany*. Boston: Franklin Press, 1879.

Weare, W. *Black Business in the New South: A Social History of the North Carolina Mutual Life Insurance Company*. Urbana: University of Illinois Press, 1973.

Weber, Max. *The Protestant Ethic and the Spirit of Capitalism*. New York: Scribners, 1958.

Weiss, Richard. *The American Myth of Success*. New York: Basic Books, 1969.

White, Gerald T. *A History of the Massachusetts Hospital Life Insurance Company*. Cambridge: Harvard University Press, 1955.

Willet, Allan H. "The Economic Theory of Risk and Insurance." Ph. D. Thesis, Columbia University, 1901.

Williston, Samuel. *A Treatise on the Law of Contracts*. New York: The Lawyers Co-operative Publishing Co., 1972.

Winter, William D. *Marine Insurance*. New York: McGraw Hill, 1919.

Woods, Edward A. *The Sociology of Life Insurance*. New York: D. Appleton, 1928.

Woodward, P. Henry. *Insurance in Connecticut*. Boston: D. H. Hurd, 1897.

Wrong, Dennis H. *Population and Society*. New York: Random House, 1963.

Wyllie, Irvin G. *The Self-Made Man in America*. New York: Free Press, 1954.

Yasuba, Yasukichi. *Birth Rates of the White Population in the United States, 1800–1860: An Economic Study*. John Hopkins University Studies in Historical and Political Science, 79, No. 2. Baltimore: John Hopkins University Press, 1962.

Zartman, Lester W. "History of Life Insurance in the United States." In Lester W. Zartman, ed., *Personal Insurance: Life and Accident*, rev. by William H. Price. Yale Readings in Life Insurance. New Haven: Yale University Press, 1914.

Index

Bei Fragen zur Produktsicherheit wenden Sie sich bitte an:
If you have any questions regarding product safety, please contact:

Walter de Gruyter GmbH
Genthiner Straße 13
10785 Berlin
productsafety@degruyterbrill.com